Working with Adult Learners

Patricia Cranton
Brock University

WE

Wall & Emerson, Inc.
Toronto, Ontario • Dayton, Ohio

Requests for permission to make copies of any part of this work should be sent to:
Wall & Emerson, Inc., Six O'Connor Drive, Toronto, Ontario, Canada M4K 2K1

Orders for this book may be directed to either of the following addresses:

For the United States:	*For Canada and the rest of the world:*
Wall & Emerson, Inc.	Wall & Emerson, Inc.
8701 Slagle Rd.	Six O'Connor Drive
Dayton, Ohio 45458	Toronto, Ontario, Canada
	M4K 2K1

By telephone, facsimile, or e-mail (for both addresses):

Telephone: (416) 467-8685
Fax: (416) 696-2460
E-mail: wall@maple.net

Canadian Cataloguing in Publication Data

Cranton, Patricia
  Working with adult learners

Includes bibliographical references and index.
ISBN 1-895131-07-3

1. Adult education.   I. Title.

LC5215.C73 1992   374   C92-093782-9

ISBN 1-895131-07-3
Printed in Canada by Hignell Printing Limited.
2 3 4 5   05 04 03 02 01 00 99 98 97 96

Contents

List of Figures

Preface

Purpose of the Book

The overall purpose of this book is to provide practical information, within a theoretical context, for educators who are working with adult learners. Almost all educators of adults practise without training in their profession. They have expertise and experience in their subject area and are keenly interested in helping others learn about their subject area, but may not have developed an awareness of education as an area of study.

Many adult educators are aware of and refer to the books, handbooks, and guides which provide "recipes" for effective practice. The intent here is to go beyond that, to foster an awareness of the complexity of adult education and of the theoretical framework within which it exists as a discipline. It is also the intent to translate that complexity into useful information for the practitioner. It is hoped that such a process will lead educators to reflect on their work and to develop their own informed theory of practice.

Intended Audience

This book is addressed to adult educators, whether they work in formal settings, such as colleges, universities, and training programs in business and industry, or in informal settings, such as community groups and special interest groups. Particularly, the book is addressed to those educators who want and expect their learners to take responsibility for their own learning. Finally, the book is intended for all students of adult education, whether they are enroled in formal programs at a university or exploring the discipline as an individual learning project.

Structure of the Book

Some assumptions are made in this book, which influence the organization, structure, and presentation of the material. It is assumed that adult education practice is bound by the cultural context in which it occurs, by the learning environment, and by the characteristics of the learners and the educator. No *one* approach is right or wrong, effective or ineffective; rather, the approach should be deliberately selected, dependent on the situation. However, it is also assumed that self-directed learning is a goal of adult education and that transformative learning is a valued outcome of working with adult learners. This assumption leads to an emphasis on approaches which encourage learners to take responsibility, question, and reflect.

Chapter 1 describes the theoretical framework within which adult education practice exists. It is essential for the educator to develop an awareness of the diverse contributions to the field; this diversity reflects the complexity and breadth of professional practice.

Learner characteristics have a strong influence on the educator's choice of approaches, methods, and materials. Chapter 2 examines some of these in detail, including self-directedness, a characteristic which we hope to develop through our work with learners.

Educators can and do play a variety of roles in their practice. These roles are often not chosen deliberately, but are based on what we have observed others doing or on our own personality and preferences. Chapter 3 reviews educator roles on a continuum from educator-directed, through learner-directed, to mutually-directed. The educator who is aware of roles, including when and why they should be used, can make careful decisions about approaches to be taken in specific contexts.

Chapter 4 outlines a process that learners go through in becoming self-directed. Ways in which educators can facilitate the process are examined in detail. In much of the adult education literature, it is assumed that adults are self-directed, yet every practitioner realizes that this is not necessarily the case. This chapter bridges a gap between current theory and practice.

Transformative learning has been introduced into the literature quite recently. Chapter 5 introduces transformative learning to the practitioner and provides several techniques which can be used to encourage the process.

The educator who is working toward self-directed and transformative learning can encounter difficult situations, constraints, and conflicts. Chapter 6 addresses some of the most common difficulties and provides concrete practical ways of dealing with them.

Every educator makes decisions daily about his or her practice—which handout to use, which activity to suggest, when to intervene in a discussion, when to give information. In other words, every educator has a *theory of practice.* In Chapter 7, it is suggested that this theory of practice should be made explicit, then used deliberately to make informed decisions. Two case studies illustrate the process of developing a theory of practice; some implications of the theory of practice advocated in this book are discussed.

About the Author

I am currently Professor of Adult Education and Director of Instructional Development at Brock University in Ontario. I have been working with adult learners at college and university levels for the past 16 years, although I have not always seen myself as an adult educator.

My own theory of practice has gradually evolved; I was not trained as an adult educator, but rather as a university instructor and researcher. I began my practice by teaching as I had been taught—a combination of lecturing and questioning. Evaluation of and reflection on my practice led over time to the inclusion of varied methods, particularly more interactive methods. I then began to recognize the power of encouraging learners to make their own decisions about their learning. It was this discovery that brought me to the study of adult education and to the development of the theory of practice which underlies this book. It is hoped that this book will stimulate other educators to engage in the same rewarding process.

1

Theoretical Framework

Adult education takes place in such a wide variety of contexts that it becomes difficult, if not impossible, to describe one unifying framework or theoretical model for the field. Included under the rubric of adult education are informal learning activities such as community action groups, patient education, self-help groups, individual learning projects, and learning networks; and formal learning settings such as continuing education centers, colleges and universities, literacy programs, labor education, and training in business and industry. Adult educators are any individuals who become involved in leading or guiding or facilitating or organizing learning activities in either informal or formal settings.

Educators, then, simply may be individuals who choose to become involved in the facilitation of the learning activities of others, or they may be trained teachers or individuals with formal academic qualifications in a subject. Adult learners, of course, can be any individuals who choose to or are required to participate in any informal or formal learning activity.

In addition, the culture or social context within which adult education takes place has a profound influence on the way in which it is viewed both by educators and by participants. A common North American model views the process as one that is "driven" by expressed learner needs and interests (see, for example, Knowles, 1980). Other writers, such as Jarvis (1987), from England, emphasize the social dimension or context of adult learning. Adult educators who have worked in developing countries (e.g., Freire, 1972) describe adult education as a freeing or liberating activity for oppressed peoples. Recent writers, such as Mezirow (1990), attempt to integrate some of these perspectives. Mezirow writes: "We know that we must respond to initial learner interests and self-defined needs, but we do so with the intent to move learners to an awareness of the *reasons* for these needs and how the learners' meaning perspectives may have limited the way they customarily perceive, think, feel, and act in defining and attempting to satisfy their needs. This is what being a professional adult educator means, a quite different role from that of a group process technician or a subject matter specialist" (pp. 357–358).

How then, can we describe a theoretical framework from which to derive tenets of practice? Although the purpose of this book is not to build theory, we cannot separate practice from theory and view techniques for working with adult learners as a "bag of tricks" or a set of isolated rules. It is essential that the work of the adult educator be grounded in what we know about how people learn and develop, about education as a philosophy and a system, and about the contexts in which we work. In this chapter, adult education will be defined and described, overviews of some common theoretical models will be provided, and an integrative model will be presented.

What is Adult Education?

The seemingly simple task of defining adult education becomes exceedingly complex when one considers the possible array of activities and settings to which we have already referred. Jarvis (1987) writes, "At the heart of life itself is the process of learning. It would be easy to assume that conscious living and learning are synonymous processes, but…this is not so. Nevertheless, they are very close to each other and constantly overlap" (p. 1). In other words, almost anything that anyone does as a part of life can be described as a learning experience, and therefore, in some sense, as adult education. The problem becomes one of what to *exclude* in defining adult education. When Tough (1979) used a liberal definition, including all individual "learning projects," he found that 98% of the adult population was engaged in adult education. This brings us very close to considering that "living" and "learning" are synonymous. If we learn from "experience" and, of course, we continually "experience" as we live, adult education becomes "everything an adult does." This approach, unfortunately, is fairly common in the literature, with the result that the area of adult education appears to be intangible, amorphous, and virtually impossible to describe within a framework, or to define. To return to our purpose, that of providing guidance for the practitioner, it is valuable to be aware of this global view, but it is not very useful in terms of selecting roles or developing a theory of practice.

Examining the components contained within the concept of adult education leads to a more manageable definition. We can define an adult as someone who has assumed the social roles of adulthood in his or her culture or sub-culture. Chronological age is relevant only to a limited extent in defining an adult. Even if we turn to legal definitions, there is considerable variance. But when an individual is independent or "grown up" in a social sense, we are usually quite comfortable in referring to that person as an adult. We can define learning in a fairly traditional manner; that is, any sustained change in thinking, values, or behavior that is brought about by an experience. Adult education, then, becomes the set of activities or experiences engaged in by adults which lead to changes in thinking, values, or behavior.

We've avoided including "everything" by stating that adult education is a *set* of activities or experiences which *lead to* learning. Of course, the definition is not as tidy as it appears. Is education no longer education if an individual does not learn? Is learning no longer learning if it is a product of an isolated but dramatic event? However, these problematic loose ends can be left to coffee break discussions, and the definition stated above will serve as the basis of the following chapters.

Overview of Theoretical Background

Why bother with theory? Many a practitioner may be tempted to skip over an introductory section with a title such as this. Yet it is an awareness of and reflection on the context of the field within which we work—its history, the thoughts of others on it, and its theoretical bases—which separate the professional adult educator from the technician. The importance of this awareness grows as adult education moves away from an emphasis simply on meeting the expressed needs of the learner and toward a responsibility for fostering questioning attitudes and critical self-reflection. Mezirow writes, "Transformative learning for emancipatory education is the business of all adult educators" (p. 357). If this statement is accepted, even in part, we must go beyond techniques—or minimally, we must think about and question the techniques we use and the bases for them. The adult educator can no longer be an automaton (or passive facilitator), merely providing the resources for the learner. We must consider what journey we are on and why we are taking it.

Adult education has had a checkered history. Its main roots lie in psychology and, within that, mostly in the psychology of learning, which had its origin only in the nineteenth century. Before then philosophers studied "knowledge" as a concept, rather than the process of acquiring knowledge (learning). This approach, too, provided some of the early foundation blocks for adult education, especially through Dewey's writings in the early 1900s. Another influential building block has been literacy education, particularly the writings of the critical theorists (those individuals who question the structure of the institutions of education and the structure of society). More recently, adult education has incorporated theoretical foundations from sociology (both the social context of learning and the study of group behavior).

As can be seen from this simplified picture of the history of adult education, there is no easy path of theory development to follow. The field has developed rather as a building would be constructed if there were several carpenters from different countries, speaking different languages, with neither architect nor blueprint. What we will do here is to describe some of the walls in the basement and some of the rooms in the building. The structure itself is not yet finished, and in fact, it may well turn out to be several buildings. Readers who are interested in this topic in more detail than is provided here can pursue the references given. Unfortunately, but not surprisingly, no integrative book on the theoretical foundations of adult education has yet been written.

In the Beginning...

Although "the beginning" of adult education is not easy to pinpoint (we could go back to Socrates), Dewey's (1925, 1933) thoughts and writings provide an accepted starting point. In addition, Dewey probably has had the most profound and lasting impact on adult education of any early writer.

Dewey can be described as a philosopher and as a "generalist"—his list of published works is as diverse as it is long. His early writings must have startled the traditional philosophers of the time who spent their days debating the concept of knowledge and the existence of reality. For Dewey ignored these esoteric debates and argued that knowledge comes through experience and that reality is defined through experience and through "action." Through this interest in experience and the *acquisition* of knowledge (or learning) through experience, Dewey came to define "psychology" as a field of study that was separate from philosophy. It was not, however, until William James wrote his book, *Principles of Psychology,* that the academic world began to accept this idea.

Dewey's thoughts on learning led, naturally, to his interest in education. One of his many endeavors was to set up an experimental school with his wife, wherein he implemented his idea that all learning came through direct experience. Dewey wrote extensively and broadly; the interested adult educator can refer to *Education and Democracy* (1916), *How We Think* (1933), or *Experience and Education* (1938), to name a few relevant works.

Many of Dewey's ideas on education are threads which can be found consistently throughout the adult education literature. He did not write specifically about *adult* education (much of his writings and the experimental school were concerned with children's learning), but because he held that learning was based on experience, he naturally regarded learning as a lifelong process and described it as such.

As learning comes from experiencing things, according to Dewey, the way in which individuals define and solve problems becomes the central process of learning. This leads to the concept of learning as a "scientific method" and to regarding all learners as "scientists." An individual is faced with a real problem to solve. Hypotheses are formed about the problem. Evidence is collected to test the hypotheses. Hypotheses are accepted or rejected, more hypotheses are formulated, the problem gets solved, and the process of learning has taken place.

Such a description may seem simplistic; however, if this notion of learning is applied to education, profound implications emerge. Dewey's ideas were considered radical at a time when schooling was almost always equated with rote memorization. For example, Dewey's students would learn about the textile industry by learning to weave, while elsewhere other students might memorize the dates of significant developments in that industry.

Most importantly, for us now, Dewey's legacy lies in the fact that any book with "adult learning" or "adult education" in the title will refer to the value of experience in learning. This concept is now taken for granted, but less than 100 years ago it was a startling one.

Another key concept in adult education that can be attributed to Dewey's work is the emphasis on "reflection." Recently, adult educators have begun to emphasize learner self-reflection and critical reflection as central concepts in adult learning (cf. Boud, Keogh & Walker, 1985; Mezirow, 1990). Although this notion may be attributed to the influential and prolific writings of Argyris and Schon (for example, Schon, 1983), fifty years earlier Dewey (1933) described "assessing the grounds of one's beliefs" (p. 9), which is the core of the process of critical reflection described in the current literature.

Before leaving Dewey, it should be noted how these ideas worked their way into the present practice of adult education. Lindeman (1926), who based his work on Dewey's earliest writings, produced the first book specifically about adult education, entitled *The Meaning of Adult Education*. It was from this basis that Knowles began his extensive writing in this area, which both defined adult education as an academic discipline and determined the course of its practice for decades to come. We will return, of course, to Knowles, but first, other early building blocks of the foundation will be examined.

Behaviorists

Even someone who has never been a student of psychology will probably have heard of Skinner and his well-known research, training rats and pigeons to perform various complex tasks. Skinner's work, beginning in the 1950s, is most commonly associated with behaviorism—the idea that we learn by being reinforced (positively or negatively) for our behaviors. If we give a dog a cookie for "good" behavior, we expect that the dog will repeat the behavior. If we pick up or pay attention to a crying baby, we guiltily suspect that we are "reinforcing" the baby's crying. If someone admires the clothes we wear, we will probably feel good when wearing them again. The behaviorist theory of learning has affected the way we think about all learning.

Although Skinner's experiments with rats are what we usually associate with behaviorism, a few early psychologists, Thorndike (1898), Watson, as described by Hilgard and Bower (1966), and Pavlov (1927), first founded and experimented with behaviorism. Watson studied the "stimulus-response" connection that determined the direction of the psychology of learning for at least the next 40 years. Pavlov, using dogs as experimental subjects, proposed the theory of "classical conditioning"—the learner associates the presence of a reward with a stimulus that occurs prior to it. Most of us are familiar with the image of dogs salivating at the sound of a bell, having "learned" that they will receive a treat when a bell rings. Pavlov's research still influences the way we think of learning.

How does this relate to adult education as we now know it? Behaviorism, through the writings of Skinner and others (for example, Skinner, 1953), provides the theoretical basis of programmed instruction, modular instruction, computer-assisted instruction, and even, to some extent, instructional design (or educational technology). In examining the idea of individuals learning as a result of the reinforcement of their responses to stimuli, we can easily see that all approaches which break learning into small steps and provide praise (reinforcement) for the accomplishment of those steps are based on the behavioral approach to the psychology of learning. Consider an individualized learning package or a module in which a learner reads a short paper or listens to a tape, responds to questions, then is told that the response is correct or incorrect, or an instructional design model in which the learner is presented with an objective, engages in some activity to reach that objective, and is reinforced with on-going feedback.

Gagné (1975, 1977), who is often included as a contributor to the theoretical foundations of adult education (cf. Jarvis, 1983), originally based his writings on a behaviorist approach.

The behaviorists, of course, overlooked the "person," or rather they ignored the cognitive and affective processes that occur within the learner. Skinner eventually ran into trouble when he could not explain the acquisition of language. And the psychology of learning reformed itself to incorporate the processes that were not explained by the behaviorist approach. Several paths of development were occurring simultaneously, and we will return to some of these in our description of the foundations of adult education.

Humanists

The practice of adult education is, and has been historically, humanist (emphasizing the person) in nature. Practitioners' guides usually discuss the necessity for creating an atmosphere conducive to learning, identifying learner needs and interests, providing warmth and support, emphasizing interaction among people, de-emphasizing or eliminating grading, and providing options and flexibility to match individual styles and preferences. These are all characteristics of a humanist approach to education. Most of these ideas are now basic principles of adult education and are primarily attributed to Knowles. Because of his profound influence on the nature of research and practice in the area, Malcolm Knowles will be discussed separately, under the heading *Andragogy*. First, examples of other humanistic influences on adult education will be mentioned briefly.

Carl Rogers (1951, 1969) wrote mainly about the self-actualization of clients in therapy, but he also addressed adult learning (see *Freedom to Learn*, 1969). Rogers completely downplayed the role of the teacher (as authority figure or leader). Malcolm Knowles tells an anecdote (personal communication, 1988) of attending a seminar of Carl Rogers, where Rogers did not identify himself as the leader until participants were ready to leave, thinking that no professor was going to attend. This approach to the facilitating of adult learning has been taken up, though to a lesser extent, by Knowles and by many writers and practitioners. Rogers saw the role of the adult educator as one of supporting personal growth, encouraging change in self-perception and self-concept, and facilitating the development of self-awareness in the learner. This trend is reflected in the recent adult education literature, particularly in discussions of adult education as "empowerment."

Maslow (1968), writing about self-development, is another humanist psychologist who has influenced adult education, particularly through the work of Knowles. Maslow described a "hierarchy of needs," beginning with physiological needs, and moving through safety, love and belonging, self-esteem, and finally self-actualization. Maslow argued that individuals cannot move toward self-actualization unless the more basic needs (such as food, shelter, a safe environment) are met. Again, one can see evidence of acceptance of this concept in current writings in which the environment and the comfort of the learner are emphasized; learning is said to be facilitated by an atmosphere of acceptance; and learning is described as best taking place when an individual's self-esteem is positive (cf. Brundage & Mackeracher, 1980).

A large literature exists in psychology and in education on learning style (and cognitive style, a somewhat different individual characteristic). Learning style will be discussed in more detail in Chapter 2, but should be mentioned here as an influential concept in adult education. Principles of adult learning nearly always include phrases such as, "employing a variety of methods to meet the needs of individual learning styles or preferences," or "being flexible in adapting to the needs of individual learners." These ideas are derived from the work on learning style. Kolb (1984), described a learning *cycle* which contains four phases: concrete experiences (for example, observing a new piece of equipment in operation), reflective observation (thinking about the experience), abstract conceptualization (understanding the new equipment in relation to other similar pieces of equipment), and active experimentation (trying to run the equipment oneself). Individuals exhibit preferences for different phases of the cycle, which when examined in various clusters (such as a preference for concrete experience *and* reflective observation), yields a preferred learning *style*. Some people prefer "doing" (accommodators), some prefer "thinking about" (assimilators), some prefer quickly focusing in and coming to conclusions (convergers), and some prefer generating ideas (divergers).

Kolb's work and his measurement of preferred learning style have been criticized (cf. Jarvis, 1987), but nevertheless, his *Learning Style Inventory* is frequently used in both research and practice.

Developmental Psychologists

In the late 1960s and 1970s, considerable research on adult development was published. As Cross (1981) points out, two different approaches were taken, though they were often mixed in the literature. Some psychologists attempted to describe the *phases* that an individual goes through during a lifetime. These phases most often are related to social or cultural activities, such as leaving home, moving into the adult world, searching for stability, becoming one's own person, settling down, mellowing, and carrying out a life review (Cross, 1981, 174–175). Many readers may be familiar with Gail Sheehy's *Passages*, a popular book about life phases. The contribution of this work to adult education has been to draw attention to the effect of life phases on learning or readiness to learn. Some later writers indicate that an individual who is in transition or moving from one phase to another (e.g., change in career, change in family responsibilities, retirement) is more likely to be ready for new learning experiences.

The other stream of developmental psychology addresses the *stages* of growth of an individual from immaturity to maturity. Some writers are interested in personality development (cf. Loevinger, 1976) and others in moral development (cf. Kohlberg, 1969) or intellectual development (Perry, 1970). Progress through these stages tends to move from simple (black-and-white, childlike) ways of being through to a complex, integrated awareness of the self. Cross (1981) provides an excellent summary of the major works in this area. Here, Loevinger's (1976) stages of ego development will be listed, as an illustration of the nature of this research.

- Presocial, symbiotic, impulsive—dependent and impulsive.
- Self-protective—externalizing blame, manipulative.
- Conformist—conformity to external rules, social acceptability.
- Conscientious-conformist—aware of self in relation to group, adjustment.
- Conscientious—self-evaluated standards, responsible.
- Individualistic—respect for individuality, differentiation of inner life from outer, distinction of process and outcome.
- Autonomous—respect of autonomy, interdependence, conceptual complexity, toleration for ambiguity.
- Integrated—reconciling inner conflicts, integrated identity.

If we recall the humanist contribution to adult education, we can see how the pieces begin to fit together. The developmental psychologists describe the *process* of individual growth. The adult educator provides the environment and the support and the encouragement to facilitate this growth. In a sense, the work of developmental psychology has served to provide goals for the humanist approach.

In recent years the work of developmental psychologists from the 1970s has been criticized on the grounds that it is based primarily on research of male development; it is argued that the phases and stages of growth of women are qualitatively different from those of men. Gilligan (1982), among others, has provided alternate views of intellectual and ego development, based on women's "ways of knowing." These writings are only starting to appear in the adult education literature and clearly will gain prominence as the academic study of women's issues grows. Recent writings on feminist pedagogy bear a striking resemblance to those on adult education; however, the link has not been made in research or in practice. Hart (1990) writes about raising consciousness regarding women's issues and discusses the implications for educational practice. Adult educators must maintain an awareness of these important issues and watch for further literature.

In summary, developmental psychologists have provided some of the cornerstones of adult education practice. The educator should have some knowledge of the phases of development and their relationship to learning readiness, and be aware that one of the roles of the educator is to support growth through the developmental stages.

Critical Theorists

So far, we have been discussing theoretical perspectives which attempt to *describe* how things are. Behaviorists and humanists offer descriptions of how learning takes place; developmental psychologists present descriptions of human growth to maturity. Critical theorists, on the other hand, criticize things as they are and write about how things should or could be. They are most often critical of society and institutions (such as education), particularly in relation to the oppression of individuals or groups of individuals. It is the critical theorist who makes us aware of our social mistreatment of people and provokes us into change. Quite often, a critical theorist who was viewed as a radical during the time that he or she wrote will seem quite "tame" a few decades later as awareness leads to restructuring and change. As was noted earlier, Dewey changed the course of education by his radical proposal that people learn best by doing.

The critical theorists are vital contributors to the theory of adult education. Adult education is inextricably linked with social change, with reform. This can be seen clearly in the move to provide literacy education for individuals in our country who have never had this opportunity, or for individuals in a developing country—the "freeing" of individuals from the constraints of illiteracy leads to change in the structure of that society. In many cultures, social reform is considered to be the primary purpose of adult education; in Nigeria, for example, where free public education is not available, adult education is seen as the only means of achieving technological change (Ume, personal communication, 1990).

Among the critical theorists, it is probably Freire (1972, 1974) who has had the most impact on adult education. Freire worked in Brazil with illiterate and oppressed people. Through this experience, he came to realize that people had accepted their oppression; in other words, they had accepted the existing power relations in their culture. The educator, as long as he acted as an "educator," was simply another power figure imposing his values on people—different values, perhaps, but within a similar power structure. Consequently, Freire envisaged and wrote of a radically different role for educators. He proposed that we must see ourselves as learners, as individuals learning about the culture of the people with whom we are working. Only when we are a part of that culture, "living with the people as they live" and understanding and accepting their values, can we engage in the dialogue and learning process that will lead to liberation from oppression. The educator is not "above" the people with whom he or she works, is not a "provider of information," but rather, is a co-learner, mutually responsible (with the people) for growth and change.

In addition to stimulating our thinking about the role of the adult educator, the concept of reflection as a vital process in adult learning is predominant in Freire's work. He (1972) emphasized the importance of dialogue in which people analyze, evaluate, and express judgments, as this dialogue can lead to a continuous re-creation of the individuals involved in the process. Freire also advocated the necessity of action based on reflection (reflection alone does not produce change). It is easy to see how critical reflection is a necessary ingredient of liberation from oppression.

This conception of adult education is quite different from the North American model of meeting learner needs by providing resources; however, as we will see in the section on transformative learning, Freire's (and other similar) writings are now being integrated into the adult education literature. Before discussing some of the works in which this integration has occurred, we will review Malcolm Knowles' work, which provides us with the commonly accepted North American adult education model.

Andragogy

Inspired by Lindeman (1926) and other early writers in adult education, Knowles introduced the term "andragogy" into American educational literature in 1968 (although the term has been traced back to 1833, in German literature). He defined andragogy as "the art and science of helping adults learn," and originally, clearly differentiated it from pedagogy (the art and science of teaching children). Twenty years ago, Knowles saw pedagogy and andragogy as opposing approaches and wrote of "pedagogy *versus* andragogy." He held that the pedagogical model gives the teacher full responsibility for all decisions about learning and places the learner in a dependent role, following teacher instructions. More recently, Knowles places pedagogy and andragogy on a continuum. The sub-title of his book, *The Modern Practice of Adult Education* (1980), was changed from "pedagogy versus andragogy" to "from pedagogy to andragogy" in later editions.

The andragogical model is based on several underlying assumptions which have been presented in slightly different forms in different publications. *The Modern Practice of Adult Education,* for example, emphasizes four basic underlying assumptions: the self-concept of the learner includes self-directedness; the learner's experience should be used; readiness to learn depends on need; and, orientation to learning is life- or problem-centered. These assumptions have consistently guided researchers, writers, and practitioners in adult education over decades.

It is important to consider some of the implications of these assumptions for educational practice. For a fuller account, the reader is referred to Knowles (1980), and for case studies of applications of the principles, to Knowles (1984).

- *Adults are self-directing.* Knowles points to five implications of this statement.
  - The learning climate should be one which causes adults to feel accepted, respected, and supported—there should exist a "spirit of mutuality between teachers and students as joint inquirers" (47).
  - Emphasis should be placed on learner involvement in a process of self-diagnosis of learning needs.
  - Learners should be involved in the process of planning their own learning, with the teacher serving as a procedural guide and content resource.

— The teaching and learning process is the mutual responsibility of learners and teacher—the "teacher" becomes a resource person and catalyst rather than an instructor.

— Learners should engage in self-evaluation, with the teacher helping the adults obtain evidence *for themselves* of the progress they are making. "Nothing makes an adult feel more childlike than being judged by another adult; it is the ultimate sign of disrespect and dependency, as the one who is being judged experiences it" (49).

• *Adults have many and varied experiences.* The volume and variety of adults' experiences has three implications for practice.

— Participatory experiential techniques should be used in order to tap the experiences of learners.

— Provision should be made for learners to plan how they are going to apply their learning to their day-to-day lives.

— Activities should be incorporated which encourage learners to look at their experiences objectively and "learn how to learn" from them.

• *Adults are ready to learn as a result of being at a developmental transition point.* This concept has at least two implications.

— Curriculum should be organized so as to meet the real-life concerns of individuals, rather than the needs of the sponsoring institution.

— The concept of developmental readiness (or tasks) should be considered in the grouping of learners. For some learning, homogeneous groups are more effective, and for other kinds of learning, heterogeneous groups are preferable.

• *Adults prefer problem-centered or performance-centered learning.* Again several implications flow from this statement.

— Educators must be attuned to the concerns of the individuals and develop learning experiences that are relevant to these concerns.

— The appropriate organizing principle for sequencing adult learning is according to problem areas, not subjects.

— Early in any adult education session, there should be an exercise in which the participants identify the specific problems they want to be able to deal with more adequately.

Malcolm Knowles has written extensively on the practice of adult education; this brief summary has outlined only a few of the assumptions and principles which he has discussed. His ideas will reappear frequently as we proceed with later chapters on characteristics of adult learners and techniques for working with them.

Beyond Andragogy?

Naturally, other writers and practitioners extend the work of the founder of an area of study. The originator's influence remains strong, but others who follow go beyond. Since the adult education movement is very "recent history," it may be difficult to develop a perspective—that is, to decide which of the current writings will result in changes in practice and thinking, and which will be relegated to the back shelves of our bookcases.

Although there are many "beyond andragogy" writers, a few stand out. Of these, Brookfield (1986) and Mezirow (1990) will be discussed here.

Brookfield (1986) does not criticize the work of Knowles himself so much as the use of Knowles' work by others. He correctly points out that Knowles always states carefully that his "assumptions" are just assumptions, and not "an empirically based theory of learning painstakingly derived from a series of experiments resulting in generalizations of increasing levels of sophistication, abstraction, and applicability" (91). But practitioners have now taken Knowles' assumptions and translated them into *rules* of practice. This, argues Brookfield, is a mistake—we should be questioning these assumptions and collecting evidence about them, in addition to implementing them.

Brookfield's analysis of Knowles' work is comprehensive and enlightening; the reader is referred to his 1986 book, *Understanding and Facilitating Adult Learning*, for details. One of his main points of discussion is the idea that adults prefer to be, or have a "deep psychological need to be" self-directed. Self-direction has become one of the cliches of adult education, yet it is an assumption that may well need to be questioned. Brookfield points out that individuals from other cultures (e.g., totalitarian regimes) are not self-directed. "Indeed, were self-directedness an empirically undeniable aspect of adulthood, then the continued existence of a totalitarian regime would be inconceivable" (94). Perhaps political events since 1990 will raise questions about this statement, but, nevertheless, millions of individuals have lived in such regimes.

Brookfield goes on to describe several applications of andragogy and includes some participants' evaluation comments from a 1985 course of his own. Included are such statements as: "Some additional input from instructor could provide insight into issues." "I would have liked more chance to hear Stephen's thoughts on a number of important issues." "You be the judge." "A little more comment on student's oral presentations would be useful." (111). Brookfield notes, "My own belief is that participants were uncomfortable with being required to assume a degree of responsibility for designing their curriculum, negotiating their assessed piece of work, and judging the worth of their efforts" (111). He goes on to say, "According to andragogical tenets, this, strictly speaking, should not happen. Instead, the adult's tendency toward an independent self-concept should ensure that participants experience this requirement to assume some control as a liberating activity, freeing them from the shackles of a didactic, authoritarian form of education. That this is most definitely not always the case illustrates just how effectively facilitators and participants have been socialized into the traditional forms of education" (111–112).

Brookfield
Not supportive
of self dir.

In addition to examining whether or not learners need to be self-directed, Brookfield questions the role of the adult educator as one of simply meeting the needs of participants. He argues that the educator is morally responsible for contributing to the direction of adult learning. "Practitioners can become technically proficient but find that without a firm philosophical rationale to guide the application of their skills, they are devoting their efforts to programs and purposes that are morally dubious" (285). Brookfield strongly opposes the role of adult educator as technician and resource person who works toward meeting the needs of learners. "If we...regard facilitator roles and responsibilities as being primarily those of technicians of design, we denude practice of any philosophical rationale, future orientation, or purposeful mission... Furthermore, if we accept the view that we should serve only felt needs, then our priorities, purposes, and primary functions will be wholly determined by others" (287).

What Brookfield does is encourage us to question andragogy as a theory of adult education rather than to routinely put its principles into practice. It is essential for all professionals to reflect critically on their practice, to be aware of their own values and assumptions, to make responsible choices based on their expertise and values, and, through critical thought, become aware of and develop their philosophy of practice. Without a thoughtful rationale to guide their practice, Brookfield states, "It is likely that most facilitators will sooner or later fall unthinkingly into patterns of facilitation that support structures of organizational convenience and confirm learners' patterns of dependency learned in the school classroom but have little to do with assisting adults to create, and re-create, their personal, occupational, and political worlds" (1986, 297).

In his early publications, Mezirow (1977, 1981), another "beyond andragogy" writer, describes a learning cycle in which a "disorienting dilemma" is first experienced, followed by self-examination, the exploration of options, and learning through planning a new course of action to overcome the dilemma. Reflection is obviously a part of this cycle, and Mezirow discusses levels of reflection, labeling his own work as critical theory (1981). More recently, Mezirow and his associates (1990) have produced a collection of descriptions of programs, approaches for encouraging critical reflection, and techniques for developing learner self-awareness. Some of the specific approaches will be returned to in Chapter 5; for now we will examine the contribution that Mezirow makes to extending adult education beyond andragogy.

Mezirow defines adult education as a process of reflection and action, and states, "From this vantage point, adult education becomes the process of assisting those who are fulfilling adult roles to understand the meaning of their experience by participating more fully and freely in rational discourse to validate expressed ideas and to take action upon the resulting insights... Rational thought and action are the cardinal goals of adult education" (1990, 354). He sees the process of critical self-reflection as leading to a reformulation of an individual's "meaning perspective" (the assumptions that a person uses to interpret experiences). This reformulation, along with acting on the reformulation, is called *transformative* learning. The effort to facilitate transformative learning is called *emancipatory education* by Mezirow.

It is apparent that transformative learning and emancipatory education take the educator beyond andragogy as traditionally defined. Mezirow's perception of the role of the adult educator is revealed in comments such as these: "Every adult educator has the responsibility for fostering critical self-reflection and helping learners plan to take action" (357). "To be an educator in this context means to be an empathic provocateur; it also means to serve as a role model for critical reflection and the ethical idea of caring and to serve as a committed co-learner and occasional guide in the exciting journey of transformative learning" (360). "Our function is to help learners critically examine the sources and consequences of their own meaning perspectives and the interpretations they have made of their own lives" (361). "The educator may know more than the learners about the subject of instruction at the outset, but he or she relearns what is known in the context of the learners' efforts to interpret these insights in terms of their own lives" (368).

Although the statements reflect views that seem to differ from the precepts of andragogy, they can be seen as logical extensions. Rather than simply accepting learners' experiences and using them as a resource, we are now to encourage a critical examination of these experiences, of the assumptions that underlie them, of the individual's interpretation of them, an examination that has, as a goal, the transformation of learner's meaning perspectives. And, as even Dewey would agree, the transformation is not complete without the learner ultimately acting on the basis of the learning. Thus, the facilitator becomes more active and also more of a co-learner than in the andragogy model. The learner's role now includes psychological change—values and beliefs are challenged, the self-concept is threatened. Mezirow states, "The axiom in adult education to 'begin where the learner is' takes on a whole new dimension from these findings" (359). In other words, we are taking a step beyond andragogy.

In addition to supporting the role of the educator in working with individual learners, Mezirow and the other contributors to his book, advocate a strong social role for the educator. Transformative learning challenges not only individual beliefs and values, but the values of the society in which the individual lives. Emancipatory education becomes a means of fighting oppression and cultural constraints. Mezirow elaborates: "As adult educators, we are committed to encourage the opening of public spheres of discourse and to actively oppose social and cultural constraints that impede free, full participation in discursive learning. Such constraints include impediments to freedom, equality, justice, democratic participation, civil and human rights, education, health, safety, shelter, and rewarding employment... Learners and educators become justifiably radicalized when societies preclude the redress of grievances, enforce unjust laws, or become oppressive in response to efforts to make institutions more responsive to the fundamental needs of learners" (1990, 375).

Through education, the "passive facilitator" that Brookfield (1986) criticized has become an active facilitator of transformative learning and a social change agent. Looking back to the ideas expressed in the beginning of this section, we see how far we have come from the educator who is primarily involved in the reinforcement of small sequential steps of learning.

In the next section, concepts proposed by various theoretical contributors to adult education will be brought together to provide a model that will guide us through the practical approaches to working with adult learners. The assumptions and principles underlying our actions as adult educators will be made explicit.

A Model for Working with Adult Learners

The previous section presented a complex array of ideas, approaches, and theoretical perspectives, and the integration of these concepts is indeed difficult. The following model is not intended to be exhaustive or comprehensive; it is not intended to be a "theory of adult education"; rather, it is meant to act as a guide to the remaining chapters in this book. It will provide an organizational framework and a means of identifying the assumptions that underlie practice (or, in Mezirow's words, our meaning perspective). The general framework within which we work can be depicted as in Figure 1.1

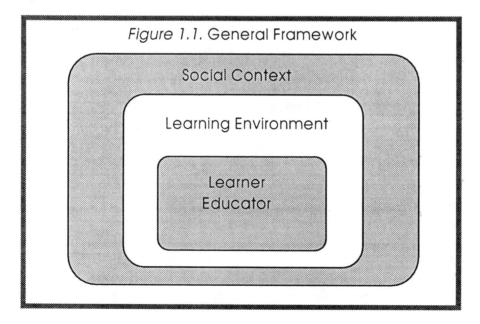

Figure 1.1. General Framework

Social Context

Learning Environment

Learner
Educator

Simply put, the learner and the educator work together within a learning environment which is itself within a social context. Not so simply, each one of these components has its own complex set of characteristics, and in addition, a process of change is continually taking place. The overall process can be depicted as in Figure 1.2.

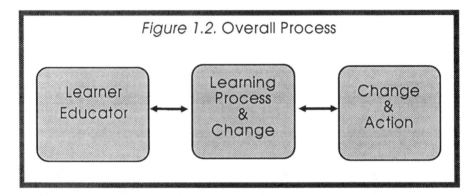

Figure 1.2. Overall Process

Learner Educator ↔ Learning Process & Change ↔ Change & Action

The learner and the educator, each with their own set of experiences, characteristics, values, and beliefs, work together in a learning process which includes change as a part of the process, with an outcome of changed thinking, values, behaviors, and actions. All of this takes place within a learning environment and within a social context.

Now, let's look in more detail at what is in each of these boxes. Both learners and educators can be described by a fairly long list of characteristics, some of which are relatively permanent, such as personality type and culture, and some of which are more likely to be affected by the learning process, such as values. The first box of Figure 1.2, which includes learner and facilitator, can be enlarged as in Figure 1.3.

The *Unaffected Characteristics* influence the learning process, but are unlikely to be changed by it. The *Affected Characteristics* influence the process and may be changed by it. "Experience" appears in both boxes, as past experience cannot actually be changed, but the learning process adds new experience and reinterprets past experience. Notice the relationships between the affected and unaffected characteristics; for example, philosophy is unlikely to change, but some of the values within it may change; life phase cannot be changed, but life stage may be changed, within that. These descriptors of learners and educators are the focus of Chapter 2.

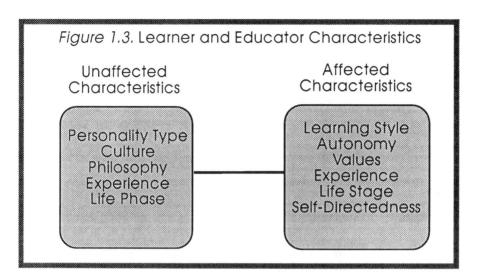

Figure 1.3. Learner and Educator Characteristics

Unaffected Characteristics

Personality Type
Culture
Philosophy
Experience
Life Phase

Affected Characteristics

Learning Style
Autonomy
Values
Experience
Life Stage
Self-Directedness

The learning process component can likewise be expanded. Though both learner and educator go through the same process, their involvement may be different. Figure 1.4 depicts the details of the process component.

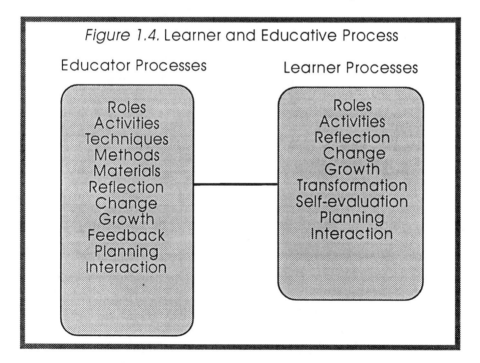

Figure 1.4. Learner and Educative Process

Educator Processes

Roles
Activities
Techniques
Methods
Materials
Reflection
Change
Growth
Feedback
Planning
Interaction

Learner Processes

Roles
Activities
Reflection
Change
Growth
Transformation
Self-evaluation
Planning
Interaction

During the learning and educative process, many different things go on. Educator and learner are engaged in various roles (co-learner, expert, model) and activities (group work, role-playing, reading). The educator implements techniques and methods, and usually provides materials or resources. Learners and educator are engaged in reflection, change, and growth. The educator provides feedback; learners evaluate their own learning. And throughout the process, all participants are involved in planning and interaction. Each of these areas will be discussed in detail in subsequent chapters.

Finally, we come to the "outcome" of the process—change and action. In the larger sense, there is no clearly defined outcome or product of learning, which is a continuous process of change and action provoking further learning and further change. However, most educators work within the confines of workshops, courses, and training sessions which do have an end and an outcome. The "change and action" box from Figure 1.2 can be expanded as is depicted in Figure 1.5.

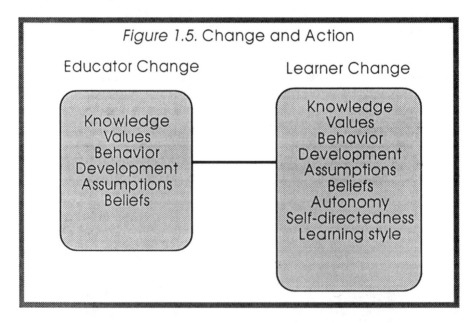

Figure 1.5. Change and Action

Educator Change

Knowledge
Values
Behavior
Development
Assumptions
Beliefs

Learner Change

Knowledge
Values
Behavior
Development
Assumptions
Beliefs
Autonomy
Self-directedness
Learning style

In this framework, both educator and learners have the potential for experiencing changes in knowledge, values, behavior, developmental stage, assumptions, and beliefs. It may be more likely that the learner will exhibit evidence of these changes than the educator, but through interaction with learners, and particularly through the co-learner role, the educator changes as well. In addition, the learner may change in autonomy, in self-directedness, and possibly in the way he or she chooses to learn (learning style). Of course, all types of changes do not take place in all learning experiences—

much depends on the content, the purpose of the session, the characteristics of the individuals involved, and the activities engaged in.

When these expanded boxes are put back into their places in Figure 1.2 and surrounded by the learning environment and social context as in Figure 1.1,

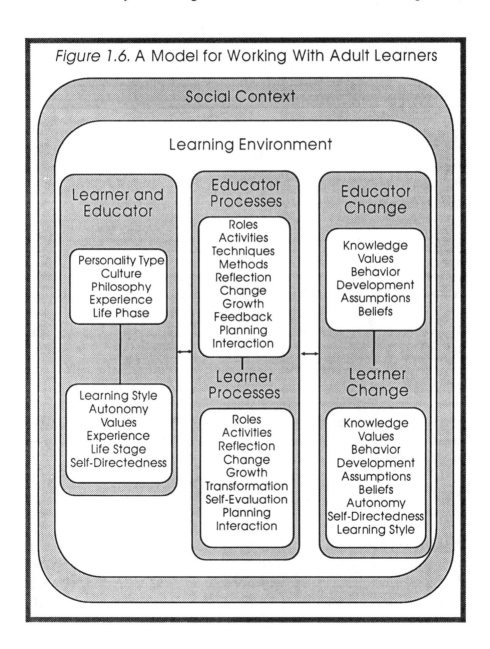

Figure 1.6. A Model for Working With Adult Learners

the complexity becomes clear. Figure 1.6 above summarizes the model for working with adult learners.

In addition, it must be remembered that each component affects the other components. For example, the characteristics of learners may influence the educator's choice of role, which in turn is related to the activities selected, and may change learner behavior, which could further influence how the educator sees his or her role. If we take the whole scenario and move it from a classroom in a college to a coffee room in a factory, it would become quite different again. Move it from rural Tennessee to downtown Toronto and it would change again.

Relation of Model to Theoretical Background

The theoretical contributions discussed earlier will be linked to the various components of the model.

Learner and Educator Characteristics

The inclusion of experience as a characteristic of adult learners is a concept that can be traced back to Dewey. The humanist psychologists discuss learning style, values, and self-directedness. Critical theorists (including Mezirow) emphasize culture, philosophy, and autonomy. Developmental psychologists point out the importance of life stages and life phases in relation to the learning process. It should be noted that behaviorism has no effect in this area, as behaviorists did not examine "the person," but rather focused on the response of an individual to stimuli. Finally, although there is a strong theoretical rationale for the concept of personality type, it was not included here as it has not previously been linked to the adult education literature. This will be discussed in Chapter 2.

Learning and Educative Process

Behaviorist psychologists advocate methods and techniques which are carefully designed to "shape" learning. The role of feedback in the learning process is also stressed by behaviorists. The humanist influence on the process can be seen in the use of group work and other interactive methods. Dewey, of course, would choose methods in which the learner is actively involved in "doing." Knowles emphasizes interactive processes, and also the mutual involvement of learner and educator in the planning process. Critical theorists stress the importance of reflection, growth, and transformative learning.

Change and Action

Different theoretical perspectives focus on different types of learning. The behaviorists are not concerned with values or cognitive processes, but only with the observable product (behavior) of such processes. Other psychologists approach learning quite differently—Rogers, for example, is primarily concerned with self-actualization and pays little attention to cognitive learning. The humanists, in general, discuss cognitive and affective learning, as well as reflection, transformative learning, and changes in self-directedness and learning style. The developmental psychologists contribute the notion that transitions in developmental stage can be facilitated by the adult educator. Questioning and changing one's assumptions, beliefs, and values are of particular interest to the critical theorists, along with the development of autonomy.

Summary

Chapter 1 has defined adult education and provided an overview of some of the major contributors to the field. In the 1990s, adult education is beginning to form an integrated body of literature, reflecting the complexity of the discipline. However, we must remember, when considering or criticizing theory development, that adult education is a very young discipline.

This chapter has also described a model for working with adult learners which will provide a framework for subsequent chapters. In Chapter 2, we turn to an examination of the characteristics of adult learners.

2
The Adult Learner

Attempting to describe the characteristics of adult learners is very much like attempting to describe the characteristics of any group of adults. Given the tremendous diversity among people, the problem seems insurmountable. Even worse, it is obviously impossible to take all learner characteristics into account when working with a group. So, it's time to be selective. The model in Figure 1.3 reminds us that there are two sets of characteristics: those that are the relatively stable traits of a person (Unaffected Characteristics), and those that are more likely to be changed as a result of experience and learning (Affected Characteristics). Among the stable traits are a multitude of experiences, cultural backgrounds, and philosophical frameworks. These are, of course, important influences on the learning process, but they are not easily categorized in a way that can guide the educator. We will return to this set of variables later in the chapter (see *Underlying Constructs,* page 57–64) and discuss them in a more general fashion. The remaining stable traits include personality type and developmental or life phase; both have a theoretical basis which will be presented and related to adult learning. Of the more changeable characteristics, autonomy (as related to culture), values, and experience are not easily categorized and hence also will be dealt with in the section, *Underlying Constructs*. Learning style, developmental or life stage, and self-directedness will be discussed in more detail here.

It should be noted that although the model lists characteristics applicable to both the learner and the educator, these are not described separately. Learners and educators are equally influenced by these variables, though the influences may have different consequences in a learning situation. In this chapter, emphasis will be on learner characteristics; the topic of educator characteristics will be dealt with more fully in Chapter 3, in the discussion of educator roles.

Psychological Type

Personality theory is a vast subject on which many divergent views have been expressed. Here the focus will be on the concept of psychological type, as introduced by Jung (1971), because of its clear and powerful influence on learning preferences and particularly on the way individuals interact with each other. As mentioned in Chapter 1, the concept of psychological type has not yet been incorporated into the adult education literature; hopefully, this section will provide an impetus for others to consider it.

Jung wrote prolifically from 1910 until his death in 1961. His book, *Psychological Types,* is the main reference here. Originally a student of Freud, Jung was an analyst whose observations of human behavior led him to break with Freud's teachings and develop his own explanation of individual differences among people. He is well known for his concept of the *collective unconscious,* our inheritance of collective ideas and feelings (e.g., God, justice, fatherland) from our past and our culture. He wrote extensively of archetypes, signs, and symbols. He produced psychiatric case studies, experimental research, analyses of Freud's work, studies of civilization, and discussions of the significance of alchemy. Written during difficult times, between the two World Wars and after World War II, and written in German, (Jung was Swiss), his work was slow to affect psychological theory. It has been only recently, with the development of instruments to assess psychological type (the best known being the Myers-Briggs Type Indicator), that Jung's work has become popular. Now, the concept of psychological type is used in training for group formation, in business and industry to facilitate people working together, and in education to increase understanding of individual differences. Some people exchange their MBTI (Myers-Briggs Type Indicator) scores upon introduction to see whether they are compatible! Within the last 10 years or so, Jung's theory of psychological type has influenced the world of training and education. Adult educators can also benefit from this understanding of human behavior.

Jung held that individuals operated in one of two basic ways within their environment. He defined "extraversion" and "introversion" as two "attitudes" (or ways of being in the world). According to Jung (1971), "extraversion is characterized by interest in the external object, responsiveness, and a ready acceptance of external happenings, a desire to influence and be influenced by events...the capacity to endure bustle and noise of every kind...constant attention to the surrounding world..." (549). The extroverted personality *constantly interacts with the environment*, an "environment" which includes people, events, objects, all that is *external* to the person. The introvert Jung finds more difficult to describe: "being directed not to the object but to the subject, and not being oriented by the object, is not so easy to put into perspective" (550). However, he states, "The introvert is not forthcoming, he (sic) is as though in continual retreat before the object...aloof from external happenings, does not join in...self-communings are a pleasure...his best work is done with his own resources, on his own initiative, and in his own way" (551). The introvert operates in an *inner world*, not through interaction with the environment. These characteristics will later be related to learning in some detail, but an example now may clarify the definitions: the extroverted person would best learn, or solve a problem, by discussing it with others or observing it take place; the introverted person would best learn by independent reflection.

Most of us have a mixture of both of these attitudes; people are never as clearly differentiated as is stated here. Yet, among our friends and acquaintances, we can easily think of the individual who cannot bear to be alone for a few days (or even a few hours) and who happily makes arrangements to fill in the time with activities. We can also find examples of the individual who prefers solitude, chooses to live in the country, and rarely turns on the television (or doesn't even have one). These are examples of extraversion and introversion as described by Jung.

In combination with the attitudes of extraversion and introversion, Jung described four "functions"—two of which are ways of making decisions and two of which are ways of perceiving the world. In one compact sentence, he defines all four: "The essential function of *sensation* is to establish that something exists, *thinking* tells us what it means, *feeling* what its value is, and *intuition* surmises whence it comes and whither it goes" (553). This requires a little more elaboration.

The decision-making functions (Jung calls them rational functions) are thinking and feeling. A person may make decisions or judgments based on a logical analysis of the situation—this is the thinking function. Or a person may make decisions based on likes and dislikes or values—this is the feeling function. The thinking type individual will say, "Give me a minute to think about it"; the feeling type individual will say, "I feel that this is the way to go."

The perceiving functions (irrational functions, to use Jung's terminology) are sensation and intuition. Sensation is the use of the five senses to perceive the world as it is. Intuition is the perception of how the world might be—the possibilities, the options, the future. The sensing type will immediately notice that you painted one wall of your house; the intuitive type will see how the house would look if you took the wall out and rearranged your furniture.

The attitudes and functions are combined. Everyone is either extroverted or introverted or some combination of the two. Likewise, every person has a dominant function. This yields eight different psychological types: extraversion with each of the four functions and introversion with each of the four functions.

The *extroverted thinking* type is an individual "whose constant endeavour...is to make all activities dependent on intellectual conclusions, which in the last resort are always oriented by objective data, whether these be external facts or generally accepted ideas" (Jung, 1971, 346–347). Interacting with the environment and using information from it, the extroverted thinking type comes to logical conclusions and brings clarity to the situation.

The *extroverted feeling* type is "likewise oriented by objective data, the object being the indispensable determinant of the quality of feeling. The extravert's feeling is always in harmony with objective values" (354). It should be noted here that by "objective" Jung means "from the object" or from the environment, as opposed to "from the subject" or from the self. This individual makes decisions based on values and feelings from the environment, or socially accepted values and feelings. He or she lives in harmony with the world and the people in it, enjoying others' company, agreeing with others, and smoothing out any conflicts that appear in the surroundings.

The *extroverted sensation* type has a "sense for objective facts (which) is extraordinarily developed. His (sic) life is an accumulation of actual experiences of concrete objects..." (363). This description may well remind the reader of Dewey. This individual operates by interacting with the environment and, in addition, uses the senses fully to perceive what *is* in that environment. Jung used the phrase "real life lived to the full" (363) to describe the life of this person.

The *extroverted intuitive* type is also "oriented by the object" but is "never to be found in the world of accepted reality-values"; instead this individual is "always seeking out new possibilities" (368) and is suffocated by stable conditions. In other words, the extroverted intuitive interacts with the environment and is focused on the possibilities for change in that environment. This individual could be a social change agent, a critical theorist, a crusader for the rights of oppressed people. (Perhaps Mezirow is an extroverted intuitive?)

The *introverted thinking* type is "strongly influenced by ideas"; however the ideas "have their origin not in objective data but in a subjective foundation" (383). This individual follows the same logical analysis as the extroverted thinking type, but does not make use of information from the environment in doing so. He or she will generate theories and come up with explanations independent of observations or data.

The *introverted feeling* type lives "principally by the subjective factor" (387). Jung finds this a difficult type to describe ("it is extremely difficult to give an intellectual account of the introverted feeling process, or even an approximate description of it..."(387)). Since the feeling process or function is primarily "inner" and not used in relationship to the environment or to others, it is not visible and one is not aware of it. Jung comments that the expression "still waters run deep" is descriptive of this individual. "As they are mainly guided by their subjective feelings, their true motives generally remain hidden" (389).

The *introverted sensation* type embodies a seeming contradiction in that the sensation function is dependent on gathering information from the environment, and the introverted attitude is inner. Jung explains, "In the introverted attitude sensation is based predominantly on the subjective component of perception" (393). This type is "guided by the intensity of subjective sensation excited by the objective stimulus" (395). We should remind ourselves here that sensation is an "irrational" function; that is, it is a perceiving function, not a decision-making function. This individual perceives stimuli from the environment, but almost as if "through a filter" (the perception is subjective). One helpful example that Jung provides is that of a painter who is an introverted sensation type—the painting would reveal the psychic mood of the painter, and only be stimulated by the environment (probably not recognizable by others).

The *introverted intuitive* type "moves from image to image, chasing after every possibility..." (400). This individual, whom Jung describes as "peculiar" (401), perceives the possibilities, the options, the visions, the "could-be" of the future, but again, because of the introverted attitude, these perceptions are subjective and inner. An example of this type is the dreamer who has endless visions of how life could be, but does not make any real attempt to bring these visions about.

The eight psychological types have been described in their "pure" form, as distinct types of people. In reality, of course, hardly anyone is a pure type. We will examine a few of the complicating factors in the theory, then relate the concept of psychological type to how adults learn. The reader is referred to Keirsey and Bates (1984) or Sharp (1987) for a fuller account. The ambitious reader is referred to Jung (1971).

Individuals have a *dominant* function. This is what has been described within each of the eight categories above. The extroverted intuitive type, for example, has intuition as the dominant function. A function for any one person may be more or less dominant; that is, I could be completely intuitive, very seldom using my sensation function; or I could be mainly intuitive, using my sensation function at some times; or I could be "undifferentiated," going back and forth between intuition and sensation. Undifferentiation is seen as a handicap or problem for the individual and those with whom he or she interacts—the switching back and forth between two opposite functions is disconcerting for all. Jung also writes of the development (in later life) of a balanced personality through the deliberate development of inferior functions; however, this is quite different from undifferentiation.

In addition to having a dominant function, each person also has an *auxiliary* function. If the dominant function is irrational (intuition or sensation), the auxiliary function will be rational (thinking or feeling). It is the second most developed function of the four functions. A person may, for example, be an introverted thinking type and have intuition as an auxiliary function. Or a person may be an extroverted feeling type and have sensation has an auxiliary function. Or any of the other combinations. Again, the auxiliary function may be strong or undifferentiated. The main point, for our purposes, is that beyond the dominant type classification of any person there is also a second function which is used for either decision-making or perception purposes. Everyone must both make decisions and perceive; these functions describe our ways of doing so.

The reader who is familiar with the Myers-Briggs Type Indicator (cf. Myers, 1960) will notice the discrepancies between this description and the results obtained from that instrument. The MBTI measures each function and attitude independently, contrary to Jung's theory of type. Jung wrote, for example, that "introverted feeling...differs quite as essentially from extroverted feeling as introverted from extroverted thinking" (387). In addition, the MBTI adds the dimension of "Judgment" versus "Perception" by means of a technique for determining whether the rational (judging) or irrational (perception) functions are dominant. The MBTI also interprets this latter factor, though Jung never refers to it as a separate characteristic.

Relation of Psychological Type to Learning

The existence of psychological type influences the way people work together in groups, solve problems, make decisions, plan their learning, and generally, learn. Overall, extroverted types will prefer to learn by interacting with their environment—talking to others or experiencing directly. Introverted types prefer to learn by inner processes, without interruption from the environment. Rational types (thinking or feeling) will learn through judgment—examining information and coming to a conclusion. Irrational types (sensing and intuition) will learn through perceptions, either of what is or what could be. We will briefly examine each of the eight types in terms of learning. The descriptions used are adapted from Cranton's and Knoop's (1990) article on psychological type and learning style.

The extroverted thinking type learns best if material is presented with logic and reason, and if this includes or is followed by an opportunity to "experience" the information in some way (doing, talking about, observing,

participating in). This individual likes to collect ideas from the world, analyze them, and present them back to the world.

The extroverted feeling type prefers interacting with others and working
in groups. This person does not work well independently and would prefer
to discuss something than to read about it. The value or the importance of
the learning may be based on the values of others or of society. Also, this
individual will try to bring harmony and good will to interactive learning
situations.

The extroverted sensation type learns by collecting information through
the senses from the environment. He or she will see learning as an accumulation of actual experiences. This person is realistic and practical, interested
in how things apply immediately to real situations. Learning for this type is
truly accomplished by doing.

The extroverted intuitive type sees learning as an active creative process.
He or she is interested primarily in the possibilities that exist in learning and
will not persist for long with routine or tedious learning tasks (such as
repetition to develop a skill). As long as there are options and possibilities,
this person will be an enthusiastic and energetic learner.

The introverted thinking type learns through an inner process of reasoning, analyzing, and understanding. External facts and experiences are only of
indirect value (e.g., to illustrate a theory developed by the learner). This
person prefers to learn by reading or listening independently and quietly
reflecting. Interacting with others is seen as a disturbance, and group work
produces anxiety.

The introverted feeling type also prefers reading or listening and does not
learn well in groups (communication skills may not be effective) unless
allowed to sit back and listen to the others interact. The subjective feeling
that guides this person's judgment may distort facts to fit the inner images.
As for the thinking type, solitary reflection time is essential to learning.

The introverted sensation type learns through perception, but perception
is distorted by the subjective element. This person may have difficulty communicating what he or she has experienced and may be misunderstood as a

learner. Group work is difficult for this person. He or she learns best by listening, reading, and experiencing individually.

The introverted intuitive type learns through inner images and visions. This person will not do well with lower level (e.g., rote) learning, and again, is not particularly good at communicating the content of the inner images to others. Hence this learner may be undervalued by others. This individual can learn by almost any strategy, as long as it triggers interest and releases images.

The reader will probably be able to see many other implications of psychological type for learning. When one becomes aware of one's own type and that of others, the possible applications become extensive. This theme will recur as we go on.

We will turn now to a more detailed look at developmental phase and its relation to how adults learn.

Developmental Phase

Although psychological type is seen to be a relatively stable individual characteristic over one's lifetime, developmental phase does change, but it changes due to age and age-related external events in a person's life. It is, therefore, a trait which is not likely to be influenced by an educational experience, but is one that has a strong influence on the learning process. Brundage and Mackeracher (1980, 52) describe developmental phase as "based largely on age-related issues in physical, social, and psychological areas." iN AppLICATioN to PROG. PLANNING.

The 1970s saw an explosion of research and writing on developmental phases. Cross (1981, 173–174) nicely integrates this work into a table, including for each phase, marker events, psychic tasks, and characteristic stance. This table is reproduced in Figure 2.1, with permission. Although one can question the particular chronological ages associated with the phases, perhaps especially for women in more recent years, the marker events and psychic tasks connected with them certainly influence the learning process. This table, used without the "phase and age" labels, in a self-awareness

Figure 2.1. Descriptions of Life-Cycle Phases

Phase and Age	Marker Events	Psychic Tasks	Characteristic Stance
Leaving Home 18–22	Leave home Establish new living arrangements Enter college Start first full-time job Select mate	Establish autonomy and independence from family Define identity Define sex role Establish new peer alliances	A balance between "being in" and "moving out" of the family
Moving into Adult World 23–28	Marry Establish home Become parent Get hired/fired/quit job Enter into community activities	Regard self as adult Develop capacity for intimacy Fashion initial life structure Build the dream Find a mentor	"Doing what one should" Living and building for the future Launched as an adult
Search for Stability 29–34	Establish children in school Progress in career or consider change Possible separation, divorce, remarriage Possible return to school	Reappraise relationships Reexamine life structure and present commitments Strive for success Search for stability, security, control Search for personal values Set long-range goals Accept growing children	"What is this life all about now that I am doing what I am supposed to?" Concern for order and stability and with "making it" Desire to set long-range goals and meet them
Becoming One's Own Person 37–42	Crucial promotion Break with mentor Responsibility for three--generation family; i.e. growing children and aging parents For women: empty nest; enter career and education	Face reality Confront mortality; sense of aging Prune dependent ties to boss, spouse, mentor Resassess marraige Reassess personal priorities and values	Suspended animation More nurturing stance for men; more assertive stance for women "Have I done the right thing? Is there time to change?"

Phase and Age	Marker Events	Psychic Tasks	Characteristic Stance
Settling Down 45–55	Cap career	Increase feelings of self-awareness and competence	"It is perhaps late, but there are things I would like to do in the last half of my life."
	Become mentor	Reestablish family relationships	Best time of life
	Launch children; become grandparents	Enjoy one's choices and life style	
	New interests and hobbies	Reexamine the fit between life structure and self	
	Physical limitations; menopause		
	Active participation in community events		
The Mellowing 57–64	Possible loss of mate	Accomplish goals in the time left to live	Mellowing of feelings and relationships
	Health problems	Accept and adjust to aging process	Spouse increasingly important
	Preparation for retirement		Greater comfort of self
Life Review 65+	Retirement	Search for integrity versus despair	Review accomplishments
	Physical decline	Acceptance of self	Eagerness to share everyday human joys, sorrows
	Change in finances	Disengagement	Family is important
	New living arrangements	Rehearsal for death of spouse	Death is a new presence
	Death of friends/spouse		
	Major shift in daily routine		

Cross, K.P. *Adults as Learners,* pp. 174–175 (Table 8). © 1981 by Jossey-Bass Inc., Publishers (San Francisco: Jossey-Bass, 1981). Reprinted with permission.

exercise for adult learners, yields useful descriptions of individuals' developmental phases. However, most often, learners' descriptions do not match their chronological ages and also do not fall consistently within one phase.

The beginning two phases include psychic tasks such as establishing autonomy, defining one's identity, defining oneself as an adult, and finding a mentor. During this time an individual becomes an adult learner, according to Knowles' (1980) definition and according to the definition from Chapter 1

(4). While passing through these phases the individual would also be taking on serious commitments and responsibilities (establishing a home, becoming a parent, starting a job) that would often interfere with or prevent participation in formal adult education settings. The next two phases involve the individual in reappraisal and reassessment, congruent with Mezirow's disorienting dilemma, which is described as providing the stimulus for learning. The *Search for Stability* phase in particular would provide impetus for learning, with its characteristic stances of: "What is this life all about now that I am doing what I am supposed to do?", concern for order and stability and with "making it," and desire to set long-range goals and meet them. Also these phases are times of searching for stability, security, control, and personal values.

The *Settling Down* and *Mellowing* periods follow the questioning phases. Psychic tasks include increasing feelings of self-awareness and competence, and enjoying one's choices and lifestyle. In addition, however, there is a reexamination of the life structure in relation to the self and a desire to accomplish goals "in the time left to live." This phase may include preparation for retirement. It is quite common to see an adult learner return to a formal educational institution for a degree, "just because it's something I've always wanted to do and now I can." Such a person is characteristic of this developmental phase. The last phase, which includes retirement in Cross's integration, has the search for integrity versus despair as a psychic task and a review of accomplishments as a characteristic stance. Increasingly, individuals pursue new careers in retirement and further their formal education.

As was discussed above and in Chapter 1, the developmental phases should not be viewed as rigid categories that everyone passes through at particular times. Although different phases are clearly related to aging and maturation, these vary considerably from one person to another, from one community to another, and from one culture to another. The developmental psychologists express varying opinions about the rigidity of phases—some arguing that while the rate of passage through the phases may vary, the sequence remains constant, and others proposing that external factors play a large part in the progression of phases. Research indicates that life transitions, such as marriage and job change, act as a prime motivator for adult learning (cf. Aslanian & Brickell, 1980). And, as was discussed in Chapter 1, theorists such as Mezirow (1977) incorporate the transition from one phase to another into the description of the adult learning cycle. Cross (1981, 235) has developed a model called CAL (Characteristics of Adults as Learners): A Conceptual Framework. In this model, under the personal characteristics of adult learners, she includes "physiological/aging," "sociocultural/life phases," and "psychological/developmental stages." The educator should be aware of the developmental phases and their influence on readiness to learn, but should never attempt to pigeonhole learners.

Relation of Developmental Phase to Learning

Some adult education literature discusses developmental phases primarily in terms of adaptation to the learner (better lighting and larger print for the older adult, and so on). However, examining how the phases might relate to learning preferences rather than "how to compensate for deteriorating physical abilities" is probably a more productive tack.

Brundage and Mackeracher (1980, 53) state, "In learning terms, these major transitions probably respond best to learning experiences which allow the individual the time to explore personal meanings and values and to transform these into meanings and values more in keeping with current reality." In addition, they suggest that during the stable times, between transition periods, individuals will be reintegrating and consolidating: learning will be related to knowledge, skills, and attitudes which enhance current roles.

The simplest way to relate developmental phases to learning is to note that the transition periods between phases produce high motivation for learning. In addition, the characteristics of specific phases may lead to particular types of learning. During the earlier phases of establishing autonomy, the learner learns how to become self-directed, explores various life and career options, builds interpersonal relationships, and is likely to model him or herself after a mentor. During the middle phases, the individual can change careers (or develop interest in further education or retraining to lead to a change); reexamine skills, interests, attitudes, beliefs, and values; determine personal values and goals; and be more likely to transform meaning perspectives. During later phases, the adult might pursue goals and interests for which time was previously lacking, adjust to the aging process, reexamine the chosen life structure, prepare for retirement (and develop interests for that period), or enter into another career and become interested in obtaining the relevant knowledge and skills.

In other words, different learning interests and processes may appear during different life phases. The use made of this information by the educator will, of course, depend on the context within which he or she is working, but in every situation, the developmental phases of learners will be related in some way to the learning taking place.

From here, we will move to explore learner characteristics which are more likely to be affected by the learning experience itself but which, at the same time, influence the process of learning. The first of these will be learning style.

Learning Style

When discussing the concept of learning style, several different approaches are apparent. Thus, the terminology used can be confusing: some authors use "cognitive style" as a synonym for "learning style," and others distinguish between the two. Here, we will take cognitive style to mean an individual's preferences for ways of intellectually processing information, and learning style to mean an individual's preferences for ways of learning. Although these clearly overlap when the content of the learning is cognitive, learning style provides a more general framework and is therefore more appropriate for our purposes.

Kolb's (1984) model of learning style represents one of the best known approaches. His work will be described, followed by some of the criticism it has received. We will then examine some approaches to learning style which are based on the way individuals interact.

Kolb's Theory of Learning Style

Kolb proposes that there are four stages involved in learning:

* concrete experience, or being involved in a new experience;

- reflective observation—observing others in an experience, or developing observations about our own experience;

- abstract conceptualization—creating concepts and theories to explain our observations; and,

- active experimentation—using the theories to solve problems and make decisions.

These four stages form a learning cycle, through which most people proceed when engaged in learning. Kolb then argues that through experience, or because of our needs and goals (or psychological type?), individuals come to emphasize or prefer one stage of the learning cycle more than the others. A nurse, for example, may most often learn through the active experimentation stage, whereas a university professor may most often learn through abstract conceptualization. Kolb found that the abilities associated with each of the stages combine to form clusters. This leads to his delineation of learning styles.

Individuals who rely on abstract conceptualizing and active experimentation are called *convergers*. When presented with a problem or a learning task, a converger likes to come quickly to a specific concrete solution. He or she is unemotional, and prefers working with ideas or things to working with people.

People who use abstract conceptualizing and reflective observation are labeled *assimilators*. They like to integrate ideas into models and theories, but are relatively uninterested in the application of the theories in real life. Assimilators learn best by reading, listening, observing, and reflecting on the information gained.

Accommodators use concrete experience and active experimentation to learn. They are the "doers," those who prefer to learn by experience. These individuals take risks and perform well in situations where they must adapt to circumstances. They would prefer to take a trial and error approach rather than read the instructions first.

People who use concrete experience and reflective observation are called *divergers*. They generate ideas, are good at brainstorming, and most often enjoy interacting with people. Divergers are not quick to come to a solution;

they like to explore all of the possibilities and may have trouble focusing in on a task.

When given a specific task and working in like-learning style groups, individuals will behave in ways indicative of their style. The convergers will quickly focus in on the task and be the first group to finish. Assimilators will often work out a model as a solution and will integrate all information given for the task. Accommodators will experiment with countless solutions; for example, they might fill the blackboard or chart paper with phrases and arrows. Divergers will talk. Quite often, divergers will not produce a written solution, nor address the task as it is presented. And all groups will inevitably have a good time and comment on the harmony of the group and the nice people that they worked with or met.

Kolb's learning style analysis seems to provide a powerful predictor of learning behavior. It also should be noted here, that although researchers have not addressed this question, learning style seems to be related to psychological type. Convergers appear to resemble thinking/sensing types; assimilators, thinking/intuitive types; accommodators possibly resemble sensing types; and divergers, intuitive/feeling types. If these relationships do exist, it would imply that there may be more than the four learning styles described by Kolb.

Learning style can be easily assessed by Kolb's Learning Style Inventory (1976). The instrument requires individuals to rank four words within each of nine sets. Each word is related to one of the four stages of the learning cycle. The sums of the ranks are then charted onto a matrix which gives the learning style profile of the individual.

It is easy to imagine the implications of this learning style model for working with learners. Convergers would enjoy solving problems with specific "correct" answers. Assimilators would prefer to observe and integrate ideas. Accommodators would be good participants in role-playing, group work, simulations, and field experiences. Divergers would enjoy brainstorming, discussion groups, and generating ideas. In fact, Kolb's research has shown that people with different learning styles can be found in different professions, matching their preferences.

Kolb has been criticized as providing a model which is too "neat and perhaps over-simple" (Jarvis, 1987, 18). It has been suggested that the stages of the cycle need not occur in the sequence which Kolb describes—active experimentation can be immediately followed by reflective observation, or the two can occur "almost simultaneously" (18). Also, Kolb does not take into account changes that occur in the learner as the result of an experience which may then influence the learner's behavior in the next similar experience. Jarvis (1987, 19) indicates that the measure of learning style may not be consistent from one time to another for an individual; however reliability studies do show a strong stability for the instrument. It could also be argued, in response to Jarvis, that learning style is not necessarily a permanent trait. For example, adult learners who have left their profession and returned to graduate school will often report that their learning style profile is different than it was "a few years ago, when I was working as..." Learning style is a *preference*, not a personality characteristic, and preferences are susceptible to change. If this is the case, the relationship between learning style and psychological type would be more complex; interesting research questions arise from this possibility.

Social Interaction Models

A valuable perspective on learning style, perhaps particularly for adult education, is to consider the ways in which learners interact with each other and with an educator or facilitator. Two approaches will be described, each of which can be assessed with a relatively simple instrument. As they were developed for use with college students, the language reflects an instructor-centered approach—both instruments use the terms "teacher" and "student."

Fuhrmann and Jacobs (1980) propose three interaction styles:

- dependence—refers to the learner's expectation that the educator is primarily responsible for the learning that occurs (e.g., the adult returning to complete a secondary school course expects the teacher to outline the requirements and provide the information);

- collaboration—refers to the learner's expectation that the responsibility for learning should be shared by learners and educator (e.g., the auto mechanic with many years of experience who attends a program to update himself on a new technological development expects to work together with the instructor and experiment with the equipment); and,

- independence—refers to the learner's expectation that he or she will set and attain individual goals (e.g., the graduate student writing a thesis proposal expects to be responsible for her own goals, using the educator as a consultant).

Data were collected on undergraduate and graduate students in fifteen higher education institutions. The authors state that no one style is "better" than another, but they do note that in their research there were few dependent older or more advanced learners. (This finding reminds us of the learner characteristic of self-directedness, which will be discussed in a later section of this chapter.)

The instrument to assess the Fuhrmann-Jacobs learning styles contains 36 items. Each style is measured by 12 of the statements. To assess the learning style, a learner is asked to consider a learning experience which was "personally positive" and then respond to the statements as they apply to that learning experience.

A model developed by Riechmann and Grasha (1974) is similar, but includes six styles:

- competition—the learner competes with others for the "rewards of the classroom" (the person who asks peers "what did you get?" when assignments are returned);

- collaboration—the individual prefers sharing ideas and working with others (the person who sets up a study group to meet once a week);

- avoidance—the individual is not interested in learning or participating (the person who arrives late, misses sessions, and sits in the back of the room with a vacant expression);

- participation—the learner takes responsibility for getting the most out of class and activities, but does not go beyond the prescribed content (the person who discusses, asks questions, and willingly engages in projects, but never looks at the supplemental reading list);

- dependence—the learner looks to authority for guidelines and prefers to be told what to do (the person who asks "how many pages?" and "single spaced or double spaced?"); and,

- independence—the individual prefers to work on his or her own (the person who rarely consults the educator or peers but is actually involved in his or her own learning projects).

To assess these styles, learners respond to 90 items on a five-point scale (agree to disagree); the scale produces six sub-scores, one for each of the six styles. Again, unfortunately, the language of the scale is not appropriate for some adult education settings, but the content of the model is interesting and has potential for use with adult learners. Undoubtedly, all of us have encountered adult learners who look to us as authority figures; as well, avoidant learners occasionally appear in adult groups (perhaps due to mandatory attendance). It is useful for the educator to be aware of these styles rather than assuming that all adult learners are self-directed and independent.

Learning style is clearly a critical learner characteristic—the way in which individuals prefer to and best learn seems to vary markedly from person to person. If learning experiences are centered around one particular style, for example, interaction in small groups, then it is likely that at least some participants will not be learning in the most effective way for them. While the available learning style models and assessment devices may not be completely comprehensive (as has been mentioned above), the concept itself cannot be ignored for that reason. Possibly, further research on psychological type will lead to the application of type to learning style and provide educators with a sound basis for consideration of individual differences in learning preferences.

We will now turn to the characteristic of developmental stage; as is becoming clear, each of the characteristics being discussed is related to the others, yielding a complex picture of the differences among adult learners.

Developmental Stage

The reader will remember from Chapter 1 that developmental stage is the movement from simple or child-like ways of being to a complex, integrated awareness of the self. Rogers (1969) talks about self-actualization; Jung (1971) writes about "individuation"; Loevinger (1976) describes ego development. There are many models of developmental stages, but all move from a simplistic to a complex understanding of the self and the world.

Many of the ideas discussed so far are related to developmental stage. Mezirow's transformative learning, for example, clearly facilitates adult development. Knox (1986) writes: "A developmental perspective helps explain how adults acquire their learning style, what prompts learning activities, and how teaching style can both accommodate learning style and guide its further evolution" (21). We will review the concept of developmental stage, as it is related to learning.

In Chapter 1, Loevinger's (1976) stages of ego development were listed; this theory is probably the best-known general explanation of human growth over the life span. Before moving to approaches that are more specific to learning, Jung's contribution will be briefly described, as it provides an interesting view of individual development within the social context and relates to the previous section on psychological type.

Jung (1971, 448) writes of individuation: "The concept of individuation plays a large role in our psychology. In general, it is the process by which individual beings are formed and differentiated; in particular, it is the development of the psychological individual as being distinct from the general, collective psychology. Individuation, therefore, is a process of differentiation having for its goal the development of the individual personality." Jung proposes that a society must maintain its internal cohesion and collective values, but at the same time must grant the individual the freedom to develop individually. The process of individuation leads to "more intense and broader collective relationships and not to isolation" (448). By putting individual personality development into the context of the social group, Jung provides a framework which better supports the work of adult educators such as Brookfield and Mezirow than do the works of other developmental theorists. Jung argues that before individual development can become a goal, "the educational aim of adaptation to the necessary minimum of collective norms must first be attained...if a plant is to unfold its specific nature to the full, it must first be able to grow in the soil in which it is planted" (449). The individual, then, cannot be directly opposed to the social group norms, but the goal of individual development is not the same as the norm of the social group.

Unfortunately, for educators and psychologists today, Jung did not articulate specific stages nor provide descriptions of this developmental process. Nevertheless, the inclusion of the "collective norm" or the social group is a concept which we cannot overlook in our consideration of developmental stage.

We will examine two more practical contributions. Perry (1970) addressed developmental stage on the basis of observations of undergraduate students; his model, therefore, is closely related to the learning process. It should be noted that Perry's description is based primarily on data collected from males. Like other learning theories, in Perry's model the learner moves from perceiving the world in black-and-white terms, through several stages, to perceiving a relativistic world. He defines nine stages or "positions." To illustrate these stages, which are listed below, one situation will be used as an example throughout (learners studying Research Methods), with reactions to this situation varying according to the learner's developmental stage.

- The learner sees the world in terms of right and wrong, good and bad. Right answers exist for everything, are known by authority figures, and can be obtained through learning. The learner at this stage says, "If I read enough and study hard, I will learn everything about research design and do well."

- The learner recognizes that diversity of opinion and uncertainty exist, but still believes that a right answer can be obtained through solving the problem and learning. The learner at this point thinks, "Though there seem to be contradictions in different research books, I just have to find the true authority."

- The learner accepts diversity as legitimate, but thinks of it as temporary in a sense—the researchers and experts have just not yet found the answers. The learner believes, "There are some differences of opinion among authorities. Some people say qualitative research is better, and others say quantitative research is better, but they will work these differences out and find the truth."

- The learner realizes that diversity of opinion is found in most areas, and comes to think of that diversity as the knowledge base (the right answer). The learner realizes, "In choosing a research method, there are no right answers; I have to work out my own opinion."

- The learner perceives knowledge and values as contextual. The learner says, "It all depends on the context in which you are using research methods; everything is relative."

- The learner realizes that he or she must "choose a side" or find an orientation through making a personal commitment. The learner says, "I can see I'm going to have to make up my own mind; I'll have to decide whether I prefer qualitative or quantitative research."

- The learner makes an initial commitment in an area. The learner reports, "Well, I've made my first commitment; I'm going to use a qualitative research design for my own thesis."

- The learner experiences the implications of commitment, particularly the issue of responsibility. At this stage the learner wonders, "But if I have committed myself to qualitative research, I may never learn about other approaches. Am I limiting myself?"

- The learner experiences an affirmation of identity and sees the commitment made as an expression of lifestyle. This learner decides, "Well, I really *do* want to be a qualitative researcher; I plan to go on to further studies and into an academic career in an area that calls for qualitative research methods."

In his research, Perry rarely observed the higher developmental stages among undergraduate students, though they occurred more frequently among graduate students. The stages have not been investigated among adult learners in other settings. The main consideration here for the adult educator is the movement away from the right/wrong perspective (with the authority figure having "the answer") toward a personal commitment to a position in a world where there are many possible opinions. This transition is rather like the fostering of self-directed learning, to be discussed in the next section.

Kohlberg (cf. Kohlberg & Turiel, 1971) is well known for his work on moral development. He also proposes a set of hierarchical levels from simple to complex perceptions of the world:

- premoral stage—"good" is pleasant, and "bad" is painful or fearful;

- preconventional level—good and bad are labeled according to punishments and rewards received for behavior;

- conventional level—expectations of the family or cultural group are perceived as valuable, and the individual is loyal to these expectations; and,

- postconventional, autonomous, or principled level—there is a clear effort to define moral values and principles which have validity and application apart from the authority of the family or culture.

Within each of these levels (except the premoral), two stages are identified which provide a more detailed description of the content of the level. A review of these stages is not necessary for our present discussion; the interested reader should consult Kohlberg's writings.

Kohlberg's model has been used extensively for research with children and has provided a basis for curriculum development for schools for many years. For our purposes, once again we have seen emphasis on the developmental process as one of moving away from accepting authority, through questioning of assumptions and values, to defining one's own values and principles in a complex world.

An understanding of developmental stages serves two purposes: providing an awareness of the characteristics of those learners we work with, and providing goals for learners' growth. We can take this latter purpose one step further and say, as does Mezirow, that it is the responsibility of the educator to challenge and stimulate learners in order to encourage transition to higher levels of development.

In the next section, we will investigate the concept of self-directedness, a key concept in the adult education literature. It has been clear, throughout the preceding sections, that self-directedness is related to a host of other individual characteristics; this relationship will be examined in our discussion.

Self-Directedness

One of the fundamental assumptions underlying Knowles' model of andragogy is that adult learners prefer to be self-directed. This concept has permeated adult education literature and practice to such a point that adult education almost is equated with self-directed learning. Unfortunately, the definitions of self-directed learning in the literature now vary considerably. Some of the "beyond andragogy" writers have questioned Knowles' original assumption, but before coming to that argument, his understanding of the meaning of self-directedness and its implications will be reviewed.

In his writings, Knowles (for example, 1980) states that self-directed learning involves the learner in: setting objectives, designing strategies to meet those objectives, carrying out a learning plan, and collecting evaluative evidence of the accomplishment of the objectives. In his book, *The Adult Learner: A Neglected Species* (revised, 1984), Knowles lists eight facets of self-directed learning, including:

- The ability to develop and be in touch with curiosities. Perhaps another way to describe this skill would be "the ability to engage in divergent thinking."

- The ability to perceive oneself objectively and accept feedback nondefensively about one's performance.

- The ability to diagnose one's learning needs in the light of models of competencies required for performing life roles.

- The ability to formulate learning objectives in terms that describe performance outcomes.

- The ability to identify human, material, and experiential resources for accomplishing various kinds of learning objectives.

- The ability to design strategies for effectively making use of appropriate learning resources.

- The ability to carry out a learning plan systematically and sequentially. This skill is the beginning of the ability to engage in convergent thinking.

- The ability to collect evidence of the accomplishment of learning objectives and have it validated through performance.

These skills are obviously not ones which the average adult brings to a learning experience. We will return to this point later.

Knowles strongly believes that adults see themselves as responsible for their own decisions and that this perception leads to the development of a "deep psychological need to be seen by others and treated by others as being capable of self-direction" (revised, 1984, 56). He is aware that this often does not appear to be the case, that when adults enter an educational setting, they associate the activity with their early school experiences and expect to be "taught." However, Knowles argues (revised, 1984, 56–57) that if educators assume that this initial behavior really reflects their learners' attitudes and behave accordingly, "we create a conflict within them between their intellectual model—learner equals dependent—and the deeper, perhaps subconscious, psychological need to be self-directing." Learning experiences must be created to help adults make the transition from dependent to self-directed learning.

It is important to note that Knowles does *not* say that all adult learners are self-directed—he is often misunderstood on this point by practitioners—but rather that adults have a *need* to be self-directed learners, and that it is our job to facilitate this process.

From this analysis, we can easily see that self-directedness is a learner characteristic that relates to the other characteristics that have been discussed previously. For example, some psychological types may be more likely to prefer self-direction than others (some beginning research conducted by Herbeson (1990) supports this). Direct connections are apparent between self-directedness and developmental phase: the "psychic tasks" listed in Figure 2.1 include establishing independence, setting goals, and setting priorities. Learning style may be related to self-directedness: it's easier to imagine self-directed divergers than convergers, for example. And the social interaction models of learning style actually parallel the definition of self-directed learning. Finally, developmental stage is clearly related—the early stages are directly opposed to self-direction with their reliance on authority, while the more complex stages require self-direction.

Self-directedness, in combination with other characteristics of a learner, is clearly an important part of the picture of an individual. Self-directedness can even be seen to be an outcome of several other characteristics. Perhaps the degree of self-directedness can be predicted from examining a combination of other variables, such as psychological type, developmental stage, and learning style.

All goes well up to this point. If we stay with Knowles' description, we can accept the need for self-directedness as a characteristic of adults, the development of self-directedness as a possible goal for adult education, and the ability of adults to obtain these skills as a predictable variable. However, in the literature and in practice several difficulties have arisen with the concept of self-directedness. These will be explored next.

Self-Directedness Dilemmas

As was mentioned at the beginning of this section, the definitions of self-directed learning .vary considerably in the literature. But this is only a symptom of the fundamental problems that exist with the concept.

Knowles' definition includes a set of behaviors exhibited by learners: writing objectives, selecting strategies, carrying them out, evaluating. In other words, self-directed learning involves the *planning* of learning, or in a sense, the planning of instruction for oneself. However, this is not included in the usual definition of learning. Brookfield (1986) points out that some of the confusion rests with the use of "learning" as a noun (change in behavior, knowledge, etc.) or as a verb (the cognitive process). He suggests that learning should only be used as a noun, which leads us to a term such as "self-directed educating" to describe the planning behaviors in Knowles' definition.

If we think of self-directed learning as a cognitive process, we would then expect it to be related to other similar variables such as "field independence" (independent of context) or "internal locus of control" (responsible for one's own actions). In the research this has not been demonstrated, and some research results imply quite the opposite trend; that is, that successful self-directed learners are "context bound" and that they rely on others extensively for information and feedback (Brookfield, 1986, 43). The view of self-directed learning as a planning process does not hold up either. Danis and Tremblay (1985) found that "successful self-directed learners" did not follow a pre-determined plan, or anything resembling the process that Knowles prescribes.

If we follow the path of defining the noun, "learning," we must then consider self-directed learning as a change in knowledge, behavior, or values. Brookfield (1986, 47) suggests that this leads to self-directed learning occurring when "learners come to regard knowledge as relative and contextual, to view the value frameworks and moral codes informing their behaviors as cultural constructs, and to use this altered perspective to contemplate ways in which they can transform their personal and social worlds." This sounds very similar to the higher level developmental stages and is far removed from the process that is implemented by most practitioners. This definition, however, should be kept in mind as we continue to examine the concept.

The next dilemma arises from the use of the word "self-directed." In a sense, all learning is done by the "self," no one can force anyone to learn, and if an individual chooses to attend lectures or to interact with a community group, this process is "self-directed." In an attempt to avoid this problem, some definitions of self-directed learning imply that it is independent or autonomous learning. These too lead us into a trap. Learning can never be truly "autonomous," as some information from the environment is required. Reading a book is receiving information from another person. Even self-reflection, alone in a quiet room, will be related to some event or experience or set of ideas that have been stimulated by the environment. Learning cannot occur in isolation—a person put into a box for several years and deprived of all stimulation would not learn very much.

Self-directed learning, then, still requires information to be obtained from and interaction to occur with others. What is left to differentiate self-directed learning from other-directed learning? We're back to the planning process that Knowles describes, except that it seems that people do not actually do this.

An individual who is planning his or her own learning first of all needs planning skills (such as the eight skills listed by Knowles), and second, enough knowledge about the subject to be learned to know what to learn. If one or both of these attributes are absent, self-directed learning cannot occur. Even if the learner has planning skills and familiarity with the area, he or she can be restricted by not being familiar with alternative perspectives or theories or approaches. For example, as a fruit farmer, I may be familiar with chemical pest-control and be able to plan my learning so as to improve my farming, be able to find resources, and judge the effectiveness of my learning by increased productivity, but I may not be aware of or consider another perspective which might lead me to learn about organic pest-control. Interaction with other learners may overcome this disadvantage to some extent, but, in the end, it seems obvious that the learner needs access to "expert" resources, whether people themselves or books written by people or videotapes made by people.

Unfortunately, in the literature, self-directedness has become an answer to the question, "what is different about how adults learn?" It is held to be a unique and constant trait of adult learners. While it may be difficult to uproot this view, the educator must be *aware* of the difficulties inherent in this description of adults. Self-directedness is not a variable which has been observed and verified as a characteristic of adults. However, we may view it as a goal of adult education, if we accept the definition from Brookfield, given above.

This brings us to one last dilemma. Most research on self-directed learning has been conducted in one of two ways: interviewing learners on the nature of the process involved in their "learning projects" (following Tough's (1979) model); or measuring self-directedness with an instrument based on Knowles' definition (such as Guglielmino's (1977) Self-Directed

Learning Readiness Scale). In addition, nearly all the research has been conducted on samples of middle-class learners with high levels of education. In other words, even the things that we do "know" about self-directed learning, based on research, do not pertain to the majority of the population and are related to specific definitions of self-directedness (which must be questioned).

A New Understanding?

Let's return to Brookfield (1986) for a final word: "At its [self-directed learning's] heart is the notion of autonomy, which is defined as the possession of an understanding and awareness of a range of alternative possibilities. Hence, self-directed learning is predicated upon adults' awareness of their separateness and their consciousness of their personal power. When they come to view their personal and social worlds as contingent and therefore accessible to individual and collective interventions, then the internal disposition necessary for self-directed action exists. When adults take action to acquire skills and knowledge in order to effect these interventions, then they are exemplifying principles of self-directed learning. They are realizing their autonomy in the act of learning and investing that act with a sense of personal meaning" (58).

We now have, rather than a mechanical process in which the adult designs a learning program, a combination of process and reflection which empowers the individual. Taking this view leads us to see self-direction not as a characteristic of a learner, but rather as a process through which a learner goes and which leads to change and growth in the individual.

Although the last thing needed is yet another definition of self-directed learning, it is necessary to untangle the ball of string with which we are working and make clear the assumptions about self-directed learning upon which subsequent chapters will be based. It will be assumed that:

- self-directedness is not "a characteristic" of adult learners;
- individuals may be more or less capable of undertaking a self-directed learning *process,* depending on other of their characteristics;

Figure 2.2. Distinguishing Characteristics of Self-Directed Learning

Self-directed learning occurs when...	Other-directed learning occurs when...
• the learner chooses to learn, including entering a formal course	• someone else, e.g. employer, family, dictates learning
• the learner consciously changes behavior, values, knowledge, etc. as a result of the experience	• the learner is brainwashed or manipulated
• the learner makes choices as to how to apply, what to read, what to observe, what to do	
• the learner is conscious of change and growth and can describe this	
• the learner is free to speak, listen, interact, consult	• the learner's freedom is curtailed by another
• the learner is free to challenge or question information received	• the learner is not free to challenge or question

- individuals may be more or less capable of undertaking self-directed *learning,* depending on their planning skills and their knowledge of the area;

- self-directed learning is a process which involves reliance on others and/or information from the environment, including, directly or indirectly, other people;

- an educator can stimulate, encourage, and facilitate the self-directed learning process;

- self-directed learning can be seen as both a process of growth (which the educator can facilitate) and a product of that growth (change in values, skills, and behaviors); and,

- self-directed learning is one goal of adult education.

Given these assumptions, what distinguishes self-directed learning from other-directed learning?

As can be seen in Figure 2.2 above, it becomes difficult to describe "pure" other-directed learning, or rather to list distinguishing features of other-directed learning. When the learner *chooses* to enter a learning situation and chooses to stay in it, regardless of the characteristics of the situation a self-directed learning process can be taking place for that individual. In this case, however, the "product" of self-directedness (an increase in this attribute) may not be enhanced.

The following summary statement will provide our working definition as we proceed:

> Self-directed learning is the process of voluntarily engaging in a learning experience, being free to think or act as an individual during that experience, being free to reflect on that experience, and being able to discern change or growth as a result of the experience, regardless of the setting in which it occurs.

And on that note, the concept of self-directed learning will be left for the time being, and we will turn, in the final section of this chapter, to a discussion of more general learner variables, including experience, philosophy, values, and autonomy.

Underlying Constructs

Each individual learner is a complex product of the variety of experiences he or she has undergone, of the philosophy which guides behavior, of values held, of the autonomy which exists in the life, social group, or culture of the individual, and numerous other influences or components of the person's background. This amorphous collection of individual characteristics cannot be categorized or typed and measured, yet its effect on learning is profound. These characteristics are rather like constructs, a synthesis or integration of numerous small pieces, which can then be used to explain the individual. And they are underlying in that they often are not visible, talked about, or even in the conscious mind of the individual. The best that the educator can hope to do is to have an awareness and understanding of the possible underlying constructs which explain and influence learner behavior. To illustrate with a simple example—an educator who leads workshops on writing skills for undergraduate students finds herself with a mixture of Vietnamese students, "mature" students (as labeled by the institution), and what appear to be ordinary first-year students concerned about their writing ability. She proceeds with self-diagnosis, group work, and peer feedback in her workshop, only to discover that the Vietnamese students cannot accept her role of "facilitator" rather than teacher, the "mature" students are too nervous to talk, and the "ordinary" students want practical hints on writing papers. It is, in this example, the past experience, philosophy, values, and expectations of autonomy that influence the behavior and learning of the participants.

Each of these four underlying constructs will be discussed briefly, with full knowledge that there are other constructs that influence the learning process.

Experience

Everyone has had educational experiences, work experiences, social and cultural experiences, personal experiences, spiritual experiences, and the practical experiences of daily living. And yet most of us have been in learning situations where no one thought to ask us if we had any experiences relevant to the topic, or where we had no opportunity to bring our own experiences into the conversation, and we felt the frustration of that missing link in the learning.

Using experience as a *way* of learning (beginning with Dewey) and using experience as a *resource* for learning (Knowles) are two fundamental concepts in adult education. As these concepts are primarily to do with techniques or the structuring of learning experiences, we will set them aside for now and return to them in later chapters. What will be summarized here are some of the ways in which experience influences or shapes the individual and hence the individual's learning. We cannot describe "experience" as it is not a trait, but rather a uniquely formed collection of events, interactions, and thoughts.

One of the most promising ways of looking at the role of experience in adult learning is through the writing and research on reflection. At first glance, this may seem to be an odd connection, but it can be argued that it is through reflection that experience contributes to learning. A book edited by Boud, Keogh and Walker (1985), entitled *Reflection: Turning Experience into Learning*, explores this approach in a comprehensive manner. An experience is seen as containing behaviors, ideas, and feelings. The process of reflection, which is a key component of learning, includes returning to an experience, using the positive ideas and feelings involved, examining and removing ideas or feelings which are obstacles to learning, and reevaluating the experience. The outcome is a new perspective on the experience, a change in behavior, and a plan of action. It is the content of an initial experience, then, and the learner's reactions to it, which form the basis for reflection and learning from the experience.

This role of experience and its influence on learning appears in many places in the literature. We reviewed, earlier, Kolb's view of learning style which, the reader will remember, included a learning cycle where concrete experience was followed by observation and reflection, abstract conceptualization, and active experimentation.

Mezirow's (1990) concept of transformative learning is based on the analysis and questioning of underlying assumptions (or meaning perspectives) which come from an individual's past experiences.

Regardless of the nature of the experiences (personal, professional, educational, etc.), they shape the way individuals understand the world around them, the assumptions they make, the beliefs they hold, and the knowledge they have. In the process of new learning, or change and growth and transformation, previous experiences form a foundation. In this sense it is impossible to "ignore" previous experiences—no matter what the learning situation, experience will underlie it. What must be recognized is the necessity of making previous experience explicit, and then working with it in any learning situation. This can be a process engaged in solely by the learner, or a mutual process engaged in by the learner and educator.

Philosophy

"We are philosophically numb, concerned with the design of ever more sophisticated needs assessment techniques, program planning models, and evaluative procedures. It seems not to have occurred to us that the perfection of technique can only be meaningful when placed within a context of some fundamental human or social purpose" (Brookfield, 1986, 289).

Although Brookfield is actually discussing the importance of the educator developing a philosophy of practice, the lack of attention to philosophy is not restricted to this area. Looking up "philosophy" in the indices of any of a stack of adult education books will yield little or nothing. And yet the philosophical framework within which the adult learner thinks and behaves is a key component of their individual make-up and therefore of their learning process.

According to Webster's New World Dictionary (1988), a philosophy is a "theory or logical analysis of the principles underlying conduct, thought, knowledge...; a particular system of principles for the conduct of life..." An individual's philosophy, whether articulated or not, becomes an important variable in the learning process. Perhaps the simplest way to integrate philosophy into what we have done so far is to view it in terms of Mezirow's approach to transformative learning.

Mezirow describes transformative learning as based on the reassessment of the perspectives or assumptions formed in childhood. What we are interested in here is the nature of the learner's "system of principles for the conduct of life" and the relevance to the educator of being aware of differing philosophies. Mezirow (1990, 14–17) describes three types of "distortions" that occur in adults' perspectives. The use of the word "distortion" refers to deviation from vision of the "ideal" perspective, and may be too strong a word. What he actually describes are the types of *influences* on a person's system of understanding the world. These influences will provide a useful way for us to examine learners' philosophical frameworks.

Epistemic influences have to do with the way the learner views knowledge. ("Epistemic" simply means "related to knowledge.") When we discussed developmental stages, we described individuals who viewed knowledge as black-and-white or right and wrong, and those who viewed knowledge as more relative and changeable. This view provides a strong influence on (or distortion of) a learner's system of principles. If someone believes, for example, that "because it is a law" it is right, or "because it has always been that way, that's the way it is" or "because the President or Prime Minister said so, it has to be that way," this yields a profoundly different way of understanding the world than does a critical and questioning approach to knowledge. In a learning environment will be the individual who wants the "right answer" from the educator, and the individual who challenges everything she or he reads or hears. (In addition, many will be found somewhere along this continuum between the two extremes.)

Sociocultural influences and distortions are those that "pertain to power and social relationships, especially those currently prevailing and legitimized and enforced by institutions" (Mezirow, 1990, 15). Assumptions or beliefs about individuals that are based on race, gender, or culture are prime examples of this type of influence. The unquestioning acceptance of any social norms would be relevant here—and many individuals' philosophies of life are based in large part on the acceptance of social norms. When over 70% of the population of Britain supported Britain's participation in the war on Iraq, the influence of social norms was undoubtedly demonstrated. In the learning environment, sociocultural influences are encountered in seemingly infinite ways—from the unquestioned acceptance of male-dominated discussion groups to the belief in the power of the educational institution or system itself.

Psychic influences are events of childhood or later traumatic events which determine the ways in which individuals conduct their present life situations. Although working with the consequences of a traumatic event may be the job of a therapist or counsellor rather than an educator, it is important that the educator have an awareness of this area as well. Changing careers or losing a job and enroling in a retraining program may well be traumatic for learners, and the educator will be in the middle of this situation. At the very least, the behavior of any learner is a product of psychic influences on his or her perspectives, and that is worth remembering when one is tempted to "force" a learner to participate in a session.

This brief overview of the influences on adults' philosophical frameworks should remind the educator of the tremendous individual differences possible among learners in the way they see the world around them and their behavior within it.

Values

Closely related to a learner's philosophy, or perhaps a part of it, are values. Values are "the social principles, goals, or standards held or accepted by an individual, class, society, etc.," as well as seeing something as "desirable or worthy of esteem for its own sake" (Webster's New World Dictionary, 1988). Values have been considered in the adult education literature in at least two different ways, which can be superficially described as the

Knowles' way and the critical theorists' way. Before continuing, though, we should be reminded that "change in values" is a part of our earlier definition of adult learning. We have values as a learner characteristic and changed values as a possible outcome of a learning experience.

North American adult education literature, up until the early 1980s, emphasized awareness, acceptance, and respect for learner values. Good examples of this can be found in some of Brundage and Mackeracher's (1980, 69) learning principles: "the adult learner needs to be aware of his (sic) own value system through which he makes decisions based on information and through which he evaluates both input and learning outcomes"; "the adult learner must be respected and must respect himself for what he is now... his current values and feelings cannot be discounted"; and "the adult learner must receive feedback which lets him know how others understand and value his feelings, meanings, and values." Learners' values are to be accepted and respected. This approach is not to be discounted—awareness and respect for values are critical to working effectively with any individual.

In addition, however, as we have been discussing, another view is that the educator has a professional responsibility to challenge the learner to question and perhaps to work toward value changes. Brookfield (1986) reviews the distinction between "felt needs" and "prescribed needs" (221–222). Felt needs are what learners say they want and prescribed needs are "premised upon educators' beliefs concerning the skills, knowledge, behaviors, and values that they feel adults should acquire" (222). Both are seen to have their place in a learning situation.

What does this mean to the educator? There may not necessarily be a conflict between the two approaches described, but rather the role that learner values play may be dependent on the situation. If I were a nutritionist responsible for giving workshops on eating habits, for example, I would of course need to develop an awareness of learner values—values about health and wellness, values about food (who is a vegetarian?) Some of these values I would accept and respect (the vegetarians) and others I would challenge (opposition to good nutrition). If, on the other hand, I were training a group of computer enthusiasts to use a new graphics program, their values may not be relevant at all. And if I were working with individuals sentenced by the courts to an alcohol rehabilitation course, value-change would likely be my primary goal. We could describe the process as a continuum, from awareness of learner values through to value change as a goal of the learning experience. And depending on the situation, we could be working at different points along that continuum. For now, awareness of the importance of learner values as a characteristic, and the varying roles of values in a learning experience are our main points.

Autonomy

Autonomy is, functioning independently, or without the control of others. Although it sounds suspiciously like some version of self-directedness, autonomy is included separately as it is also a social and political phenomenon and as such is the focus of the writings about emancipatory learning and empowerment in adult education. The degree to which learners have or expect to gain autonomy through the learning experience is a vital consideration for the educator. Consider, for example, the differences between learners who (1) have been forced, by their directors, to attend a session on performance appraisal; (2) see gaining literacy skills as a way of escaping from a tedious assembly line position; (3) realize that they cannot survive independently without gaining some marketable skills; (4) have enroled in a literature course for the intrinsic love of literature. There are issues of autonomy or expectations of autonomy in many learning situations.

The important issues for the educator to recognize include: that some learners are independent or autonomous and others are not; that some learners see the process of learning as a means of gaining autonomy; and, that it is sometimes the responsibility of the educator to "free" learners or to challenge them to become more autonomous. Autonomy is, of course, closely related to many of the learner characteristics discussed in this chapter. It is related to psychological type, particularly introversion versus extraversion. It is a part of self-directedness, both as a process and as an outcome. Clearly, philosophical frameworks are connected to autonomy, particularly in terms of sociocultural and psychic influences.

In a sense, gaining autonomy is a key concept in adult education—from the critical theorists who view empowerment as the goal of learning to the North American model of meeting the "felt needs" of learners.

Summary

In this chapter, a wide variety of learner characteristics have been reviewed, ranging from fairly specific categories of psychological type and learning styles through to a consideration of underlying philosophies and values which guide an individual's life. These characteristics are related to each other, overlap with each other, and interact with each other to yield the unique individual. The reader may have looked through the chapter headings, in search of motivation, anxiety, self-esteem, or others of the usual "characteristics of adult learners." These characteristics have not been deliberately ignored, but rather have been set aside as being more situation-specific, or more a part of the learning process than the variables we have discussed. As we follow the model presented in Chapter 1 into the process, these factors will surface.

As educators, we cannot hope to understand completely the social and psychological composition of the adults with whom we work. (Some days it seems impossible to begin to understand oneself or one's child or a close friend, let alone our learners!) Yet without an awareness of the make-up of individual differences, we may as well give a lecture to an empty lecture hall and call it education. The adult educator works with individuals to stimulate, facilitate, encourage, support, and challenge people to change and grow. This cannot be done without an awareness of how people are. It was the purpose of this chapter, in part, to increase that awareness and also to stimulate questioning about and reflection on the nature of our work.

In the next chapters, we will turn to the process of working with adult learners. In Chapter 3, the roles of adult educators will be discussed in relation to the learning process and the characteristics of both learner and educator.

3

The Roles We Play

When a group of adult educators engage in a "brainstorming" activity aimed at generating a list of their instructional roles, they inevitably run out of paper. Most groups begin with words such as instructor, expert, designer, teacher, evaluator, and after a while, someone will suddenly remember "facilitator"! This will lead to many similar terms, such as resource person, discussion leader, catalyst, nurturer, counsellor, model. The list sometimes includes role descriptions that imply equality: friend, co-learner, colleague. Then, at last, the suggestions usually return to an emphasis on the role of educator, but in a noticeably different way, with words such as learner, researcher, professional, writer, critic, reformer. Oddly, the progression of this activity seems to mirror both the progression of ideas in the literature and the individual growth of adult educators. We will return to this notion shortly, as a means of organizing the roles we play; but first, some clarification of terms, assumptions, and background is presented.

The language used in adult education to describe the role of the adult educator identifies the approach used, or the professional philosophy adhered to. Brookfield (1986, 123) writes: "The concept of the facilitator of learning now exercises something of a conceptual stranglehold on our notions of correct educational practice, and to talk of the role of the teacher or of teaching as a function, is unfashionable and distasteful to some educators of adults." The terms "facilitator" and "resource person" have been commonly used in the last fifteen years or so in order to de-emphasize the instructor-centered approach, and to break away from the associations with "school" or pedagogy. In some ways this has been a valid change—many adults associate the term "teacher" with misery or boredom or fear; "instructor" can be equally intimidating with its connotations of expertise and authority. This does leave us in a bit of a dilemma, however, since "facilitator" is also strongly associated with a particular approach to the learning process, and does not include other, equally valid, roles. In this book, the fairly general term, "educator," has been used to describe those individuals who work with adult learners. This practice will be continued, based on the assumption that "educator" *is* a general term that includes all of the roles to be discussed.

Roles are different from methods, which are again different from techniques. A role will be defined as a function or a "part" played by the educator in a learning situation or environment. There is no intention to imply that a role is "fake" or artificial in any way, though in some sense, it is similar to a performance. What the educator does is a role in that it can be deliberately started, adjusted, changed, and stopped. Some individuals may be better able to play those roles which are closer to their own characteristics, but we could say the same for actors. An effective educator can play roles that are quite dissimilar to the way he or she would behave in other settings.

A method, on the other hand, is a procedure or a strategy for doing something, in our case, for working through the learning process. Within any one method (for example, discussion groups), the educator can play a variety of roles (manager, challenger, catalyst, leader, listener) and can switch from one role to another, based on the nature of the interaction. For a full discussion of methods, the reader is referred to Cranton's (1989) *Planning Instruction for Adult Learners*. For our purposes here, it will be enough to be aware of four methodological categories:

- instructor-centered—where the communication tends to be in one direction, from instructor to learner;

- interactive—where the communication is between facilitator and learners and among learners;

- individualized—where the learner works independently at his or her own pace; and

- experiential—where the learner works and learns in a real or simulated situation.

As these definition reveal, it is clear that certain roles are more appropriately used with certain methods; hence methods will come into play in this chapter, but will not be the focus of it.

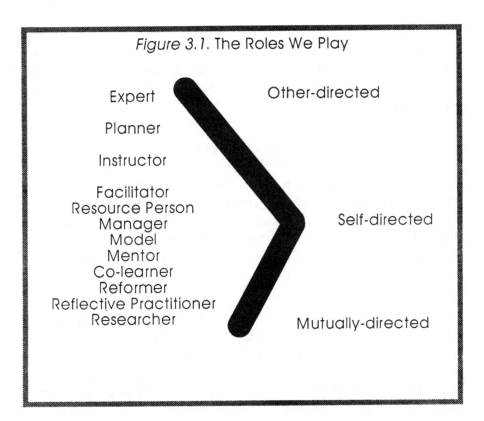

Figure 3.1. The Roles We Play

Expert
Planner
Instructor
Facilitator
Resource Person
Manager
Model
Mentor
Co-learner
Reformer
Reflective Practitioner
Researcher

Other-directed

Self-directed

Mutually-directed

Although the dictionary definition of "technique" may seem to be synonymous with that of "method," the former term will be used in a slightly different sense here. Techniques are specific practical skills leading to a desired "whole," including behavior, change, or learning. Techniques are the "details of methods." The technique of an artist's brushwork offers an analogy. If, for example, the educational method employed was large group discussion and the role assumed was facilitator, the facilitator might use the technique of making or avoiding eye contact with individuals to encourage or discourage their input, or the technique of waiting silently to encourage participation.

Now, to return to the roles we play. One of the most common means of organizing a discussion of roles (or methods) is to arrange them from other-directed learning (for example, instructor-centered) to self-directed learning. Renner (1983) provides a good example of this in his practical *Instructor's Survival Kit*, using a continuum which goes from total teacher control (lecture) through to total learner control (self-help groups). However, the recent literature, which emphasizes the educator's role in transformative learning, and just as importantly, the results of the brainstorming activity described at the beginning of this chapter, have inspired a modification of this approach. The figure above demonstrates how we will travel from other-directed learning, through self-directed learning, to mutually-directed learning in the rest of this chapter.

Figure 3.1 depicts this progression, along with representative roles for each stage. Fewer roles are listed at the other-directed end of the figure, as they are often less appropriate for adult educators. However, the segment of the line in the figure is shown longer to represent both the common adoption of these roles and the length of time that they have been a part of educational literature. The shape of the line intentionally resembles a boomerang with the roles of the educator coming back to a place nearer to where they started out.

Although many more roles could be listed, and have been listed in the literature, the discussion in this chapter will concentrate on those named in Figure 3.1. Rather than emphasize the *quantity* of roles available to the educator, the intent here is to examine selected roles within a theoretical framework. It is essential for the educator not simply to carry a "bag of tricks," but to have developed a practice founded on a clear philosophical rationale. Other related roles will be mentioned only as they are relevant. For each, the behavior and style of the educator will be described, along with situations in which the role is commonly and appropriately used. The chapter will conclude with a brief look at the research on educator roles, particularly in relation to learner characteristics and effectiveness.

The Expert Role

The majority of adult educators begin in their profession as subject experts rather than as "educators." At universities and colleges, instructors have studied chemistry or English literature, the subjects they teach, not education. In business and industry, trainers have particular skills or expertise to impart to others. In continuing education centers, teachers have a particular interest or expertise which matches the demand for or interest in courses in an area. In community groups, the organizer has a cause he or she wishes to promote. And in similar fashion we could go on through the diverse adult education settings. One of the few places where we can expect adult educators to have a background in adult education is where they are "teaching" adult education itself.

It is natural enough, then, for educators, especially those beginning in their profession, to assume an expert role. In this role, the adult educator transmits information about the subject to an "audience" and answers questions that they might have. Most commonly associated with this role are instructor-centered methods, such as the lecture or demonstration. Additionally, in his other role as expert, an educator can prepare materials with which learners work individually, or can simply respond to a series of questions or problems or case studies that learners have prepared. The main characteristic of the expert role is the perception of oneself as having information or skills which are then passed on to others. Attitudes or values are often incidental to this role, except perhaps for the demonstration of enthusiasm for the subject or the provision of a model for the profession.

The role of expert is commonly assumed by individuals who do not know any other role. We have the tendency to act, as educators, as we ourselves were taught, and so this role is perpetuated. We will examine, shortly, when the role of expert is appropriate, but first, let's examine some common misuses. The educator who assumes an expert role and transmits information through a lecture format is often misapplying the role. We are *not* arguing that lectures are never appropriate, but rather that the expert role is often wrongly assumed, and the lecture provides a common example of this. During lectures, adult learners are provided with little opportunity to interact, to do, to question, or to relate the information to their own experiences. Any learner's attention span for absorbing information through listening is limited to 15 minutes or so at one time. We've probably all had the experience of tuning in and out of a lecture, often unintentionally. In a talk that goes on for an hour, about one-third of the information may be retained, and even that recall often is short-term, unless the information is used in other ways. However, moving beyond the lecture example (for expert does not equal lecturer), the implications of the expert role automatically assign the learner to the role of nonexpert and hence to powerlessness. Learners can be intimidated, frustrated, passive, angry, or bored. Dependent behaviors are encouraged. The learner can be afraid of appearing "stupid" in the face of the expertise of the educator (and who has not had that reaction, even temporarily, upon meeting someone well known or whose work we admire greatly). A bleak future for the expert? No, not really. All educators *are* (hopefully) experts and can assume this role in effective ways. In combination with other roles, the expert role is important, and, even alone, has its place. After facilitating a discussion, the expert can summarize and integrate the ideas, elaborate and expand, or provide new insights. In working with small groups, the expert can redirect learner activities that are confused or floundering. In the expert role, the educator can detect underlying assumptions and help the learner make those assumptions explicit, then examine their validity. As an expert, the educator can provide helpful feedback for the learner. However, in these examples, the expert hat alternates with other hats and never stays on too long.

At other times, the learner wants and needs an educator who remains in the role of expert for some time. It can be just as frustrating going to someone whom you know knows the answer, and have them say, "and what do you think?" as it is going with your own ideas, hoping to discuss them, but finding no one to tell them to. When learners are new to a subject, as was discussed in Chapter 2, they may need an educator willing to assume an expert role. If time is short, if the content is knowledge (rather than values or skills), and if learners are unfamiliar with the content, the expert role will be most effective. Also when learners have not had experience taking responsibility for their learning, an educator in a directing role, if not an expert one, is required at least at the beginning of the course. And finally, in the development and writing of learning materials, an expert role is necessary. (Wouldn't you feel cheated if this book contained only questions for you to think about?)

Because of psychological type and learning style, some educators prefer to talk and some learners prefer to listen. If this happy combination exists, why not just "go with it"? Unfortunately, it is rare that a whole *group* of learners prefers to listen. And even if this were the case, it is mainly information that can be transmitted in this fashion, and not skills (doing things) or values.

The Planner Role

Most educators would describe themselves as planners of learning experiences or planners of instruction. When preparing a course outline, developing a program, or making an agenda for a workshop, we assume the role of planner. Systematic planning can also be viewed as comprising the design of instruction, an area which abounds with practical texts providing guidance for the educator. The theoretical foundation for instructional design stems from behavioral psychology, as was discussed in Chapter 1, with its assumption that learning is facilitated by the organization of content into hierarchically organized units of information. Setting this issue aside for the moment, but keeping it in mind, the role of planner will be examined in a more general way. In the role of planner, the educator makes decisions about the learning experience. Activities could include, for example, topic selection, setting objectives for learners, determining the sequence of objectives, selecting methods and activities to be engaged in, selecting materials and readings, assigning projects or papers to be written, selecting evaluation methods, constructing tests, and assigning grades to learners. In defining "directing teacher behavior," Brundage and Mackeracher (1980) include, among other behaviors: "set the objectives, define the material, divide the material into segments, organize it into sequences and hierarchies, and provide it in a ready-to-use form to the learner" (58). Making such decisions about learning is part of the responsibilities of the educators in their role of planner.

The planner role can also be more informal than the examples above suggest, and can take place while actually working with learners, as well as before class contact. If the educator goes through files and selects an article to give out or puts an agenda on a flip chart or decides, in a session, to regroup learners, these are all planning activities.

The role of planner is essential to being an educator, just as the role of expert is. It is not often that we would work with learners in an area about which we know nothing, and it is not often that we would make no decisions about or in a learning situation. However, as with most other-directed roles, the planning role also can be misused. We will examine this aspect first, then look at when the role is appropriate.

It has been stated in the literature that instructional design and adult education are conflicting areas—the former prescribes that the educator be completely responsible for the design of the process, and the latter prescribes that the educator's role is to meet the expressed needs of the learner. One is behaviorist in origin and the other is humanist. As mentioned, adult education has grown beyond both frameworks, yet many educators still see themselves as completely responsible for the planning aspect of the learning process. In her recent research with university faculty, for example, Wilcox (1990a) found that only a very small percentage of them considered that learners could contribute to planning. When the educator makes *all* or even most of the decisions, learners' needs, interests, and experiences can be neglected, the level and pace of the process can be inappropriate, the styles and methods used can be wrong for the group, and the evaluation can be unfair or invalid. Then learners can easily become bored, apathetic, frustrated, angry, or intimidated. This can lead to, for example, a situation where learners take turns going to the three-times-a-week class "in case he says something about what's on the exam." Otherwise, they see no reason to attend, the situation has virtually nothing to do with their learning, and they have had no part in forming the experience.

There are, of course, appropriate uses of the planning role. As with the expert role, when learners are working in an unfamiliar area, when they have little or no experience with planning learning, and when time is short, the educator should naturally assume a larger share of the planning function. If not, learners will be justifiably frustrated by the process of trying to make decisions when they do not know the alternatives or when they have neither time nor expertise. Even in these situations, however, the educator can share the planning role. This will be discussed in detail in Chapter 4. In other situations, where learners have more background and expertise, the educator will move in and out of the role of planner, as was discussed with the expert role. The degree to which the role is assumed depends on the characteristics of learners; however, it is never completely abdicated. In keeping with our theoretical model from Chapter 1, the educator and learner both maintain a role in the planning component of the learning process.

The characteristics of some educators lead to a natural assumption of the planning role on their part. For example, the thinking type is a natural planner, as is the educator with a convergent learning style. Their value systems and beliefs about their professional responsibilities lead many educators to believe they must plan the process. However, all adult educators must examine critically their practice and the rationale for the planning role in that practice.

Just before we leave the discussion of this role, one key constraint must be mentioned. Often institutions, professional bodies, or other groups have varying degrees of control over the planning of learning. "Required curriculum" is a familiar phrase to many adult educators. And the need to "cover the material" is a common explanation for not having learners engage in planning. Thus, very real constraints often influence the educator's planning role. Nevertheless, numerous decisions remain to be made about the learning process in any situation. (This topic will be returned to in Chapter 6.)

The Instructor Role

Although the term "instructor" is commonly used to describe anyone working with learners in a higher education setting, the term has connotations which make it a useful role descriptor. Perhaps the connotation comes from the word "instruction": knowledge or information given; details on procedure; directions. The word "lesson," too, is often associated with "instruct." Someone who "instructs" tells someone else what to do or how to do it. The instructor role is a directive role and is often used in combination with an expert or formal authority role. There is no intention of implying that all people in higher education adopt the instructor role; however it *is* commonly assumed, for much the same reasons as the expert role is used.

Stephen Leacock wrote, in 1914: "'Dr. McTeague, it seems had just entered his ten o'clock class (the hour was about ten-twenty) and was about to open his lecture, when one of his students rose in his seat and asked a question. It is a practice,' continued Dr. Boomer, 'which, I need hardly say, we do not encourage; the young man, I believe, was a new-comer to the philosophy class. At any rate, he asked Dr. McTeague, quite suddenly it appears, how he could reconcile his theory of transcendental immaterialism with a scheme of rigid moral determinism. Dr. McTeague stared for a moment, his mouth so the class assert, painfully open. The student repeated the question, and poor McTeague fell forward over his desk, paralyzed'" (151).

The instructor role, as used in this book, includes the following behaviors: making decisions about the learning experience; structuring the learning process; providing feedback and guidance; explaining and elaborating on the content; giving assigned readings, projects, activities; and evaluating learner progress. To some extent, the instructor role overlaps with the role of planner, particularly in terms of decision making or designing the learning experience. But the instructor role, during the learning experience, is somewhat different. The instructor directs, guides, defines, determines what is "right" and what is "wrong," and overall has *control* of the learning experience. One is reminded of Malcolm Knowles' early "assumptions of pedagogy": the role of the learner is dependent; the instructor's experience, not the learner's experience, is the basis of the interaction; people learn what "society" says they ought to learn; and education is a process of acquiring subject matter (Knowles, 1980, 43–44).

As do the roles of expert and planner, the instructor role has its appropriate uses. Anyone who has attempted to learn to operate a new piece of equipment without direction will attest to the value of this role! The instructor role is important and necessary in many learning experiences, and is valuable in almost any adult education setting on some occasions. However, as with the previous other-directed roles, it can be misused.

When used inappropriately, the instructor role can foster dependency among learners, create a fear of failure, ignore learners' experiences and unique individual characteristics, allow few opportunities for interaction (between educator and learner, or among learners), and give the dissatisfied learner no option except to exit from the experience. Given the potentially serious consequences, it is important to know when the role is unsuitable. As the role which dominates the learning experience, the instructor role is inappropriate when learners have experience in the subject, when they have experience planning their own learning, when the instructional goals are related to values or to more complex cognitive learning, and when learners have heterogeneous backgrounds and interests. Even when used temporarily, in combination with other roles, the instructor role can still be inappropriate, depending on the context within which it is used. If, for example, learners are moving toward self-direction and are trying to make a decision about their learning or trying to come to a consensus on an issue, nothing is more destructive than putting on the instructor garb and announcing that "we'd better move on to the next activity." After learners have worked through a problem or come to some closure on a values issue, the educator who uses the instructor role to give feedback can invalidate the work that learners have done. It is difficult, if not impossible, to make rules about when to take on the instructor role—at times it is necessary to direct or redirect, to assume control temporarily, or to instruct learners. Perhaps an overall guideline is to think of yourself as working with a colleague whom you respect and admire. At times it is fine to explain or direct or control the interaction—when your professional expertise tells you that things are going in the wrong direction, or going nowhere at all, then intervention is necessary. The same holds true when working with adult learners: at times the instructor role is valuable, and at other times it has negative consequences.

There are many situations in which the instructor role is effective. Training programs with specific skill-related objectives require the use of the instructor role. The staff of a company who are learning a new software package need direction. Professional education, with skills objectives predetermined by a professional association, demands, to some extent, the instructor role. The nursing student learning to administer medications wants to be instructed. In a different vein, any adult learner entering a new environment and beginning to study a new subject feels more comfortable when the educator initially assumes the instructor role. And when time is a constraint and everyone who is attending a session is there to learn the same thing, the instructor role is the most efficient way for that learning to take place. This, of course, is not true if the learning is complex or related to values.

Preferences for the instructor role are related to individual characteristics. Those (educators and learners) who have experienced only the instructor role will feel uncomfortable with different roles. Those learners and educators whose culture supports the value of the instructor as one in control will be resistant to change their opinion. Extroverted, thinking type educators will prefer to assume the instructor role. Introverted individuals may prefer to be quiet learners; the educator may assume that they prefer the instructor role, though this may not be the case. Learners with a converger learning style may tend to prefer an educator in the instructor role. Likewise, educators with a converger learning style prefer to instruct.

The Facilitator Role

Just as the role of instructor is associated with higher education, the role of facilitator is associated with adult education. Many adult educators routinely label themselves as facilitators in order to avoid the terms "instructor" and "teacher," which connote educator control. This extensive use of the term has led to confusion as to its meaning, as one might expect. To "facilitate" means, simply, "to make easy or easier." A facilitator is a person who makes things easier. A facilitator of learning is a person who makes learning easier.

Examining this more closely, but staying within the boundaries of the definition, the role of a facilitator is to encourage and support learner growth and change by responding to the needs expressed by the learner. In the role of facilitator, an educator does not direct, control, or impose his or her ideas of what or how learners should learn, but rather helps learners do what they want to do. Behaviors associated with the facilitator role include, for example, interacting with learners, clarifying, supporting an effective group process, providing resources, providing encouragement, building a trusting relationship with learners, being nonjudgmental, asking questions, summarizing learners' interactions, and accepting and respecting learners as they are. This list has been extensively expanded in the literature. Brundage and Mackeracher (1980, 59) include, among other items, "... behaviors which include being a catalyst, resource, reflective mirror, alter ego, and co-inquirer, and provide support, guidance, and encouragement" and then add, "the structure, objectives, and direction of the learning activities are negotiated; the content, in the form of personal meanings, comes from the learner." The picture that emerges is quite different from the instructor role previously discussed. And it is easy to see that the theoretical foundations of the facilitator role lie in humanism. Carl Rogers, one would suspect, would use the facilitator role exclusively.

It sounds ideal. We all want to be supported and encouraged in a nonthreatening, nonjudgmental way, to have someone "make easier" the attainment of our own goals. The facilitator role *is* a vital one for the adult educator. But first, let's examine some possible difficulties.

As discussed in Chapter 2, self-directedness can be seen both as a characteristic of the learner and as an outcome of the learning process. When

learners are not self-directed, or have no experience with self-directed learning, the facilitator role is not effective. Its use will provoke frustration,
anger, lowered self-concept, and little learning. This is not to say that self-
direction should not be a goal of the learning experience, and that the facilitator role should not be used at all, but it cannot be used as the main role. As
will be discussed in Chapter 4, the educator should move gradually into the
facilitator role, making the process explicit and giving learners the opportunity to learn to be self-directed.

The nature of "expressed" versus "real" needs is a crucial issue in the
selection of the facilitator role. The heart attack victim may express a need
to return to work immediately so that his business does not disintegrate; the
abuse victim may express a need to learn how to do things right so that her
husband does not beat her; the new college instructor may express a need to
learn how to discipline his students so that he feels in control. The educator
knows that a change in lifestyle is the real need of the heart attack victim; an
awareness of the syndrome of abuse is necessary for the victim of abuse; and
the college instructor needs to learn about working with adult learners. Although the examples may seem obvious, every educator faces the contradiction between expressed and real learner needs. It can be as simple as the
learner who says, "I don't see why I need all this theory, I just want to know
how to *do* it," or as complex as a learner who is working within the context
of an oppressive culture. All learners are working within the boundaries of
their own background, experiences, and values. When only expressed needs
are addressed, those boundaries are unlikely to be stretched or broken. The
educator must step in and out of the facilitator role in order for change to
take place. The facilitator role "makes things easier," and stretching boundaries is painful, not easy.

The tricky aspect of this decision, though, is determining when the expressed needs are unsuitable, and being sure that the educator's perception
of real needs is accurate. The educator, too, is constrained by background,
experiences, and values. There is the dangerous possibility of working
toward our own causes, promoting our own beliefs, to the detriment of
learning. Every educator has the professional responsibility to question his
or her own assumptions critically, and to examine perceptions of real needs
carefully. There are no easy answers to this one.

Finally, the facilitator role does not suit every learning situation. If learners are gaining specific skills or absorbing basic facts, the facilitator role is time-consuming and frustrating for them. Learning how to operate a new piece of equipment, how to improve your tennis serve, or about new accounting procedures required by the tax law require an educator who assumes the instructor role more than the facilitator role. Imagine attending a session in the shop to learn about a new computerized diagnostic system where the session leader begins with, "And how do you think we should proceed?" or "What would you like to learn about this system?"

Conversely, independent learners, self-directed learners, and learners with relevant backgrounds and experiences will benefit from an instructor who assumes the facilitator role. That is not to say that such learners should not also "break boundaries"—it is rare that the facilitator role should be used exclusively. But in these situations, spending considerable time in the facilitator role can be the most effective way to promote learning.

Recalling our characteristics from Chapter 2, we can see that the facilitator role will come more naturally to some educators and be received more positively by some learners. It is essentially a role that matches a North American middle-class culture of consumerism and meeting needs. Individuals from that culture naturally will be more comfortable with the role. In terms of individual characteristics, the feeling type (who prefers harmony and making others happy) will be at home in the facilitator role (both as educator and learner); the intuitive type (who wants to follow all the possibilities and options) will be free to do so; and the individual with a divergent learning style (who generates ideas and hates coming to closure) will have the opportunity to roam. In the same vein, the thinking type, the sensing type, the converger, and the assimilator are likely to prefer other roles, both as educators and as learners.

The Resource-Person Role

The term "resource person," for a time, was considered to be almost synonymous with the term "facilitator" and was in favor among adult educators attempting to escape from school-based models. However, the role of facilitator includes much more interaction with the learner, and encouragement of group processes and action as a catalyst for the learning process. The facilitator is simply more active in the learning process. While there is no directing or controling, the facilitator is a participant in a way that the resource person is not. In the role of resource person, the educator provides resources for the learning process. These resources may be materials, such as readings or audio visual materials; "real things," such as equipment, machinery, field sites; or human resources, including the expertise of educators and others. The resource person responds to the expressed needs of learners and assists the learning process by providing the information and experiences required for the attainment of goals. Although this role overlaps that of facilitator, in some ways it exerts less influence on the learner as a person (hence it is placed one step further down on the continuum toward self-directed learning).

A common example of the resource-person role is found in modularized or computerized courses. The learner works directly with materials and media; each learner is independent; all learners are at different places in the process, depending on their own rate of work. The resource person is there to provide information and to answer questions. Other individualized learning experiences, such as a university independent study course or the preparation of a graduate thesis, may (but not necessarily) include an educator who assumes the resource-person role.

Most educators must act as resource persons at some time. As subject experts, they provide appropriate materials and information to learners who request them. However, the exclusive or dominant use of the resource-person role leads to the same difficulties as described previously for the facilitator role. It is assumed that learners have the expertise in the subject to know what they need to know; it is assumed that expressed needs are the goal of the learning experience; and quite often it is assumed that learners have planning skills. The latter point is not the case in modularized or computerized instruction where a mixture of the planner role (the designer of the materials) and the resource-person role (the educator who is present in the situation) can be seen. In addition, the resource-person role involves less interaction between educator and learner and hence less guidance, support, questioning, probing, and encouragement of reflection. The facilitator probably often raises an eyebrow at a statement made by a learner or conveys in some way that she does not see this as the best direction to take. In a "pure" resource-person role, the educator does not have the same opportunity to do this—he may say, "No, I think you should read this, instead," but with less interaction inevitably there will be less guidance and more independent learning.

Independent learning is not, by any means, ineffective, and this impression should not be created here. But this kind of learning is appropriate in some situations and not in others. Let's look first at the individualized programs of study and the resource-person role in that context, keeping in mind that this role is combined with the planner role (the educator who developed the materials). If learners are obtaining basic skills and are very heterogeneous in background in these basic skills, this approach can be useful and efficient. Early 1960s and 1970s research clearly showed that learners could pick up missing skills in this way in mathematics, for example, in a much shorter time than with "traditional" instruction. And, in these settings, the resource-person role is invaluable. However, following this model and based on this research, modularized instruction was introduced into many settings where it produced only frustration on the part of both educator and learner. Entire technical programs at the college level were "modularized" at great expense to the educational system. Learners found they wanted interaction with others; educators found they had to use other roles (instructor, facilitator) in settings which were not designed for these roles. In other situations, educators found that they had a large proportion of learning disabled adults in their groups (e.g., in remedial programs) and that working with these learners demanded the instructor role. When individualized methods are used carefully in combination with the resource-person role, they can be extremely effective. But, in other situations, their use can be detrimental to learning.

Other appropriate uses of the resource-person role include working with advanced and experienced learners. For example, an educator who is responsible for providing information on teaching and learning to faculty (instructional development) often will be most effective in a resource-person role. An educator who works for the department of agriculture, providing information to farmers, again often will find the resource-person role most commonly and effectively used. Even in these situations, of course, other roles sometimes are required. And this inevitably depends on the characteristics of the individual learner. Some faculty, some farmers, some graduate students, some managers will need to be questioned, challenged, redirected, and the educator then slips into a different role.

This brings us back to the professional responsibility of the educator in determining when to give what is asked for and when to say, "No, I think you need to question what you're doing here; why don't you..." All educators are resource persons at times, just as they also may be experts, planners, and facilitators. And all educators must examine and question each situation in order to determine the appropriateness of the role.

Some educators and some learners will prefer the resource-person role. The introverted type, in particular, would rather be a provider or a receiver of resources than to be a participant in a group process. In terms of learning style, the convergent learner would probably be pleased at being able to go to the educator to "get what he or she needs." Educators who are either convergers or assimilators would undoubtedly be comfortable in this mode.

The Manager Role

The manager role grew out of the development of modularized, computer-assisted, and other individualized learning approaches in much the same way as did the role of resource person. The manager, however, has little to do with the provision of resources; it was initially assumed with individualized instruction that all resources were supplied with the instructional packages. Learners worked completely independently, at their own pace, with pre-packaged materials, including printed and audio-visual materials and computer-administered materials.

The theoretical foundation of this approach lies in behaviorism—content is divided into small manageable chunks, carefully sequenced, and learners receive continual feedback from the material itself. The earliest example of this method was a "teaching machine," designed strictly on Skinnerian principles of learning. With the advent of computer-assisted instruction, in the late 1960s, that same model was followed, with the computer presenting both chunks of information and feedback in response to the learner's reactions to questions or problems. At that time, individual pacing and on-going feedback were cited as the primary advantages of the method.

Educators initially responded with alarm to individualized instruction, fearing that machines would replace human teachers and arguing that this development would be detrimental to learning. But no, they were told, educators did have a role—they would be the managers of the learning. As managers, they were to keep track of which learner was where in the programs, record the results of evaluations, hand out the next learning package—in short, "manage" the details of the interaction between learner and material. Although the role of computers in education has changed dramatically since that time, the manager role still exists in individualized and distance-education programs. The positive and negative aspects of this role are similar to those of a resource person, with the added factor that even less interaction is possible between educator and learner. The manager role is appropriate when independent learners are attaining basic skills or knowledge. Even so, the educator probably often will assume other roles at some time during the instructional process.

The manager role appears in other adult education settings as well. The use of learning contracts (whereby the educator and learner negotiate and agree on what is to be learned and how it is to be learned, and sign a contract to that effect) necessitates a manager role. In a sense, learning contracts are a "humanized" version of the individualized instruction approach described above. With or without learning contracts, the educator who is implementing a self-directed approach to learning will be managing, keeping track of people. The manager role is deliberately placed at the apex of the line in Figure 3.1: in its pure form, this role assumes that the learner is completely self-directed. The educator provides no input other than making sure that things run smoothly and keeping track of the specifics of the process. The learner makes all decisions regarding the learning experience. This, of course, is not the case when pre-packaged materials are used; there the planner role of the author of the materials is strongly influential, and decisions are made for the learner within the materials.

In a different form, the manager role is assumed by almost every adult educator working in a formal setting. The characteristics of the setting often necessitate a certain amount of management: keeping track of class lists; sometimes keeping track of attendance (e.g., in training programs where learners are required to be there); recording which learners are working on which projects; sometimes arranging rooms, field sites, laboratory time, placements, etc.; and often grading and recording grades for institutional requirements. Most of us perform these functions routinely and do not think of them as an educator role. Yet they are functions which may have a direct influence on the learning experience, and it is important to acknowledge and understand this role. The manager role, in this form, can become directive or authoritarian (attendance, grading) and can come into conflict with other roles, such as that of facilitator, without the educator being aware of it. If I support self-directed learning through a facilitator role, then take over the grading process or report absentees to the administration, learners will not take self-directed learning too seriously. The manager role must be employed carefully, and educators must be conscious of when and how they are playing it.

Three different types of manager roles have been discussed. In its "pure" form, the manager role allows for maximum learner control. The educator is rather like an administrative assistant to the process. When combined with the planner role, as when pre-packaged materials are used, the learner is directed by the planner, and the educator still acts as an administrative assistant. In formal settings, the manager role may be required to meet the requirements of the setting and may conflict with other roles and their underlying rationale.

Keeping in mind educator and learner characteristics, we can speculate about some preferences. The educator who is a sensing type would probably enjoy managing the details of the learning process. Intuitives and feeling types probably would neither like this function nor do it well. Learners who are intuitive types would appreciate the freedom to go their own way while someone else "keeps track." Learners who are sensing types or thinking types would probably feel comfortable with the structure of the individualized learning programs. Feeling types, one suspects, would not be particularly enamoured by any aspects of this role. Values and experience, too, would come into play. The pure manager role would not be appreciated by those individuals who expect the "teacher to teach," based on their past experiences or beliefs about the responsibilities of educators. In the same way, educators and learners alike often expect the educator to be responsible for class lists, attendance, grading, and reporting to the institution.

The Model Role

The pure manager role has minimal influence on the learning process and allows for maximum learner control. We have now turned the corner on the continuum and are looking at roles which not only have more influence, but also are different from an expert or instructor role. In other-directed roles, the educator directs and controls, the learner makes few decisions. Now, we will examine roles in which the educator *influences*, while the learner makes choices about the nature and degree of that influence. We are moving in the direction of learning that is "mutually-directed" by educator and learner.

A model is a person (or thing) to be followed or imitated because he, she, or it has attained a high standard of excellence or worth. Adult educators act as models within their subjects or professions and within the educational process. Every educator serves as a model for some learners, but unlike other roles, we may not be aware of this one. As important learning takes place through modeling, it is essential that the educator make this role explicit in the learning experience. All too often the message is "don't do as I do, do as I say."

First, we will briefly examine the process of modeling, then turn to some ways in which the role of model is enacted. Modeling occurs when a learner watches behavior, imitates that behavior, then incorporates that behavior into his or her own repertoire. The power of modeling is demonstrated in the way we learn language and social behavior. Research on modeling tells us that the more important the model is to us, the more likely we are to imitate the behavior (cf. Bandura, 1971). Consider the common example of a parent who complains of his child being influenced more by friends than by the parent—peers are important and act as models. Modeling can contribute to any kind of learning, including knowledge, values, attitudes, and skills. Psychologists also tell us that learning takes place much more quickly when a model has been provided. Imagine learning to ski without ever having seen someone ski! Even photographs and drawings in instruction booklets provide models as to how something looks or should be done. If you have ever tried to operate a new piece of equipment without referring to the diagram in the manual, you know the value of a model. Particularly for the "intangibles"— interest, enthusiasm, values, communication skills, behavior in groups, etc.— the role of model is critical in adult learning.

Can there be any inappropriate uses? The educator is an important person in the life of the adult learner, and modeling *will* occur whether or not it is the intention of the educator. Any demonstration, therefore, of unethical or unprofessional behavior can be imitated by the learner. The nurse educator who casually passes on a patient's confidences in conversation or who remarks that "we only need to include this step of the procedure if the head nurse is nearby" is inadvertently acting as a model. The mechanic who is discourteous to a customer is in effect telling the apprentice that it is acceptable to be rude to customers. The point is that we are important to our learners and are always providing a model of behavior whether intentionally or not. Behaviors that we are unaware of can be imitated by learners.

Many times we deliberately challenge people to examine new possibilities or to break out of the constraints of their own value system. The role of model plays an important part in this process. As has been discussed previously, it is our professional responsibility to be sure that we are leading in a direction that is not harmful or destructive to the learner. A misuse of the role of model can be, with all good intentions, taking a learner in a direction that she or he is not yet ready for. Determining the real needs of others is a dangerous pursuit, and we must take this responsibility seriously.

On a somewhat lighter note, the role of model can be ineffective if the model is "too perfect." The educator who never makes a mistake (or never admits to making a mistake), who is too much the expert, or is in some other way too far removed from the life of learners will not encourage modeling. Learners may feel that such behaviors are unattainable or beyond their skill or ability. Lowered self-esteem and fear of failure can result from working with a perfect model. Consider the computer expert who comes in to help you with a problem, quickly demonstrates the correct behavior, marches off, and leaves you feeling that you had better not even try to turn on your computer again. Or the swimming instructor who glides through the water to demonstrate a technique while you shiver in fright on the edge of the pool, deciding that it really isn't that important to learn how to swim after all. In part, this is the expert role interfering with the role of model; in order to be an effective model, the educator must also be human and take care not to intimidate learners.

Generally, however, use of the role of model is appropriate and effective. It is important to be conscious of the model role at all times, to be aware that the educator is an important person to learners and that behaviors will be modeled. Depending somewhat on the situation, the process of modeling can be made explicit. This can be as simple as pointing out that you are demonstrating the best technique for operating equipment, or as complex as discussing your own professional values with learners.

At times the educator can be most effective by providing other models—people or films or videotapes which provide examples of the skills or values for learners. Within a group of learners, too, some will have experiences or skills and be able to act as models for others. It is interesting to note, in this regard, that some of the effectiveness of peer teaching (learners teaching each other) comes from the lack of "distance" between the individuals.

It is difficult to relate the role of model to personality or learning style characteristics, as we are all models and learn from models. One would expect, though, that the extroverted type of learner would be more receptive to modeling as he or she is more likely to pay attention to information from the environment. Possibly the extroverted feeling type with the desire to bring harmony into the environment would be most prone to learning from a model. In terms of learning style, one might expect that the assimilator would be most receptive to a model, and the accommodator (with a preference for "doing") least receptive. It also seems probable that learners would choose as a model an individual of the same type and style as themselves.

The Mentor Role

In Greek legend, Mentor was the loyal friend and advisor of Odysseus. Here, we will look at the mentor as that combination of advisor and friend that can be part of the relationship between educator and learner.

As with the role of model, the role of mentor is not often deliberately chosen. It can be a surprise when a former learner comes back to announce, "You were my mentor when I was..." Adult educators are in a unique position to assume the mentor role, encourage its development, and thus facilitate learner growth. It is better then, not to completely "leave it to chance," but rather, as suggested for the role of model, to have an awareness and understanding of the process involved and to foster it carefully.

It is quite possible to work with groups of learners and never assume a mentor role; it is just as possible to act as a mentor for several adult learners simultaneously. However, it is an individual-to-individual relationship and not a role used with a group. There, one can act as a model, but not as a mentor. The mentor relationship is based on mutual interests, respect, and liking. It usually includes a compatibility of learning style and personality type. The relationship can evolve into friendship as the educator/learner aspect of the connection is ended. Unfortunately, there is little research on the nature of mentor role, as defined here, and even less mention is made of it in the practical adult education literature. Mentors who are assigned to or imposed on learners have a clear-cut role, and the relationship consists of a fairly well-defined process, but this is more similar to the facilitator role. In the continuum at the beginning of this chapter, the mentor role is moving back away from self-directed learning, toward more mutually-directed learning. Both educator and learner have choice and influence within the process. Both have control over the relationship itself and the learning that occurs within it. The educator neither instructs, nor simply meets expressed needs, but rather *works with* the learner to move in directions that *both* choose. Thus the mentor role is assumed by both participants. If the educator is not aware of being in a mentor relationship with an individual, it really has not been that role, but rather one of model.

It all begins to sound a bit like "falling in love" and just about as difficult to define or consciously work with. However, educator awareness of and reflection on the roles being assumed can make the process more conscious, and to some extent, deliberate. The relationship is a longer term one, not likely to occur in a workshop session, but quite possible if sessions or interactions go on for several weeks. In the beginning, the individual learner is likely to be the one who comes asking for advice or extra readings related to the learning or to talk about"something of interest. It is easy to mistake him or her for a dependent learner—one must be careful not to make this assumption and decide to encourage independence by not being accessible. As the relationship develops, there is often considerable interaction, sharing of ideas, discussion of common interests. The educator will be aware of the potential influence that he or she has as the learner will ask for advice on professional or career goals, sometimes on personal goals. Misuse can occur if the educator is unaware of the nature of the role, with its delicate balance between dependence and learner growth. Quite often, within institutionalized education (e.g., course structures), the mentor role has a clear-cut ending.

However, if there is an opportunity for continued interaction—in more informal learning contexts, such as community groups or working with graduate students or in business or industrial working environments—the mentor role will evolve into a collegial role. The educator remains the individual with more experience and background, but begins to learn from the learner and his or her expanded expertise or growth. Eventually, if it continues, the relationship can become one of friends or colleagues, and the educator/learner roles are terminated.

There are really no inappropriate uses of the mentor role; one cannot force oneself onto an individual as a mentor because of the mutuality of the relationship. Misuse can occur if the educator misunderstands the beginning of the relationship and rejects the learner. Abuse can occur if the educator assumes the role and then guides the learner in directions which are wrong for that person or unethical. At this level, the same issues that were discussed in regard to the role of model are relevant.

The role of mentor is an important and powerful one. If the educator is aware of the role and its development, it can be a very satisfying professional experience. For the learner, it can be one of the most profound influences on growth and development.

Examining the mentor role in relation to educator and learner characteristics is a different process than with the other roles. As noted earlier, the basis of the relationship is one of mutual interests, respect, and liking. Educator and learner will be compatible in terms of psychological type, learning style, values, and to some extent, cultural background and experience. The introverted thinking type educator may well be the perfect mentor for an introverted thinking or introverted intuitive learner, but not for his or her opposite, an extroverted feeling type learner. The educator with very different values or background from the learner probably will not appeal to the learner as a potential mentor. The selection of this role for a particular learner has a different basis from the selection of other roles (because it is more like friendship); and we can work effectively with a variety of learners in a variety of roles, without assuming the mentor role.

The Co-Learner Role

In the co-learner role, the educator moves another step in the direction of mutually-directed learning. As was seen in the discussion of theoretical foundations in Chapter 1, it was Freire who most strongly advocated the use of the co-learner role, particularly to learn about the culture and values of the people with whom we are working. Freire saw the educator and learner as mutually responsible for growth and change. It is this approach, in which the educator acts as a true learner (with learners), that provides the basis for our discussion here. In much of the adult education literature, the educator is considered a learner, especially when she or he reflects on instructional practice, but rarely is the role of co-learner discussed outside of reference to Freire's critical theory.

The co-learner role can provide the primary philosophical rationale for working with adult learners (as for Freire), or it can be deliberately chosen for a specific situation. Unlike the roles of model and mentor, the educator can slip in and out of the co-learner role as appropriate. When acting as a co-learner, the educator becomes a full member of the group. He or she participates as a learner and has the same responsibilities and rights as the other members of the group. Leadership functions are shared, dependent on the nature of the activities. Goals and objectives are mutually negotiated, with the educator having the same responsibility as learners for input. Materials and resources are sought out by all members of the learning group.

It can be seen from this description that learners must be self-directed, to some extent at least, for this role to be assumed. There also must be a high degree of trust and comfort between educator and learners. The educator, as well, becomes vulnerable and can feel threatened by the situation. (It's easier to be in control!) Moving in and out of the role must be done with great care so as to not be, or appear to be, manipulative. In fact, changes from the co-learner role to other roles, along with the rationale for doing so, should be made explicit. The educator may also see this as taking a risk.

Typically, the co-learner role is effective in informal learning situations where all participants have an equal stake in the process. A community action project in which a common concern or issue is explored and action taken to make changes is an example of a situation where the co-learner role is often used. Similar examples include workers' education, informal professional development activities, self-help groups, consciousness-raising groups, and computer conferencing networks. Quite often in such learning situations, the educator is as involved in the exploration and learning as are the learners. What we have a tendency to do, and what tradition suggests we do, is to hide this process from learners. Asked to give a professional development session for her peers, the educator may spend weeks preparing so as to assume an expert role. The co-learner role, however, can enhance everyone's involvement, growth, and development in these contexts.

The co-learner role used in conjunction with other roles takes on a slightly different look, but is equally useful and effective. It has the side benefits of increasing learner trust in and respect for the educator, and also of facilitating learner self-directedness. Consider the scenario in which learners in a session express an interest in a topic about which the educator is not familiar or well informed. In the expert role, the educator might offer to bring in the information later; in the planner role, the educator could remind learners that the topic is not on the agenda; in the facilitator role, the educator could suggest that learners investigate the topic on their own; however, in the co-learner role, tasks would be divided up, with the educator participating fully in the investigation of the suggested topic. Even during a session, for very short time periods, an educator can slip into the co-learner role. If, for example, a problem comes up in a discussion, the educator can work along with learners as a group member to solve the problem. It is *not* wise, however, for the educator to pretend he or she does not have information or know how to solve a problem—this could put the relationship of trust with learners at risk. In that situation, the educator can assume a facilitator role, saying, for example, "I worked that one out last year... why don't you give it a try here."

Inappropriate uses of the co-learner role? The educator who is a dishonest co-learner, as just mentioned, is likely to be seen as manipulative and lose the trust of learners. The co-learner role is also time-consuming and energy-burning; in situations where time is a prime consideration, it will not be efficient (though it may still be effective). Learners who are dependent or low in self-directedness will become frustrated with the co-learner role and will often question the credibility of the educator. (Why are you the teacher if you don't know?) In some subjects, the co-learner role is ineffective. Technical skills, basic knowledge, literacy skills, and psychomotor skills are areas where the educator is not likely to be a co-learner. And finally, the cultural background and values of both learner and educator will influence the choice of the co-learner role. With a group of learners (or part of the group) who expect the educator to possess and dispense knowledge or skills, the co-learner role should be used sparingly, or introduced gradually over time. As well, some educators may not be comfortable in the role; again, it should then be little used or experimented with carefully and slowly.

In terms of learning style, convergers would be very frustrated with an educator in a co-learner role (the converger educator would also dislike it)—convergers like to focus in quickly on solutions. Divergers, on the other hand, both learners and educators, would enjoy this opportunity to explore ideas. Accommodators, who like "doing," would probably welcome the opportunity to "do" together with the educator. Psychological type is also likely to be relevant in similar ways. Introverted types would not enjoy the "groupy" aspect of the co-learner role. However, intuitive types (both learners and educators) would be interested in the exploration of possibilities that is a part of this role. Feeling types who particularly enjoy working with others may also appreciate this role.

The Reformer Role

In the most recent literature the view is presented that it is an obligation of the adult educator to be involved in emancipatory education. The transformation of individual perspectives is the "business of all adult educators" (Mezirow, 1990, 357). Following Mezirow's arguments, the reformer role can just as easily be labeled the "transformer role" or the "liberator role." However, the notion is not new—although adult education has been influenced for decades by the ideas of Malcolm Knowles, historically the concept of the educator as reformer was clearly linked with political movements (cf. Selman, 1989). The label, *reformer,* best reflects this original source. A reformer is interested in the correction of political or social injustices, improvement by removing abuse and oppression, and the development of character, values, and consciousness.

The view of adult education as a process of social transformation is not commonly accepted in North America. Brookfield (1985) writes that in Britain and Europe, "it is quite usual to regard education as a tool of social reform..." (64), whereas in North American "a good adult educator...is one who gives adults what they say they want" (69).

As was the case for the co-learner role, the reformer role can provide the primary focus of the interaction with learners, or it can be used in specific situations and in conjunction with other roles. In the reformer role, the educator challenges the learner to make explicit and then examine his or her assumptions, to assess the validity of presuppositions and their sources, to engage in critical self-reflection, and to reformulate perspectives. The educator actively employs techniques which question, challenge, raise consciousness, and transform. Such methods as journal writing, role-playing, free association, and brainstorming are often used by the educator in the reformer role. Social norms and the cultural context of the learner's experiences are made explicit, examined, and questioned.

The reformer role seems most natural to assume in situations such as community action groups, labor education, self-help groups, consumer education, religious education, human relations training, women's studies groups, health education, and so on. What these settings have in common are goals of social change and of increasing individual awareness and development within the social context. Such goals are more likely to be achieved by an educator in the reformer role (perhaps in conjunction with other roles) than through either instructor-centered or learner self-directed approaches. In higher education, the most visible example of the importance of the reformer role is in the development of women's studies programs where "scholars must analyze the structure and conditions of women's oppression and contrasting models of and for self-determination" (Nemiroff, 1989, 3). Here, we see expressed the clear combination of social change and individual growth within a social context, and feminist pedagogy describes a combination of humanist and reform approaches to education.

For the educator who is working in a context which does not involve social reform as an explicit goal, is the reformer role relevant? Within Mezirow's framework of transformative learning, it can be argued that the reformer role does come into play, as every individual's assumptions are based on the social context of their experiences and these assumptions need to be examined. When the educator questions, challenges, and encourages critical self-reflection, he or she is assuming, during that situation, the reformer role. It should be noted that Mezirow argues that individual transformation

precedes social transformation. In this process, the educator can use a reformer role with other roles and move into and out of it, depending on the
learner and the issues under discussion. Exercising the role can be as simple
as asking a learner to explain why he or she holds a certain view during a
discussion and probing the response or using exercises designed to clarify
learners' values, or as complex as designing a series of sessions to raise
consciousness and transform learners' perspectives of issues. Chapter 5 is
dedicated to an examination of these approaches.

The potential for abuse of the reformer role is immediately apparent. One
can easily think of historical examples of social change that became destructive for individuals or groups. In the reformer role, the educator must be
aware of the line between indoctrination and transformation. Mezirow
(1990, 361) makes the crucial point that transformative learning involves
"helping adults construe experience in a way in which they will more clearly
understand the reasons for their problems and the options open to them, so
that they may assume responsibility for decision making." In other words, in
a *mutually-directed* approach the educator works with the learner to help
clarify and question assumptions, to expand horizons, *and* to assume responsibility. The goal is empowerment of the learner, not indoctrination. Mezirow also makes the point that the "neutral" adult educator is also taking a
stance on issues by remaining neutral—he or she is maintaining the status
quo. Nevertheless, the danger remains a real one; the educator, too, works
within the constraints of his or her social norms, cultural context, and value
system. In the powerful role of reformer, it is easy enough to influence adult
learners in ways that are not appropriate for them. The educator, too, must
consider, clarify, and question values and actions.

The learner who is stimulated by the educator's use of the role of
reformer may well undertake a painful process as a result. If the timing is
wrong—if the learner is simultaneously dealing with other issues or if support is not available—the process can harm the individual. The educator
must be aware of this possible misuse of the role and be prepared both to
provide support and to switch out of the role. This can be particularly tricky
when working with a group. If one individual in the group shows a strong
emotional response to an activity or discussion, the temptation is either to
ignore or to blame the individual, rather than to recognize a valid reaction to
the reformer role.

The educator's use of the reformer role and learners' receptivity to it are probably related in some ways to psychological type. Jung describes the extroverted intuitive type as a "social reformer"; the combined interest in seeing all the possibilities and in interacting with the environment lead naturally to the reformer role. Other educators who are extroverted types, particularly feeling and sensing, would be less likely to be drawn to this role as they are less interested in change. Introverted types with intuition would be interested in the change aspect, but would withdraw from the proactive component of the role. The same relationships would likely hold true for learners. Intuitive types would be open to the questioning and challenging process and willing to examine the alternatives. It should be noted that Jung describes the introverted thinking type as being especially hostile to criticism or questioning—this learner would resist the implied "criticism" in the educator's reformer role. It is also quite likely that developmental stage would be related to learners' acceptance of reform. An individual in a transition period developmentally would be more open to transformation of his or her perspectives or be already engaged in the process.

The Reflective Practitioner Role

We move, here, to a slightly different type of role, more of a "meta-role," one which can be used simultaneously with all other roles. At the same time, to be a reflective practitioner is also to be a learner.

It has been stressed that the adult educator must be aware of the rationale behind the use of a particular role in an instructional situation. This awareness can be a part of a continual development and revision of a theory of practice. Without engaging in this process, the educator is simply a technician, responding to the expressed needs of the learner or of the organization. Unfortunately, adult education literature abounds with practical guidelines and maxims that are not grounded in a theoretical framework. And educators, many of whom have not studied education as a discipline, fall into the understandable trap of applying principles and guidelines without thinking about what they are doing or why they are doing it. This constitutes the nonreflective practitioner role.

How does one assume the role of reflective practitioner? Reflection implies a conscious consideration of experiences, ideas, feelings, and values. Boud, Keogh, and Walker (1985) suggest that the process of reflection has three stages:

- An experience is "returned to" and recaptured in as much detail as possible. It is useful to do this in writing or through discussion with others. A Practitioner's Journal may be a helpful device for reflection.

- Feelings attached to the experience are reviewed, again in writing or through discussion.

- The experience is reevaluated, a stage that should contain several components. Ideas and feelings about the original experience are associated with ideas and feelings that occur during the reflection process. The meaning of these associations is examined, and the associations are integrated or grouped. For example, one might have felt angry during an experience, but upon reflection felt no anger; or an idea that seemed logical during the experience might seem silly in retrospect. Next, validation occurs through examining new ideas or knowledge or feelings in relation to previous experiences or existing knowledge. Finally, new knowledge becomes a part of how we act and feel (referred to as "appropriation" by the authors).

Described in this fairly abstract way, the process of reflection may seem difficult or time-consuming. However to review experiences is a natural human activity; here, the suggestion is simply that the process be made conscious and systematic. It is usual for a workshop leader to think again about a session after the end of the day or for an educator to consider the group of learners from one meeting to the next. If this normal "thinking about" our work becomes more focused and part of the process of developing a theory of practice, then we are adopting the role of a reflective practitioner.

Another approach to reflection has emerged from the work of the organizational psychologists Schon (1983) and Argyris (1982). They point out the discrepancy that inevitably exists between "espoused theories of practice" (for example, the principles of adult education) and theories-in-use (what we actually do). Educators who have effective theories-in-use base their practice on valid information or information from the participants involved in the activity; they exercise free and informed choice over the activities of their practice; and they exhibit an internal commitment to their chosen course of action while monitoring it. Argyris and Schon propose that practitioners should realize that they are actually building a theory of practice *while they are in the situation,* and that they reflect on and make explicit this theory-building activity. Rather than attempting to implement the "principles" or the espoused theory of practice, practitioners can be engaged in developing their own continuing theory of practice (Argyris & Schon, 1974).

The role of reflective practitioner can be made explicit in working with groups, and learners can participate in the process of defining the philosophical rationale of practice. For example, all members of the group (educator and learners) can keep track of roles being used, when they are used, and can discuss their reactions to the roles. Again, the use of journals is particularly effective for analyzing a process. If this kind of activity is not appropriate for the subject in which the educator is working, a short time can always be spent during or at the end of a session in which participants talk about what happened, what worked for them, what did not work, and how they felt about the interaction. Even conducting a more systematic formative evaluation of a session (e.g., questionnaires or learner comments) and discussing the results with the group can be a part of making the educator's reflective role explicit within the group. The educator who is open about being a reflective practitioner with his or her learners is also acting as a model for reflective learning for the group. Despite feelings of vulnerability or fear that the risk is too great (don't let them know that we're not sure of ourselves), the reflective practitioner role can be introduced gradually, and inevitably both the educator and learners benefit.

There are really no inappropriate uses of the reflective practitioner role. Thinking about one's practice with a view to continually developing a theory of practice can only be beneficial. Mistakes may be made in the analysis, but the process itself remains essential.

Some psychological types are more naturally drawn to the role of reflective practitioner than others, and some learners will be more receptive to the process being made explicit. Thinking or intuitive types are likely to enjoy the analysis and the examination of possibilities and alternatives. Feeling types will go about the reflection in a way that is related to their preferred function—using judgment based on values or feelings—and will benefit equally. Sensing types may have some difficulty, preferring to get on to the next experience and not to dwell on the past. Cultural values and expectations may make it difficult for some educators and some learners to risk making the reflective process "open."

The Researcher Role

In the researcher role, we go one more step beyond the reflective practitioner role. Research is, in general, the systematic investigation of phenomena in order to develop or establish principles or relationships which can be generalized to other situations. In research, observations are conducted and attempts are made to say that "this causes that" or "this is related to that" or "this can be predicted from that." The goal of research is to develop a theory (an explanation) for a set of observations. The educator who assumes the role of researcher attempts systematically to establish explanations for or principles about the interactions with learners which can then be applied in the next situation. To some extent, we all do this informally—"that exercise worked well last time, I'll use it again"—but this role can be made explicit and conscious.

This is not to suggest that all practising educators begin writing articles on adult education, although the combination of subject-area and education expertise has produced some extremely valuable insights. Rather, it is suggested that educators view themselves as researchers in order to develop their own explicitly stated theory of practice. As Argyris points out, when questioned about their practice, or why they chose a particular action at a particular time, educators refer to "hunches" or to intuition ("I knew it was the right thing to do"). The data are there, and by deliberately assuming a researcher role, educators can untangle what is the "right thing to do" for them, in varying situations.

In the role of researcher the educator may: systematically observe learner behavior and reactions, educator behavior and reactions, and characteristics of the environment; formulate hypotheses about the connections among observations; test hypotheses by observation (which can include any kind of information or data); reject or accept hypotheses based on observation; formulate rules or principles; and develop a theory or explanation of practice. Two characteristics distinguish research from other activities: it is *systematic*, and it has the goal of *generalization* to other situations.

How does one go about performing this role amid the other numerous and more pressing responsibilities of the educator? We obviously cannot conduct a full-scale investigation of educator effectiveness (unless we happen to be in that academic discipline). It is, however, possible to make many systematic observations that are not inordinately time-consuming. Depending on the environment, some examples may include: the results of group activities recorded on flip chart paper; copies of learners' papers, projects, journals, and learning contracts; responses to evaluation questionnaires; agendas, activity descriptions, and educator notes; video or audio tapes produced within a session for other purposes; and any other written material produced within or for a session. The very collection of such observations will naturally lead most educators to formulate hypotheses about what happened and why. If these hypotheses are written down in some form (this need not be formal— questions or ideas in any format are useful), they will lead to greater awareness of behaviors and reactions, and hence to further observations. It is the process of making this "researcher thinking" explicit that will cause the educator to consider practice in a new way and consciously develop a theory of practice.

The role of researcher is at the final point on the continuum toward mutually-directed learning. Learners are actively involved in the contribution of data to the development of educator practice. It is here, in essence, that the learner has the most power for influencing education.

As was said in relation to the role of reflective practitioner, the role of researcher is always appropriate and relevant for the adult educator. Two cautions should be stated, however. First, research should not be conducted which either detracts from the learning process (spending all one's time making observations and forgetting about learners) or is any way unethical (learners must always know that you are making observations and must give their permission for you to copy their work or make records of their behavior). Second, the educator must be cautious about making generalizations. As was seen in the model in Chapter 1, the educating/learning process is an exceedingly complex one, influenced by numerous factors. Conclusions drawn from one set of observations will not always apply to another situation; the educator who insists that they "should" apply and attempts to impose certain behavior on another group could be engaged in an unproductive activity.

Interest in the researcher role will naturally appeal more to educators and learners with certain characteristics. The thinking type, with a preference for logical analysis, will be most likely to assume the researcher role. The feeling type will have a tendency to formulate hypotheses based on "gut feelings" rather than on logic. The intuitive type will be intrigued by the possibilities and will produce dozens of versions of a model to describe the relationships among factors, but may not get around to making systematic observations or analyzing the information. The sensing type has great skill at collecting and organizing data, but may have difficulty with drawing conclusions, formulating hypotheses, or developing generalizations. In terms of learning style, the assimilator is the ideal researcher, with the combined preference for observation and reflection, and the formulation of abstract concepts and generalizations.

The Roles We Play: A Summary

Twelve educator roles have been discussed along a continuum from other-directed (expert role) through self-directed (educator as manager) to mutually-directed learning (educator as researcher). Figure 3.2 below presents a summary of these twelve roles. For each, the major educator behaviors or characteristics are listed, along with when the role can or should be used, and possible dangers inherent in the use of the role. As has been emphasized throughout this discussion, the selection of roles is based on educator and learner characteristics, subject or discipline, the learning environment, and the social environment in which one works. Each of the components of the model presented in Chapter 1 interacts with the other components to produce an almost infinite variety of learning situations. It is the use of the reflective practitioner and the researcher role which provide the educator with the opportunity to make choices based on a sound theory of practice.

Research on Educator Roles

Limited research exists on the use of various roles in adult education. In part, this is due to the nature of adult education—its newness as an academic discipline, the diverse nature of practice in the discipline, and the complexity of the phenomena to be investigated. The latter point becomes apparent as soon as one example is examined: say we wanted to determine the effectiveness of the co-learner role. First of all we would have to define co-learner in a clear enough way to be able to tell reliably when it was being used within any situation and when it was not. Then we would have to determine and

Figure 3.2. Summary of Educator Roles

Role	Major Characteristics	When to Use	Dangers
Expert	• Transmits expertise	• To provide elaboration and insight • With inexperienced learners • For materials development	• Little interaction • Dependent, powerless learners
Planner	• Designs	• With inexperienced learners • For materials development	• Powerless learners
Instructor	• Tells what to do • Directs, guides	• With specific skills-related objectives • With inexperienced learners	• Dependent, powerless learners • Limited interaction
Facilitator	• Responds to needs • Encourages, supports	• With self-directed learners • With experienced learners	• Learners may not have the skills • Real needs may not be met
Resource Person	• Provides materials	• With individualized packages • With advanced learners	• Real needs may not be met
Manager	• Keeps records, evaluates, arranges	• With individualized and distance education • With independent learners	• Less interaction • Real needs may not be met
Model	• Models behaviors and values	• In most situations especially with values and complex learning	• May be inappropriate behaviors
Mentor	• Advises, guides, supports	• In longer-term relationships • With compatible individuals by mutual consent	• Inappropriate directions • Lack of educator awareness
Co-learner	• Learns, mutually plans with learner	• When educator and learners share goals • With advanced learners	• Manipulation Dishonesty • Learners not ready
Reformer	• Challenges, stimulates questions, transforms	• With goals of individual transformation or social change • For empowerment	• Indoctrination, manipulation • Painful process
Reflective Practitioner	• Examines and questions practice • Develops philosophy and theory	• Continually	• Can be threatening and difficult
Researcher	• Makes observations • Formulates hypotheses • Develops theory of practice	• Continually	• Time away from Learner • Overgeneralization

assess all of the relevant learner characteristics. Next, we would have to determine and assess all of the relevant environmental characteristics. And most importantly, we would have to decide what "effectiveness" meant and find a way to measure that.

Nevertheless, particularly with the increasing numbers of graduate programs in adult education in North America, researchers have begun to tackle some of these complex issues. Prior to the late 1970s, many investigations were conducted into the numbers of adult learners participating in programs and their reasons for entering or reentering education. These works are nicely reviewed by Cross (1981) and will not be included here. In addition, it should be noted that research in higher education (college and university) is viewed as a separate literature in most cases; oddly, very little overlap exists between this area of investigation and adult education. The interested reader should peruse such journals as *Journal of Higher Education, Canadian Journal of Higher Education, Higher Education,* and *Review of Higher Education.*

In the last 10 years, the most commonly researched area in adult education has been self-directed learning and, consequently, the role of the facilitator. We will turn to a summary of that research after looking briefly at some of the work in higher education which is related to other roles.

Higher Education Research

In higher education, the emphasis has been on instructor-centered roles, especially the use of the lecture method. Unfortunately, years of research have concentrated on comparing the effectiveness of the lecture method (expert role or instructor role) to other methods. However, as was discussed in this chapter, different educator roles are more suitable in some contexts than others and are more effective with some learners than others. Not surprisingly, some researchers found one method to be superior, some found another method to be superior, and most found no overall differences between methods. Some survey research, such as that done by Brown and Bakhtar (1983), examined the perceptions of the instructor-centered roles by educators and learners; it is interesting to note that both groups place a high value on clarity of presentation, structure, and interest, and also complain that there is not enough opportunity for involvement and response. Learners from different disciplines tend to view the role in different ways; for example, individuals from the sciences value the structure characteristics more highly than instructors from the arts. As we have discussed, the learning environment is one of the critical factors in the selection of educator roles.

Extensive research on instructor-centered roles has been conducted through analyses of learners' evaluations of instructor effectiveness. This literature is far too voluminous to review here; however, there is a remarkable consistency in the factors that are associated with effective use of the instructor role. Reviews of the literature (cf. Cohen, 1981; Marsh, 1987) inevitably include factors such as presentation skills, rapport with learners, structure, and evaluation among the dimensions related to effectiveness.

The type of research that has been carried out on instructor-centered roles tells us what learners see as effective *for that role*, but gives no indication of when the role itself is effective. Cranton and Smith (1986) found that learners' perceptions of the effectiveness factors varied dramatically from one discipline to another, from one program year to another, and from one class size to another, all within the context of higher education. Learners' perceptions across settings have not been investigated.

Research on the effectiveness of groups in the learning process (moving toward the facilitator role) has also concentrated primarily on comparing one method to another. As one would expect, the reviewers (cf. Bligh, 1980; Jaques, 1984) conclude that there are no differences overall between methods. Of course, when individual differences among learners and educators, and differences across settings are "averaged out," there is probably not *a* best method or role. It is worthwhile to note, however, that group interaction has been found to be more effective when problem-solving and attitudinal change are the goals of the process.

The examination of group interactions *per se* has tended to show that discussion skills and more complex cognitive learning are facilitated by the process (Kulik and Kulik, 1979). The problem we have in interpreting this kind of research is that there are endless types of group interactions and studying them as one phenomenon does not tell us very much. Luker (1987) found, in small group settings, that the proportion of time the educator spent

lecturing varied from 7 to 70 percent, and that considerable variation occurred across disciplines.

Looking at the seemingly fruitless years spent investigating the effectiveness of various methods and roles, the reader will wonder why we haven't
spent our time looking at how learners with different characteristics respond
to different roles. About 20 years of research went into that direction as well,
but with little result. In his Presidential Address to the American Psychological Association in 1957, Cronbach (1957) suggested that we should forget
about comparisons of methods and examine the interaction between individual characteristics and "treatments" (or methods). From then until the late
1970s, educators looked for these interactions. Finally, Cronbach and Snow
(1977) concluded that the search was leading nowhere—most likely because
learner characteristics were not being adequately assessed, or because other
factors could not be controlled or accounted for. This research was conducted not only in higher education, but also with younger learners.

Adult Education Research

In the adult education literature, we also find research which attempts to
delineate "good" educator behaviors. Zerges (1984), for example, surveyed
continuing education learners in business courses and found that they
valued: educator knowledge of materials, clear statements of expectations
and objectives, sequential organization, and prompt and fair evaluation. In
terms of interpersonal skills, learners selected responsiveness, animation,
humor, and friendliness, but rated these characteristics lower than the
structure-related ones.

In another example of this type of research, Schmidt (1984) examined the
preferences of adult learners returning to university and found that they
preferred independent learning and noncompetitive activities, but that they
wanted educator direction. They did not particularly value the importance of
social relationships or interaction.

On the other hand, other researchers have come to the conclusion that
adult learners respond positively to "andragogical methods" and that these
methods are related to increased learning, as perceived by learners (cf. Bowers, 1977; Knights and McDonald, 1977). And when educators are asked to

give their perceptions, they most often indicate that they do use different roles with adult learners more than they do, or would, with younger learners (cf. Beder and Darkenwald, 1982; Gorham, 1984). Whether or not these perceptions are accurate is questionable; Gorham continued her investigation by observing some educators and did not find that they did what they said they did. Likewise, Wilcox (1990a) found discrepancies between stated beliefs about practice and actual practice. One is quickly reminded of Schon's (1983) espoused theory versus theory-in-use.

What can we make out of this tangle? Findings from the adult education literature are not much different from those in the higher education literature. And as we could have predicted, perceptions of "best" roles vary from one situation to another, from educator to educator, and from learner to learner. This type of research cannot hope to come to general conclusions, given the complexity of the process and the lack of theoretical bases for most of the investigations.

Also parallel to higher education research, adult educators have looked for links between learner characteristics and preferred educator roles. McKeachie (1970) reviews some of the earlier work in this area and comes up with such general conclusions as sociable learners prefer discussion and more motivated learners prefer independent study. Moore (1982), without collecting data, proposes links between Kolb's learning styles and various educator roles. In her thesis, Herbeson (1990) finds some evidence of relationships between psychological type and preferences for self-directed approaches to learning. Thiel (1984), in a study of successful self-directed learners, determines that the majority displayed the accommodator learning style. In an analysis of the assumptions underlying the use of self-directed approaches, Candy (1987) discusses numerous learner characteristics which may be related to preferences for certain roles (for example, locus of control, self-efficacy, field dependence, self-concept, and learned helplessness), but without research evidence to support the suggestions.

The difficulty, of course, with this type of research is that whatever characteristics are selected for study, there are dozens more which are not considered and have just as strong an influence on preferences for educator roles or the effectiveness of roles. In addition, the learning and social environments are clearly related to role selection. Although it is important to continue to investigate such relationships in the educative process, it is unrealistic ever to expect rules to be formulated which the educator can follow in order to arrive at the "correct" role for the situation.

In this light, the most valuable roles for the educator to be aware of and to use are those of reflective practitioner and researcher. Through these roles, the individual educator can formulate his or her own informed theory of practice, as will be seen in Chapter 7.

4

Working Toward Self-Directed Learning

An overview of educator roles has been provided, including those used in instructor-directed, learner-directed, and mutually directed learning. Different roles are more or less appropriate in varying contexts; however, adult educators and theorists have traditionally emphasized learner self-direction. In this chapter that approach will be explored in depth, with an emphasis on how the educator can effectively implement self-directed learning in practice.

The idea that self-directed learning is *the* essential ingredient of adult education has led to some difficult and even destructive experiences for both learners and educators. Any learner who has been "dropped into" a self-directed course, or any instructor who has assumed that his or her learners must be self-directed and has proceeded on that basis will identify with this statement: learners *expect* "teachers to teach"; everything in their experience with education and in their society leads them to expect that when they enter an educational environment, there will be a teacher who will tell them what to do. They may be completely independent and self-directing in their professional and personal lives; they may happily go about learning about a new interest or hobby in a self-directed way; but they expect the workshop leader, the course instructor, or the staff developer to know more than they do and to impart that information in as painless a way as possible. If this does not happen, they will become confused, disoriented, and angry, and feel that their rights as learners have been ignored.

The adult educator, on the other hand, is aware of the literature of the past 45 years in which it is repeatedly stated that adult learners are self-directed, prefer to be self-directed, or at least, have the potential to be self-directed.

Therefore, they naturally expect that when they announce the use of a self-directed approach, learners will respond enthusiastically, saying in effect: "At LAST we've found a situation in which we can really learn what we want to learn!" If this does not occur, the educator also becomes confused, disoriented, or angry, and will be ready to drop the approach.

To do them justice, many practical guidelines for educators do mention that self-directed approaches should be introduced "gradually" or that learners need to *learn* to be self-directed or, sometimes, that not all learners are self-directed. These cautions, however, are generally forgotten in the practicalities of implementation. Many self-directed programs, such as that offered at the McMaster Medical School (cf. Ferrier, Marin and Seidman, 1981) or various programs in nursing (cf. Ash, 1985) or management development (cf. Thorne and Marshall, 1984) have not taken these cautions into account. Educators generally do not include a transition period as part of the process; as a result, learners often react with fear and anxiety. And while little consideration is given to the transition process in the practical literature, even less emphasis is placed on it by researchers. Investigators have spent some time trying to determine who is self-directed or what other characteristics self-directedness is related to, but almost no time examining the process of becoming self-directed.

The centrality of the concept of self-directed learning in adult education cannot be denied or overlooked. And, as almost anyone who has survived the process will agree, being a self-directed learner *is* a freeing experience. The very nature of learning changes—from trying to figure out what the teacher wants and repeating it, to exploring, growing, and breaking free of boundaries. In this chapter, a description of the process of becoming self-directed will be offered and the roles, methods, and skills involved in working toward self-direction will be discussed in some detail. First, however, the concept itself will be reviewed briefly.

In Chapter 2, it was concluded that self-directedness is not a characteristic of an adult; that is, it is neither a stable trait nor a way of being in the way that, say, psychological type is. Learning is a *process*, and self-directed learning is a particular way of going through that process. Individuals may be more or less capable of undertaking self-directed learning, just as they are more or less capable of undertaking any kind of learning. It is a process which involves others, and one of those others is the educator; it is not equivalent to independent learning. The educator has a role in stimulating and encouraging self-directed learning.

Self-directed learning is an *outcome*, as well as a process. An individual gains the skills of engaging in self-directed learning, which involves a change in attitude and behavior; this results in an outcome which then enables that person to engage further in self-directed learning activities with more ease and expertise.

And finally, self-directed learning is a *goal* of adult education. Regardless of the theoretical perspective, some form of self-direction is seen as a valued goal. The humanists talk of self-actualization; Jung describes individuation; developmental theorists describe a postconventional, autonomous stage of functioning; and critical theorists see empowerment as the goal of education. We cannot work as adult educators without accepting this goal as an important responsibility.

The Process of Working Toward Self-Direction

Very little has been written about the process of becoming self-directed. Knowles (revised, 1984) lists the skills that a learner must have in order to engage in self-directed learning (see Chapter 2). Brookfield (1986) describes some methods and techniques, such as learning contracts and peer networks, that are commonly used by educators to encourage self-directed learning. Other authors list the characteristics of "ideal" educators (cf. Tough, 1979). But aside from several studies which describe the anxiety experienced by learners in self-directed learning situations (cf. Ash, 1985), the process itself has rarely been addressed.

One exception to this is a qualitative study of a graduate level course in adult education at the Ontario Institute for Studies in Education (Taylor, 1987). Based on an analysis of fourteen interviews with the eight learners in the course, Taylor describes four phases and four transition points involved in the process of moving toward self-direction.

- *Disconfirmation*—a discrepancy between expectations and experience. For example, the learner expects to receive an agenda and objectives, but instead she is asked what she wants to learn.

- *Disorientation*—discomfort and confusion, accompanied by a crisis of confidence and withdrawal from people associated with the source of confusion. The learner thinks "I don't understand this—am I the only one? No one else has said anything."

- *Identification of the problem* (a transition phase)—naming the problem without blaming self and others. The learner begins a transition by thinking, for example, "This must be what adult education means. The problem is I didn't realize that before."

- *Exploration*—an intuitively guided, collaborative, and open-ended exploration leading to insights, confidence, and satisfaction. The learner may discuss the approach with classmates, realize that everyone was confused, and begin to feel better about the course.

- *Reflection* (a transition phase)—a time of private review of the process. The learner thinks about and perhaps writes about the process as a part of a transition to acceptance.

- *Reorientation*—a major insight or synthesis experience occurring simultaneously with a new approach to the learning (or teaching) task. The learner feels, *"Now* I understand what's involved here, I really can select my own readings on the topic."

- *Sharing the discovery* (a transition phase)—testing out the new understanding with others (as a part of returning to a state of equilibrium). The learner may, for example, explain the approach to a co-worker, checking to see if it "makes sense" to him.

- *Equilibrium*—elaboration, refinement, and application of the new perspective and approach. The learner now may implement the approach in another course (Taylor, 1987, 183).

This description follows, in general, other learning cycles (e.g., Mezirow, 1977) where a discrepancy between expectations and experience produces disorientation, followed by an exploration of the alternatives, reorientation to the new experience, and, finally, integration. As such, it provides a useful overall framework for the process of becoming self-directed. However, Taylor's study data were collected from a small homogeneous group (adult education graduate students), and it seems probable that more diverse groups of learners would react in other ways. The experience of working toward self-directed learning requires, for most adults, a radical change in beliefs and values. Long-held assumptions about the nature of education must be examined, questioned, and revised. In this sense, the process is an example of Mezirow's transformative learning and usually is a complex and painful process.

Figure 4.1 below presents a model of the process of working toward self-directed learning, incorporating Taylor's suggestions, but expanding on the stages in the process and including a variety of "possible paths" which individual learners might follow. Possible paths are indicated by dotted lines; the most common paths are indicated by solid lines. The outcomes of the process (indicated in double-lined boxes) include rejection, acceptance and equilibrium, or advocacy of self-directed learning.

We will examine this process in more detail, then turn to the needs of learners and educators in the process. It should be noted here that the model which will be discussed in this chapter involves working towards a *fully* self-directed approach to learning (learners actively involved in the full planning process). In practice, many variations and compromises exist.

Learner Reactions in Working Toward Self-Directed Learning

Learners enter into any educational experience with a set of assumptions and expectations about their upcoming experience and about learning experiences in general. Assumptions are usually based on past experiences, including formal schooling and exposure to any other adult learning environments. Expectations may be based on the particular reasons for choosing to participate—advertisements or publicity about the course; knowledge of the program, workshop leader, or subject; knowledge of self-directed learning; and comments of colleagues or peers. In addition, each learner enters the situation with personal and cultural characteristics—psychological type, learning style, developmental stage, values, attitudes, beliefs, and social norms.

The usual collection of individual differences with which every educator works? Yes, but now we are presenting a different approach to learning, one that may clash with the expectations of learners and possibly with some of their individual characteristics. Learners who have prior experience with

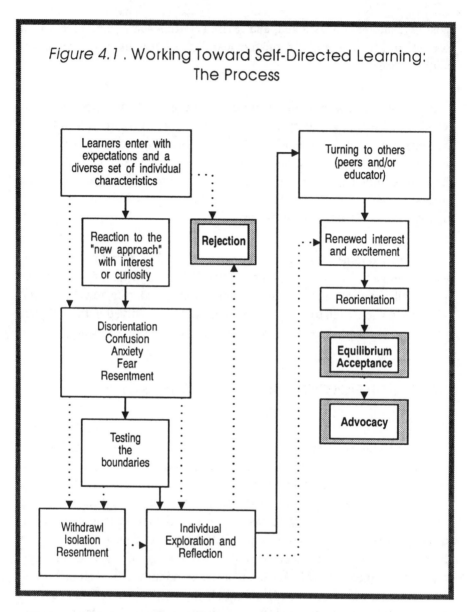

Figure 4.1 . Working Toward Self-Directed Learning: The Process

self-directed learning will begin this educational experience at one of the later points in the process described below.

Curiosity

Most individuals display some interest, curiosity, and a questioning attitude to this new approach. Typical learner behaviors include:

- asking questions about requirements, textbooks, and evaluation activities;
- commenting on expectations; and,
- relaying any previous personal experience with self-directed learning.

However, on some occasions (and this would happen probably only rarely for any one educator) a learner will immediately, and without questioning, reject the process. He or she may leave the session or simply not return if it is a longer course. If attendance is required by employers or other agencies, this individual will withdraw mentally. Also, other learners may skip the stage of interest in a new approach and immediately display disorientation and confusion.

Confusion

During the stage of disorientation and confusion, learners display a variety of behaviors and reactions including:

- questioning the credibility of the educator;
- demanding that the educator impart his or her knowledge and expertise;
- displaying anxiety;
- expressing fear of failure;
- feeling "cheated";
- imposing a personal structure on the situation;
- meeting and discussing the situation with peers and colleagues; and,
- withdrawing from participation.

Some learners go through this process without comment, giving no outward indication; others consult individually with the educator or peers; still others openly discuss their concerns both in and outside the session, possibly with program administrators or employers. Disorientation and confusion last for varying periods of time for different individuals.

Testing

Many learners go from confusion to testing the boundaries of the situation. It appears that individuals try to cope with their confusion by determining what is and what is not allowed within the new approach. This testing differs from the exploration stage (which usually follows) in that it is still based on the assumption or expectation that the educator has unstated requirements, hidden agendas, and final control over the situation. Trust in the educator is not yet established; the learner must check out his or her original assumptions about educators and educational experiences in order to determine where and how this new one fits.

When testing occurs, typical learner behaviors include:

- missing sessions;
- arriving late;
- asking permission;
- doing nothing;
- suggesting banal or trivial learning projects;
- trying to manipulate the educator into the expert role;
- checking out the reality of self-evaluation;
- asking to have parameters re-stated;
- consulting with the educator and peers;
- asking for more structure; and,
- asking for feedback.

At times the behaviors are negative and aggressive, at other times they are positive, but overly dependent, and some individuals exhibit a mixture of several approaches. This is a decidedly difficult stage for the educator; we too are working within our own assumptions and expectations, and the temptation is strong to decide that this approach simply doesn't work and to give learners what they want. Ways for the educator to deal with this stage will be discussed in the section on educator skills.

Not all learners go through this part of the process. And, in some groups, manifestations can be quite subtle, with only a few behaviors exhibited, such as asking for confirmation and seeking guidance.

Withdrawal

Some individuals move directly from confusion to withdrawal, and some test boundaries before withdrawing. But for many, withdrawal and isolation do not occur at all. It appears that the varying ways of going through the learning process can be related to psychological type; for example, introverted types have a tendency to withdraw into themselves in uncomfortable situations. Some behaviors exhibited during this stage include:

- lack of participation in discussions and group activities;
- actual physical withdrawal, such as sitting outside the circle or at the edges of groups;
- nonverbal indications of withdrawal (body posture) and resentment (facial expression);
- outbursts of apparently aggressive comments during discussions; and,
- not engaging in social interaction with others before or after the session, or during breaks.

Again, facing these behaviors is difficult for the educator, who usually expects that he or she can make everyone happy or meet all learner needs. This stage can also easily be confused with rejection of the approach, particularly if the withdrawal behaviors continue over several meetings, as is sometimes the case. However, these learners are sorting things out in their own way and will inevitably move onto the next stage of exploration and reflection. If learners are keeping journals, it is often interesting to note that during the withdrawal process they themselves do not perceive the process as negative, but are simply questioning their own assumptions and values, and trying to reorient themselves to a new situation.

Exploration and Reflection

Once sure of the boundaries, or rather sure that there are no hidden boundaries, learners tentatively begin to explore. This stage may overlap with "testing," but it takes on a more positive tone. For example, a learner who has never been to a library or used a computer may skip a session and tour the library or try the computer, checking that he can really "get away with it," but also exploring with a beginning sense of excitement. At this stage, learners may:

- bring in articles or newspaper clippings that they have found;

- discover and read a book related to a topic discussed;

- write extensively in journals about new ideas and connections and conflicts;

- relate their experiences to the group and/or educator;

- explore learning projects that interest them;

- read extensively;

- apply new ideas to their work and want to share this with the educator or peers; and,

- discuss ideas with their colleagues or co-workers or family.

The stage of exploration and reflection may still contain conflict and questioning, rejection and acceptance, and some elements of testing. However, renewed interest begins to show, and the experience begins to be very satisfying for both learner and educator.

Turning to Others

Most learners turn to others to check out and discuss their explorations. Some of the behaviors listed under exploration are also included in this component; however, an identifiable stage in the process now often emerges (more so for extroverted learners, and even more so for extroverted feeling type learners). Learners meet each other socially, going to each other's homes and out for meals; they arrive at sessions together and make plans for meetings after the session. Discussion and sharing of ideas and projects becomes animated and intense. Some decide to work together on projects. The educator will find his or her office crowded with learners, many of whom appear to be more interested in talking to each other than to the educator. Considerable educator time will be spent in meeting with learners and discussing their ideas (they no longer tend to ask for guidance, but rather want to discuss). They ask for additional resources and exchange resources with each other. This stage in the process inevitably leads to the next, that of interest and excitement, fuelled by interactions with peers and with the educator. It should be noted, though, that while some learners do not participate in the "turning to others" stage, they nevertheless do move on to the excitement stage.

Renewed Interest and Excitement

Finally, the joy and excitement that we thought we deserved from the beginning emerges. By this stage, learners have chosen projects or activities and areas of interest. Most are actively involved in reading, writing, or doing and applying. And most are at least interested in, and often excited about, what they are doing. There is no longer any question of whether they will be allowed to choose their assignments or whether they will fail. Learners still need educator approval, but it takes on a different tone; in fact, if criticisms are made at this stage, most learners will stoutly defend the approach they have chosen or the work they are doing. They may work with each other and still congregate outside the office door, but it is no longer for validation and confirmation—it is collegial; it begins to resemble the approval we seek when we go to a colleague to discuss a new idea. It is at this stage that the educator can really become a co-learner or a mentor.

As strange as it may sound, even though this stage has been the goal, it also can be a difficult stage for the educator, for here is where we "let go." We no longer have control, authority, or responsibility for the learning, and that seems to violate societal expectations, as well as past experience and values. This will be discussed in more detail in the section on educator skills.

Reorientation

As various projects and learning activities are worked through and as the excitement of the new experience begins to die down, learners will reorient themselves. They will integrate this new experience into their set of educational experiences; they will resolve the issues that led to the initial disorientation and confusion. For some individuals, this process takes considerable time and may occur well after the learning experience. For others, it seems to come as an insight, an "aha" phenomenon. Learners now see themselves as responsible for their own learning, a transformation in perspective has taken place.

Some learner behaviors which indicate that this stage is reached include:

- putting together what happened in the experience (saying "Now, I understand why you did ... at the beginning");
- a lessening of emotional reactions and of excitement;
- stating, as an *assumption*, that other learning experiences should follow this format; and,
- writing or discussing the process in an integrated fashion.

Equilibrium

The reorientation stage, or the integration of the process of self-directed learning into the individual's experience, finally leads back to equilibrium. The learner entered the situation "in equilibrium" with a set of expectations about the educative process. The final outcome, for most learners, is to return to equilibrium, but with some of the expectations changed. One consequence of this, of course, is that the learner then enters the next situation with those expectations, which may or may not be met. He or she may go on to "advocacy" or may return to the old set of expectations. For the learner who is also an educator, the equilibrium stage will most often lead to the adoption and application of self-directed techniques to his or her own teaching. Learners also report that they have revised the way they interact with others outside of the educational environment (e.g., with patients, clients, co-workers, friends, children, spouses). The revision of assumptions and expectations leads to changed behavior.

Advocacy

Some learners may adopt a position of advocacy which may be exhibited in different ways. Learners who go on to other experiences in which they are given no responsibility for the learning process may insist that the educator make changes in his or her approach. Learners who are in administrative positions may attempt to make changes within their institutions or organizations. Individuals who are undertaking graduate work may choose to conduct research on self-directed learning and even make career decisions based on their experiences with the approach. Learners who are also educators may implement the approach in their own situations and try to convince their peers to do the same. They may go on to give workshops to others on the topic, or produce written materials for others.

Needs of the Learner in Working Toward Self-Directed Learning

Given the complexity of adult learning styles, motives, and orientations to learning... it is clearly unrealistic to claim for the self-directed learning style (or indeed any learning style) some form of commonality across the spectrum of adult learners and settings for learning (Brookfield, 1986, 67).

And yet, if we accept self-directed learning as a key process in adult education and if we accept the ability to be self-directed as a valued outcome of an educational experience, we must continue to look for ways to meet learners' needs as they go through the process. In this section, we will review some learner needs. Needs will be related to stages in the process of working toward self-directed learning; however, it must be remembered that individuals go through that process in different ways and exhibit different behaviors.

Emotional Needs

In the earlier stages of the process (disorientation, confusion, testing), the learner experiences a loss of frame of reference or perspective. The old ways of doing things no longer work and therefore must be questioned and possibly discarded. This produces a variety of emotional reactions, such as anger, anxiety, fear, loss of self-confidence, and resentment toward the instigator of the loss—the educator. The learner needs a safe and secure way of dealing with these reactions; for some, this is a private affair and may include writing or reflection; others will discuss the situation with a support group outside of the educational environment, including colleagues, friends, or family; still others will need an opportunity to discuss their reactions with their peers in the group; and, finally, some will need to vent their feelings to the educator. Regardless of the way in which learners choose to express their emotional needs, acceptance, support, trust, and respect must be provided. Within the learning situation, the educator should ensure that there are opportunities for this kind of interaction among learners (small group discussions, role-playing, informal interaction). Emotional reactions addressed to the educator must be accepted and respected as a part of the process. This is not the time for challenging; the initial challenge has already been made, and the learner is responding.

Later in the process (exploration and reflection, turning to others), emotional reactions include excitement, intense interest, joy, and a sense of liberation or autonomy. Learners begin to believe in their ability to direct their learning and gain confidence. Some learners experience this quietly, preferring to write or to reflect on the process; it may appear that the outcome is an intellectual one (e.g., an outpouring of writing) for them, but an underlying emotional response exists. Most learners have a need to share their excitement with others, both inside and outside the educational setting. Other members of the learning group play a vital role here. Access to an effective peer network or interactive group process is often an emotional need of learners. Also needed is approval, affirmation, and positive feedback from the educator.

In the final stages of the process (reorientation and equilibrium), learners' emotional needs are more similar to those of our colleagues or co-workers: acceptance, respect, and perhaps critical feedback. If the educator has assumed a mentor role with a learner, there may be more need for support and encouragement than with other learners. Usually, however, learner needs at this point are intellectual or skills-related rather than emotional.

Intellectual Needs

The distinction between intellectual needs and skills for self-directed learning is to some extent artificial. Knowles (revised, 1984) includes both in his list of learner characteristics. However, they require different educator responses and tend to occur at different times, so therefore will be treated separately here. Intellectual needs will be defined as those pertaining to understanding the process of self-directed learning and its rationale, and understanding the relationship of the process to other approaches to learning.

Skills, on the other hand, will be defined as the abilities involved in carrying out the process—planning, finding resources, and evaluating.

The primary intellectual need of the learner is to understand self-directed learning. In its comprehensive form self-directed learning requires individuals to:

- set their own objectives;

- design strategies to meet those objectives;

- carry out their learning plan; and,

- collect evaluative evidence of the accomplishment of the objectives.

In order to accomplish these ends, the learner must be able to:

- describe what an objective is;

- understand the rationale for using objectives in learning;

- list a variety of strategies to meet objectives;

- recognize an appropriate strategy for an objective;

- list sources of materials and resources;

- describe methods to evaluate learning;

- describe the rationale for evaluation; and,

- recognize appropriate evidence for attainment of an objective.

Before the process begins, learners must understand *cognitively* what is involved. This applies equally to learners involved in academic upgrading, professional training, staff development, informal learning contexts, or any setting in which the self-directed process is used. In some contexts, of course, some components are other-directed (e.g., objectives may be set by others, but learners are self-directed in selecting strategies to meet objectives). In these situations, learners still require an understanding of the full process so that they can place their own experience within that framework.

In addition to an understanding of the process of self-directed learning itself, individuals also need to recognize their own abilities and skills. Learners should be aware of:

- their interests and needs;

- the relationship between their previous experience and the current learning;

- their preferences for ways of learning;

- their need for support and structure;

- their emotional responses to change; and,

- their assumptions about the educating-learning process.

Although the learner's intellectual needs should be addressed throughout the entire process, focus should be directed on these particular needs primarily during the curiosity stage (with an introduction to the nature of self-directed learning) and at the exploration stage (in more detail).

As can be seen, meeting the intellectual needs of learners who are working toward self-directed learning is no small task. It is important to remember that not all of the responsibility lies with the educator—the learner, other group members, and people outside the class or session all play a role in the process. However, the intellectual needs of learners can not be neglected, nor can it be assumed that they have been met by others. The role of the educator will be discussed after we have examined the skills required of the learner.

Skills Needed

In order to direct his or her own learning effectively, the learner must become, in essence, a designer of instruction. In fact, in a paper which addressed the apparent conflict between instructional design and adult education (self-directed), Geis (1987) argued that the resolution was to see the learner as the designer. And this is really what the present approach to self-directedness suggests. However, this resolution requires numerous skills of learners that most do not have. Some learners survive and do quite well in the process, even without preparation or guidance; others drop out or struggle along, never really getting the most out of their experience. Even learners who appear to adapt quickly are likely to waste time and to go through unnecessary frustration.

It may be justifiably asked how the time can be found to provide learners with design skills when they have so much material to cover. No educator of auto mechanics or basic electricity or anatomy wants to spend precious time on topics such as "how to write objectives." There are two answers to this: first, learners will not learn auto mechanics if they do not know how to plan their learning; and second, the design skills can be obtained within the context of the subject (more on this when we get to educator roles). First, let's look at the skills needed by the learner.

In order to be completely responsible for his or her own learning, the learner must be able to:

- diagnose learning needs and interests;

- write observable objectives for each learning need;

- sequence the objectives so as to facilitate learning;

- select strategies for the achievement of each objective;

- find resources and materials related to each objective;

- consult with others as necessary during the process;

- collect evidence as to the learning of each objective; and,

- judge the effectiveness of the learning process.

In reality, the educator is often responsible for some of these skills and is at least involved in facilitating the process with learners. The degree to which learners need all the skills listed obviously depends on the degree of self-directedness in the sessions and on the amount of educator involvement. Most commonly, the educator assumes more responsibility for objectives and evaluation, and the learner assumes more responsibility for strategies and resources. This arrangement is sometimes necessary because of institutional or professional constraints, or it may be due to the educator's perception of real learning needs as opposed to expressed needs.

In addition to design skills, some learners need practical skills as well. Examples of these include the ability to:

- use a library;

- use community resources;

- use technical or business resources;

- use a computer;

- arrange transportation and/or finances;

- arrange a suitable environment in which to learn;
- find day care or babysitting; and,
- arrange time in which to work.

Although the educator clearly cannot meet all the practical skill needs of all learners, an awareness of these needs is essential (and not only in self-directed learning, although they usually become more apparent in this situation). The educator who realizes that the lack of such skills is interfering with the learning process can arrange library assistance, provide access to resources, and offer guidance in other, more personal, areas. This assistance *is* part of the role of the facilitator who is working toward self-directed learning.

Learners need both the design skills and the practical skills before they can effectively work in a self-directed way. These needs must be addressed as early in the process as is feasible. Sometimes, during the disorientation stage, learning these required skills eases the anxiety and confusion; however, at other times, it only serves to exacerbate it, depending on other characteristics of the learner. (Imagine that you are feeling angry and resentful and someone tries to "cure" you by showing you how to write objectives!) By the time learners reach the exploration stage, they have had the opportunity to develop the needed skills, hopefully within the context of the subject. In the next section, an exercise will be described which assists learners in this process.

Summary

It will now be apparent why many reports on self-directed learning programs note the anxiety experienced by learners. In order to be successful in this endeavor, learners must become their own educators. In fact, Little (1979) presents the argument that we should talk of self-education or self-directed education in order to convey the nature of the process. For most educators, it all seems simple enough; we have been doing it for years. But, if we put ourselves in the position of the first-year nursing student or the learner in a management development series or even the new graduate student in adult education, we quickly can see how overwhelming the process must seem. The educator must remain constantly in tune with the emotional, intellectual, and skills needs of the learner. This requires a lot of the educator! In the next section, educator needs will be examined.

Needs of the Educator in Working Toward Self-Directed Learning

As will be clear by this time, working toward self-directed learning is as complex and difficult for an educator as it is for a learner. Emotional and intellectual needs and skills required will be discussed, but as these are closely related to the stages that a learner goes through, the process depicted in Figure 4.1 will serve in general as a framework.

Prior to the Process

Before entering a self-directed learning session, the educator must have a thorough understanding of the process and must have planned the implementation of the particular situation. Intellectual needs are the same as for the learner near the beginning of the process; in other words, the educator must know what the components of self-directed learning are, as well as learner reactions and learners' required skills—without that understanding the process is doomed from the start.

Pre-session planning requires that several sets of decisions be made. Examples of key questions that need to be answered are listed below.

- *How ready are learners likely to be for self-direction?* Will they have experienced it before? If not, what evidence is there about their independence, maturity, or other related characteristics? How much structure and guidance will be required at the beginning?

- *Will all components of the experience be self-directed?* If not, which ones will be and which not? What constraints come into play here? Are there institutional or professional requirements? Can any of these be circumvented? To what degree?

- *Will learners determine the objectives totally?* If so, will this be done as a group or individually? What boundaries or restrictions will be placed on their choices, if any? If objectives will not be determined totally by learners, how much input will they have? How flexible are the objectives that will be used?

- *Is the sequence of learning predetermined by the nature of the content?* Will learners have control over this? As a group? Individually? If learners follow individual sequences, who will keep track of their activities?

- *Are there restrictions on the strategies that learners can employ?* Do they have to be in certain places at certain times; are there institutional or employer constraints, such as required attendance or number of hours spent in the situation? Are there some strategies that are obviously more appropriate than others? If so, will learners be encouraged or required to use these strategies?

- *Are resources and materials available?* Are they accessible for learners? Do any arrangements need to be made to ensure accessibility? Is there any expense to learners? Do learners require transportation or special times to access resources? Will this be a problem for any learners? Are there any constraints regarding resources?

- *To what extent will learners evaluate their own progress?* If they are totally responsible, are there any constraints on this? Are there restrictions on the type of evidence of learning considered acceptable? Are there restrictions on the range of results? If learners are not completely responsible, what input will they have into the evaluation process? Who will have the final say in cases of disagreement? Will anyone else be involved in the evaluation—peers, employers, field supervisors, professional associations? If so, what will be their responsibility? Who will have the final say in cases of disagreement?

- *How will the effectiveness of the overall learning experience itself be determined?* Will learners have responsibility for this? Will they have input into it? Who else will be involved and what responsibilities will they have? Are there institutional requirements regarding evaluation of educational activities?

The specific decisions to be made will vary in different contexts. However, each of the *areas* included in the questions above must be addressed: learners' entering characteristics, objectives, sequencing, learning strategies, resources and materials, evaluation of learning, and evaluation of the effectiveness of the process itself. The reader who is familiar with instructional design will recognize these headings. The learning experience must still be designed, but when using a self-directed approach, the question to be answered becomes who is responsible for planning and/or implementing what aspects of the design.

Prior to entering the self-directed learning experience educators should also consider some of their possible emotional and psychological needs. Educators have a long history of associations and experiences with educational environments on both sides of the desk. For most of this history the educator has been in *control*: telling others what to do, explaining, managing, directing, and evaluating. There is a certain heady power in being in control which is not easy to give up. Often, upon being introduced to a learner-directed approach, the educator will say, "But *I* know what they need to learn"; "How can they evaluate themselves—they'll just give themselves all A's"; thus stating, either explicitly or implicitly, "I'm not giving up control." The educator responds emotionally to this perceived loss of control in the same way as the learner responds to being given control. It is important to be aware of and prepared for this reaction.

To be successful in implementing self-directed learning the educator should:

- truly believe in learners' abilities to direct their own learning;
- be able to give up responsibility and decision making to learners when it is appropriate;
- be prepared to accept emotional responses from learners, including those that appear to be directed against the educator personally;
- be able to listen to learners with interest and enthusiasm without directing; and,
- accept that he or she remains an important figure in learners' experience even though responsibility has been shared or given to learners.

Early Stages

The early stages of working toward self-directed learning are probably the most trying for the educator. It is difficult to deal with learners' emotional reactions and testing of the boundaries of the experience. Quite often, the first time through, the educator will compromise or even give up at this early stage and provide the direction that learners are asking for. In some cases, and to some extent, this reaction can be appropriate, provided that it is not the end of the process.

Intellectual Needs

In the early stages the educator needs to be knowledgeable about learner characteristics and their relationship to self-directed learning, and to understand learner reactions to the process. Although it is difficult to separate this intellectual understanding from the actual skills needed, effective use of relevant skills will be based on knowing what is happening to the learner and why. It is to be expected, for example, that a learner from a culture which values the teacher as an authority will react quite differently from a learner with some self-directed experience, and this learner again will be different from one who has spent the last three years sitting in large lecture classes. It is also to be expected that individuals with different learning styles or personal characteristics will react in different ways. It seems, at times, that there are about as many responses as there are learners; the educator must know and understand this, and recognize that varying responses are part of the change process.

Skills Required

A fairly complex set of skills are required of the educator at the beginning of the process. These skills are difficult to describe generally, but also are closely related to the nature of the individual educator and group of learners. These skills include the ability to:

- provide the right degree of structure and guidance as needed;

- provide consistent and clear information about the process; and,

- provide the appropriate environment in which learners may deal with their confusion or anxiety.

Providing Structure

In the beginning, with a learner group that is new to self-directed learning (or when the majority of the group are new to it), no attempt should be made to have learners select objectives or topics. They will react with understandable fright and indignation. Rather, the educator should propose topics and/or objectives and invite learners to add, delete, or revise. Most often, very few or even no suggestions will be made at this point. But after continued invitations and immediate action taken on suggestions, as they become more comfortable, learners will begin to contribute. It *is* feasible and advisable to indicate to learners that they have complete freedom over choice of projects, papers, assignments, or whatever is relevant to the context of the course. It is also possible to introduce self-evaluation, but do not emphasize it. The educator should make it completely clear that requirements, such as meeting deadlines, maintaining attendance, and working on various projects or activities, are the total responsibility of each learner, unless outside constraints prevent this. Otherwise, the beginning sessions or the start of a longer session should be fairly well structured by the educator—that is, learners are invited to participate in, say, group work or discussion, but the educator provides the structure and usually the content. Slowly, as many decisions as possible should be turned over to learners. These may be small to begin with (e.g., the composition of groups or concrete, practical decisions, such as the length of the break). As time goes on, learners can make more important decisions. The educator can make offers such as, "We could do this in small groups or work on it individually; which do you prefer?" or "We can easily spend more/less time on this topic; the agenda is flexible; what would you like to do?" If no one responds, the educator can simply wait until someone does, then check the suggestion with the rest of the group. As learners see that they have the power to make decisions about the nature of their learning, they will become more and more involved in this process. Quite often, though, this does not occur in the early stages, and it is best to turn over only smaller decisions. It is important to provide just enough guidance and direction to ease learners into the process while, at the same time, challenging them to assume responsibility for their own learning.

Providing Information

The provision of information about self-directed learning is an on-going process. In the early stages, the concept itself should be defined and its major components described. The educator should make clear which aspects of self-directed learning will be available over the session or sessions. In addition, and, just as importantly, the process should be made explicit as it occurs. In other words, the rationale for the nature of the learning experience should be made clear. For example, the educator can say, "I'm providing you with suggested topics and objectives since this area is new to you, but I expect that as time goes on, you will want to make your own contributions to our agenda," and "We have the goal of your becoming responsible for most of the decisions here, I'd prefer that you make this decision—you're the ones who will be doing it."

The educator also needs to be skilful in dealing with learners' confusion, fear, resentment, and testing of the boundaries of the situation. Confusion will be minimized by providing initial structure and explanation as described above. But learners will still worry about making their own choices, particularly about evaluating themselves, if that is incorporated into the session. Most often, they do not believe that educators really mean what they say. One must clearly, consistently, and positively repeat that the learner is capable and competent to make his or her own decisions. When anger or resentment is expressed, the educator should respect and understand that and must not see it as a personal attack. Simple statements such as, "I understand how you feel, but I really believe that you're the one who best knows what you want to do," or "I know that this is a difficult process, but I think you're a better judge of your own learning than I am," are usually effective. In addition, opportunities should be provided for learners to discuss these issues with each other and to write about them. If learners keep a journal, it allows them to reflect on their experiences, and they may be willing to share this with the educator, which provides valuable comment and feedback. This can begin a dialogue between educator and learner which increases understanding on both parts.

Providing the Environment

It is important to create an environment which provides for the comfort of the participants and also makes clear the role of the educator. For example, learners should sit so that they can see and interact with each other. The educator should be part of the group, physically, sitting *with* learners and never standing above or behind them or behind a large desk or podium. It is interesting to note, here, that if the educator sits in the same location throughout a session, or over a series of sessions, that place will become just as much "teacher's desk" as any real desk. It is important to move locations, to move with the group. When joining small groups, it is essential to sit with them and not lean over someone's shoulder, as this creates the impression of checking a student's work.

Learners who are testing boundaries need to be respected. Someone who misses a session and behaves sullenly afterwards, giving an excuse, should receive a cheerful but relatively disinterested, "Oh, no problem." Whatever the "test," an educator must accept it and not revert to "requirements." Outside constraints should have been made clear from the beginning—these, of course, provide real boundaries. If a learner disappears altogether, he or she has completely rejected the process. The educator must be consistent with all learners; preventing someone from doing something will quickly destroy the self-direction process. It is interesting to observe that testing behavior is frequently contagious—if one learner decides he is not interested in the topic being discussed and goes off to investigate the computer lab, the next day will see a group in the computer lab. This makes it difficult for the educator who wants to keep his or her flock in control.

Emotional Needs

Two important emotional issues face the educator: the need to deal with the resentment or anger of learners; and the need to relinquish control. In working with learners' emotional reactions, particularly anger or resentment, the educator must remember that the attacks are not personal. Learners are experiencing a *loss*, and some people react to a loss with anger. The educator initiated, or seems to have initiated, that loss.

Giving up control and letting learners test the boundaries may be even more difficult for some educators. A common reaction is fear—What if they all leave and don't come back? What if they all go off in different directions? What if we don't cover the material? What if they don't want to learn anything? If, in fact, all the learners do leave and do not return (it *has* happened!), then the educator probably made decisions about content or process that were not right for those learners; this outcome is *not* the result of giving up control.

Skills Required

Although each individual and situation is different, some of the following techniques may be useful in dealing with the negative reactions of learners:

- Express understanding of the feelings revealed.

- Relate learners' feelings to the process of becoming self-directed.

- Focus the learner on his or her assumptions about the role of the educator (stating them, writing them).

- Suggest that the learner examine where these assumptions came from (previous experience, societal norms, personal values).

- Provide opportunities for learners to work with each other to examine their assumptions and feelings about them.

- Suggest that learners keep journals of their reactions to the process.

- Provide an opportunity for learners to meet with an individual who has gone through the process.

Each of these techniques returns attention to the process, while, at the same time, accepting the feelings involved. The educator, though, may also respond with anger or resentment or decreased confidence or anxiety. This can be expressed to learners only to a limited extent—they have enough to deal with, without an angry educator. The educator can try the following:

- Discuss the situation with peers, particularly those involved in the same process.

- Keep a journal of the process.

- List, examine, and question his or her own assumptions about the process.

This type of exploration will lead to better understanding of emotional reactions and perhaps to the continued development of a theory of practice. Reactions to the process of giving up control also should be carefully examined through discussion, writing, and reflection.

Middle Stages

During the middle stages of moving toward self-directed learning, exploration, reflection, turning to others, and interest and excitement emerge. An easier time for the educator? Emotionally, yes, but now the learner must be guided through the design process.

Intellectual Needs

The educator needs to be knowledgeable in two areas: he or she must have an understanding of the design process described previously under learner needs, and an awareness of content resources and materials. A complete description of the design process is beyond the scope of this book; the reader who is unfamiliar with it could consult Cranton (1989) or Knox (1986) for details on designing adult learning experiences, or any one of a host of general instructional design references (e.g., Gagné and Briggs, 1970). Content expertise is not normally an issue of concern for the educator; however it is also important to be aware of the availability and accessibility of a variety of resources and materials.

Skills Required

The skills required of the educator during the exploration and interest stages are quite different from those needed in the early stages. The educator must be able to assist learners with:

- planning or designing;
- group processes; and,
- evaluation.

Planning

The learner who is exploring interests, selecting topics, settling on a project, or planning any aspect of his or her learning will need guidance at this stage. Wilcox (1990b) describes a six-step exercise, entitled *Planning for Learning: A Self-Directed Strategy*, which provides a useful framework for this process. The learner proceeds through the following steps as he or she:

- decides on a focus for the learning;
- establishes objectives;
- plans activities for learning;
- plans the sequence;
- communicates learning; and,
- plans for evaluation.

It is immediately obvious that this procedure follows the steps of a design model; what the educator must be able to do is to take the learner through a planning process in a systematic way. Without it, exploration can go on forever, and the learner can become frustrated and resentful, feeling that she is "getting nowhere." Such an exercise can be made available when appropriate to individuals, small groups working together, or the whole learning group if the majority are at this stage.

Group Processes

Another important component of this stage is the support provided by the peer group. Brookfield (1986) includes a peer network as an essential component of successful self-directed learning programs. In the process of working toward self-direction, learners almost always turn to each other for support, interaction, ideas, and, possibly, the development of joint learning activities. The educator plays an important role in facilitating the development of the group or smaller sub-groups. A great deal of literature exists on group dynamics and on fostering effective group processes; this literature comes from counseling theory, social psychology, organizational behavior, and from education. Based on the literature, Knoop (1990) provides several guidelines for encouraging effective group behavior, including the following:

- Set a relaxed, non-stressful, supportive tone within the group.

- Support original and unusual ideas, independent judgments, humor, and openness in communication.

- Encourage the group to satisfy individual members' needs.

- Give prompt feedback in a nonjudgmental, descriptive (rather than evaluative) manner, considering others' readiness to receive feedback.

- Practise supportive listening, conveying the feeling that what is said is of interest and importance, valuing the speaker regardless of whether you agree or disagree with the ideas.

- Prevent "group think," that is, group norms that interfere with critical thinking or the expression of diverse views.

- Encourage group development through diagnosis and awareness of the factors that affect the group's performance.

- Stress group maintenance activities—encourage, be friendly, warm, responsive, involve all, reconcile differences, compromise, be flexible.

- Avoid self-centering activities such as dominating by talking too much, blocking, devaluing, or distancing yourself from the group.

Self-Evaluation

One of the most difficult aspects of self-directed learning for both learner and educator is learner self-evaluation. Even the most independent individual will balk at this component of the process. This is particularly interesting considering the amount of self-evaluation in which adults engage in the rest of their lives; we constantly examine our effectiveness at work, in personal relationships, in sports, in hobbies, and even in mundane daily activities. Yet, when it comes to learning, the teacher is supposed to judge. Actually, two distinctly separate phenomena are evident here—in informal learning contexts, participants would be outraged if the workshop leader or the group leader assigned grades at the end of the session, but in a formal learning context, learners are just as outraged when it is suggested that they should evaluate their own learning. There is a long and strong association between educator and evaluator, one that is difficult to break for both educator and learner.

Two sets of skills are involved here: one breaks the strong association of instructor with evaluation, and one allows learners to develop the necessary skills to evaluate themselves. The latter set is much more tangible than the former and will be addressed first. The process can be described in a series of steps:

- Before learners have begun to work on projects, activities, or papers, they should be discouraged from thinking about what such work will be worth. At this point they do not know how much they will learn from the activity, how much effort they will put into it, or even whether they may later consider a completely different approach.

- Learners should be encouraged to develop specific observable objectives for each activity they are involved in. These may be revised, of course, but should exist. They will form criteria for evaluation.

- When learners have selected and are working on activities, the educator should provide as much feedback as is requested, but *not* succumb to questions about their worth.

- When learners have completed or nearly completed all activities, it should be suggested that they assign a "weight" to each one (a weight can be precise, say 40 percent, or imprecise, such as "about one-half"). The weights should be based on the amount of time and energy spent on the activity and the amount of learning from the activity. If a learner has difficulty here, some direction can be provided: "Does it represent more than one-quarter of your time and learning?" "Does it represent more than one-half?"

- Returning to their original expectations and objectives, learners then describe the degree to which these were met. It is usually useful to do this first in writing, then "translate" this written description into the format required by the institution. Again, the educator can provide direction through questioning. By this time, many learners will easily assign a value to their work, but some others will benefit from carefully structured questions: "Is it acceptable?" "Is it outstanding?" "Were all objectives completely met?"

- Only in the most unusual circumstances should the educator interfere with the learner's decision. But now and then the educator has to disagree, justify the disagreement, and negotiate a new value with the learner. For example, a learner may still be testing and provide an obviously outrageous value, or a learner may be so lacking in confidence that he or she notably undervalues the work. Usually, through questioning, this can be dealt with.

An alternative approach used by many educators is that of learning contracts. Here, learner and educator negotiate from the beginning what work will be done and what grade it will receive. Knowles (1975) provides a detailed description of the use of learning contracts; the interested reader should consult this reference. There are a few problems with the use of learning contracts. Even though they are described as flexible, most learners feel bound by them, and rarely are they changed. When a learner enters a new situation, he or she does not usually know what will be of interest and, particularly, how much time will be involved or how much learning will take place. And perhaps most importantly, self-evaluation skills are not necessarily learned during the process.

Other approaches to evaluation are also sometimes recommended in the literature: the use of "blanket" grades, where all group members receive the same grade so that the evaluation issue is put aside; or the implementation of a pass/fail system. There are some advantages to such systems (e.g., relieving anxiety), but again, evaluation skills are not learned.

Sometimes simply going through the self-evaluation process will break the learner's association of educator with evaluator. However, this is often not enough. A few suggestions for facilitating this process will be listed.

- The educator should provide descriptive feedback, but not evaluative feedback. The descriptive feedback can be questioning and challenging (e.g., "Have you thought of looking at it this way?"), but not judgmental.

- Comparisons should never be made among learners in a group; competition for the educator's approval should be discouraged and eliminated if possible.

- Learners should be encouraged to provide feedback to each other. They may even wish to participate in each other's evaluation process in some circumstances (e.g., the evaluation of a presentation or an activity designed by a learner).

- Attempts to have the educator engage in evaluation should be met with questions about what the learner thinks of the activity.

- The evaluation process should be made as objective as possible and should always be related to the criteria developed by the learner.

- Comparisons with other sessions, courses, programs, or educators should be discouraged—the focus should be on what value this activity has at this time for this individual learner.

Situations inevitably will arise which are not addressed by these suggestions. The educator's underlying assumption is that the learner knows better than anyone else what he or she has learned and of what value it is. This assumption will need to be expressed repeatedly in many different ways throughout interactions with learners.

Emotional Needs

The middle stages of the process are usually filled with interest and excitement for learners, although anxiety about the evaluation process often remains. The educator needs to be able to share the enthusiasm of learners, facilitate group processes, and deal calmly with evaluation worries. Also, at times, a learner in this stage will become isolated (see Figure 4.1), and this may pose difficulties for the educator, particularly when the rest of the group are excited about their new autonomy.

When learners become enthusiastic about their choices, activities, and discoveries, they often want to share this with their peers and with the educator. As well as a desire to simply share, this also represents a need for educator approval. As has been mentioned, the educator remains an important figure for learners, regardless of the degree of self-direction achieved. The educator must consistently display interest in and support for learner activities.

The group or a peer network plays a vital role in the process for many learners. At times the educator needs to smooth out group differences, resolve conflicts, and work with a group or sub-groups to ensure an awareness of group development. If one thinks back to the descriptions of psychological types and learning styles, it can be seen that this is not always an easy task; in fact, the educator must often behave in ways which may not be natural for his or her own type. However, the importance of the group and the educator's role in it cannot be underestimated. It may be useful for the educator to discuss difficulties with colleagues, to reflect on the process (perhaps in writing), and to encourage group members to take on various responsibilities for the "health" of the group.

The skills required in encouraging learner self-evaluation have been discussed. However, this can be as difficult a process for the educator as for the learner—we are used to being responsible for evaluation! The educator should list, examine, and question assumptions concerning evaluation. It may be that the individual who is new at facilitating self-directed learning will need to introduce this aspect of it more gradually, beginning with a negotiation process rather than full learner self-evaluation. Again, discussion with colleagues is useful, as is reviewing and analyzing the writings of, for example, Knowles and Brookfield. It eventually becomes difficult to insist on the retention of the "power of evaluation" over learners.

When learners withdraw or become isolated from the group and the process, it is not always easy to sort out what is happening. It could be that these individuals have remained in the confusion stage (people do take varying amounts of time at different stages), but isolation is usually a somewhat different phenomenon. Learners may have gone through testing the boundaries and then have withdrawn, or simply moved from more vocal resentment to isolation. They may finally reject the process altogether. What makes this difficult for the educator is that it may occur at a time when many others are enthusiastic. Who wants to worry about the sullen person in the corner when everyone else is enjoying themselves? This learner should not be "pushed," but consistent checking and support should be available. The educator response should be similar to the response to the anxious or confused learner: an expression of understanding, gentle questioning, encouragement to keep a journal or to discuss the process with others, and respect for learners' reactions.

Later Stages

Reorientation, equilibrium, and, possibly, advocacy occur in the later stages of moving toward self-directed learning. Learners' assumptions and expectations about the educative process have been revised and integrated into their own set of experiences and values. In a short-term educational interaction, these stages probably will not be reached; even in a longer term course, only some learners will reach this point. But when this stage occurs, the educator must now "let go," perhaps becoming a co-learner or mentor.

Intellectual Needs

The educator who has enabled learners to travel this far probably has an understanding of the necessary change in roles that must take place at this time. However, some find it difficult to let go. Knowledge that the educator now should have includes:

- how to recognize when the learner has reached the reorientation stage (comments such as, *"Now,* I see why you insisted on..." are sure signs);

- an understanding of the roles that are appropriate to assume at this point (resource person, model, mentor, co-learner, reflective practitioner, researcher); and,

- how to recognize when support and educator approval are still required by the learner.

Skills Required

When these later stages have been reached, the educator must be able to employ techniques to put into effect the points above. In other words, the educator must be able to let go in a way which "works" for both learner and educator; assume the most appropriate roles and be able to use different roles with different individuals (learners will not reach this point at the same time); and provide support as it is needed by learners.

Relinquishing Control

It seems that it should be easy to "let go"; after all, that has been the goal throughout the process and now it has been reached. However, the entire process has been an intense one and involves much more personal reaction and interaction than remaining in an instructor or expert role. Sharing learners' transformation can result in an attachment to individuals which makes letting go difficult. In addition, to let go is finally to step away from traditional educator roles and may reawaken the old assumptions about being an educator. Clearly, a part of this process is an emotional one—this will be discussed in the next section. But another part involves a set of skills to be practised. Although this process is very much dependent on the personality of both educator and learners, some guidelines follow.

- Now and then, one should move out of the educator role altogether; for example, discuss other topics of mutual interest with an individual. This tends to disassociate the individual from the "learner."

- The educator can use appropriate self-disclosure, such as comments about interests, family, or lifestyle. This has the tendency to make one more of a person and less of an educator and, again, the old associations begin to break down.

- Any attempts of the learner to put the educator back into the discarded roles should be discouraged. Providing resources, support, and advice are still appropriate, but "teaching" no longer is; the learner should be reminded that he or she knows how to direct learning.

- Ideas should be discussed with the learner on an equal level; for example, ask for the learner's opinion, advice, and suggestions on how to proceed or what to read on a topic.

- The educator should continue to encourage the peer network which has developed. As much as possible, requests for information or resources should be referred to other learners who are likely to have the answers.

- Learners can be encouraged to write or talk about how their assumptions have changed. The educator must be clear in his or her response to what they say.

- The educator should encourage integration by suggesting learners discuss or write about their experience and compare it to other experiences.

Assuming Appropriate Roles

The above guidelines make clear the change in roles that takes place during this stage. The educator is no longer facilitating the development of self-directed learning, but rather is reinforcing the outcome of the process. Different roles will be appropriate with different individuals, but those of co-learner and reflective practitioner are most often appropriate. The difficulty here, of course, is that learners will be at different stages and so the educator must play different roles, almost simultaneously. For some educators, adept at switching roles, this may not present a problem. If it does, learners can be grouped according to their stage of development, with the more self-directed learners working individually or together on their projects, meeting with the educator less frequently and primarily for support and approval. The educator's attention can then be focused on those learners who are not as far along in the process so that he or she will not have to switch roles as often. Sometimes, depending on the characteristics of learners, it is also useful to group more advanced learners with less advanced learners—the former group may act as models or resource people for the latter. However, if there are remnants of competitive behavior, resentment, or any other conflicts within the group, this technique will not be effective.

The educator must be very careful to interact with *individuals*, rather than the group; there is probably no other time in the process when this is as crucial (though it is always important). Focusing on the individual and being aware of which stage that individual is in will make it easier to use the appropriate role.

Providing Support

The final skill required of the educator at this stage is the provision of support without direction. Somehow, being supportive comes easily enough when one can also guide or direct. But now, guidance is no longer needed. Nevertheless, learners still look to the educator for approval and support—rather like the independent son or daughter who no longer wants to be told what to do, but who still hopes that the parent is pleased. The educator can compare this stage to working with a colleague, perhaps a new colleague, where it is important to discuss ideas critically and also to provide support for that individual's work, but not necessarily to tell him or her what to do. Another way of viewing the relationship is to think of the person as a former learner—not implying that they have stopped learning, but rather that the educator's role in their learning is coming, or has come to, an end. The educator is pleased at the transformation, and, beyond that, has nothing more to say. This is, of course, in large part an emotional issue, and that aspect will be discussed next. With practice, the skill of providing support without direction becomes easier, but letting go of the more directive role may always be an emotional struggle.

Emotional Needs

As has been mentioned, for the educator in the later stages two emotional aspects are paramount. One is letting go of the learner as a person after an intense and rewarding interaction; the other is letting go of the role of providing guidance and direction.

The guidelines suggested under "Skills Required" will facilitate the process of letting go—quite often practice of behaviors, even though they do not "feel right," will lead to a change in the underlying feelings. And, in a sense, one does not need to "let go" of or lose the learner as a person—the learner may enter into a mentoring relationship, a collegial relationship, or even a friendship with the educator. Keeping this in mind in the later stages will help. Most often, of course, learners-as-people whom one does not want to "lose" are simply replaced by the next group and the process begins again. It is important to remember, though, that the educator's influence stays with them, and they may well show up at the office door in a few years to express thanks and provide information about the changes in their lives. The intense emotions involved in leaving learners may never disappear. But this personal reaction is not negative; the fact that the educator *cares* is a part of the job.

Letting go of the role of facilitator of self-directed learning is a slightly different story. Most educators are in their profession because they enjoy helping others change and develop. All our past associations reinforce the idea that the educator is a "teacher." And, it must be admitted, this role often brings a sense of power which is difficult to give up. When the learner has "grown up," an equality exists between educator and learner which did not exist before; equality may be difficult to accept after one has been in power. Again, the suggestions under the heading of "Skills Required" will facilitate this change, even though they may seem artificial at first. The educator must think of the goal as having been reached and the journey as over. Continuing to direct learners or encouraging them to remain dependent only defeats the purpose of the work that has been done.

Summary

A process has been described which began with learners entering into an environment where self-directed learning was one educational goal. It was assumed that individuals would have a variety of backgrounds and characteristics, including differing experiences with self-directed learning and differing capacities to become self-directed. The stages that learners most commonly go through were described (recognizing that some learners will reject the goal from the outset or part way into the process). Several different paths through the process can be taken, and individuals will spend different amounts of time in various stages. The use of such a framework allows the educator to anticipate probable events and better meet varying learner needs. Unfortunately, most adult education literature neglects this process, giving the practitioner the impression that learners will respond with the joy of prisoners finally released from the tyranny of their captors. Not necessarily so. And even if so, prisoners, too, experience a profound psychological adjustment to their freedom. When restrictions are lifted, when power is given, when rules change, human beings must adapt and change. This change may be as difficult for the individual as when restrictions are imposed and power is taken away.

Even more neglected in the literature has been the change process which most educators undergo as they work toward learner self-direction. Self-directed programs are often implemented with no provision made for professional development. It is *expected* that anyone who works with adult learners is willing and able to work within this framework and to adopt the various necessary roles. In fact, as we have seen, there are many skills required of the educator. Most complex are the changes in beliefs, values, and assumptions that must often be undertaken to work effectively in this process. Many adult educators have guiltily felt inadequate after being "introduced" to the learner self-directed approach. Hopefully, it has been made explicit in this chapter that the process is difficult and complex for both educator and learners; that it contains many new skills to be obtained; and that if it requires the abandonment of long-held assumptions about education, it can produce strong emotional reactions. Chapter 7 will return to this issue with a discussion of the educator's development of a theory of practice.

The reader will recall that self-directed learning as a concept was critically analyzed in Chapter 2 and that the role of facilitator was questioned in Chapter 3. It was concluded that there are many situations in which a self-directed approach is not adequate and occasions on which the educator must be more than a facilitator. Yet, in Chapter 2, the assumption that self-directedness is a goal of adult education was stated. If so, how can we say that it is not always appropriate? Well, there is a notable difference between saying that the adult learner should know how to direct his or her own learning and saying that the individual must or will always be self-directing. Self-direction must be a goal of adult education so that the learner can choose to learn, choose what to learn, and choose how to learn it, including the selection of other-directed learning environments. There will be many times when the learner will prefer the educator as expert or instructor, just as we prefer to go to an expert mechanic rather than figure out how to repair our cars ourselves. On the other hand, we must be free to choose to learn how to repair the car, not forced to go to the expert because we do not know how to learn.

Likewise, the educator must have the knowledge and skills to guide learners toward self-direction, to know when to engage learners in that process and when to adopt other roles. It becomes the responsibility of the educator to develop a theory of practice which incorporates learner self-direction as a goal and includes a means of deciding when that goal is relevant.

5

Working Toward Transformative Learning

Recently, the concept of transformative learning has been introduced into the adult education literature (as was discussed in Chapter 2). Using this approach, the educator goes beyond simply meeting the expressed needs of the learner, as in self-directed learning, and takes on the responsibility of questioning the learner's expectations and beliefs. In this chapter, the process of transformative learning will be described, and practical techniques for working toward transformative learning will be presented.

It should be noted that transformative learning is not relevant in all adult education settings. In many situations, the acquisition of knowledge or skills form the learning goals, and transformative learning is neither relevant nor appropriate. On the other hand, one of the primary differences between education for adults and education for children is that children are "forming" and adults are "transforming." The adult learner has an established value system, a set of beliefs, certain expectations about the way things will be, and basic assumptions about the way in which the world operates. Often, these values, expectations, and assumptions match those of the environment in which the individual learns and hence facilitate learning. If you have always wanted to learn word processing skills, and you are finally attending a workshop on the topic, it is not likely that there will be any conflict between your assumptions and your learning. In fact, your previous experience as a typist will prove to be a useful base upon which to build new skills. However, at other times, learners' values or assumptions can inhibit, be in conflict with, or act as a constraint to learning. If I am a woman and I believe that only men are able to repair cars, I may never learn about auto mechanics, no matter what my actual facility. If I grew up in an illiterate community that did not value fancy book learning, it may never occur to me that I could go to college. If I am nervous when faced with rapidly changing technology and do not really believe that a computer can make much difference, I may be a reluctant learner of word processing skills. If I am an autocratic manager, I may find it difficult to see the value of learning about participative leadership skills.

A purely self-directed approach usually will not offer learners the opportunity to go beyond their current assumptions (except, perhaps, in accepting the self-directed approach, as we saw in Chapter 4). Expressed learner needs are based on the values, beliefs, expectations, and assumptions of that learner. The educator who works only with expressed needs does not challenge the learner to question the assumptions underlying the need.

Transformative learning is a process of critical self-reflection, or a process of questioning the assumptions and values that form the basis for the way we see the world. Values are not necessarily changed, but are examined—their source is identified, and they are accepted and justified or revised or possibly rejected. Transformative learning may occur as a result of a life crisis, such as a change of job, retirement, death of a spouse, a move, divorce. However, it may also be precipitated by challenging interactions with others (including an educator), by participation in carefully designed exercises and activities, and by stimulation through reading or visual materials. Most of us will remember a particular educator who changed the way we saw the world, a course or workshop which forced us to rethink something we valued, or a book or movie which had a profound and lasting impact. These are examples of transformative learning.

Emancipatory education (Mezirow, 1990) is the organized attempt to produce transformative learning in others. And as such, it has as its goal not only individual change, but also social change—the removal of the oppressive conditions which may have produced distorted assumptions and values.

Transformative Learning

Transformative learning and its theoretical foundations are described in detail by Mezirow (1990); the reader who is interested in a complete account

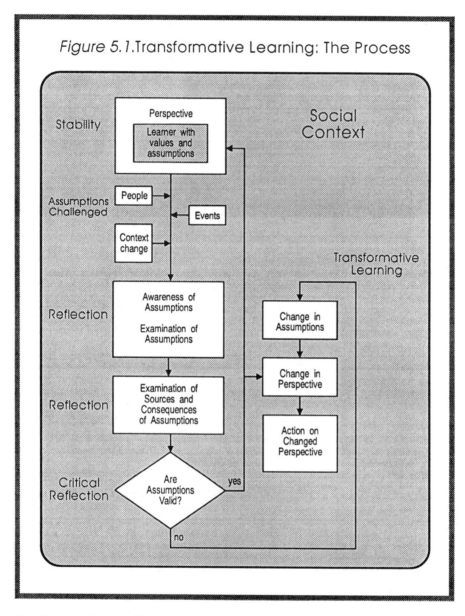

Figure 5.1.Transformative Learning: The Process

should consult that reference. It is interesting, as well, to trace the development of Mezirow's thinking by examining his earlier writings on learning cycles (cf. Mezirow, 1977). Some of those concepts will be incorporated into the following summary.

Figure 5.1 depicts a general model which describes the general process of transformative learning; however, it must be remembered that this process is likely to vary from one individual to another. It is also a process about which very little research evidence has been gathered, or even very little has been written. Emotional reactions have not been included in the model, as they were in the analysis of self-directed learning, but will be included in the discussion as we proceed.

We begin the process with a learner who has a value system and a set of assumptions which form his or her perspective on life. The learner exists, of course, in a social context which, at least in part, contributes to or reinforces this perspective. The individual may or may not be in a formal learning environment.

The transforming process can be stimulated by people, events, or changes in context which challenge the learner's basic assumptions. In Mezirow's (1977) language, this is a disorienting dilemma—a situation in which our views of reality do not match what we now encounter. Mezirow (1990) provides an example of a woman who finds that the other women in her evening course do not rush home to cook dinner for their husbands as she does. This presents a challenge to her assumptions. The following hypothetial situations provide some further examples: Mezirow's book provides a challenge to the assumptions of an adult educator; a publicity campaign about abuse challenges the assumptions of an abused woman; a drinking-and-driving accident of a friend challenges an individual's assumptions about drinking; a television program on Dewey's educational theory challenges the assumptions of a teacher; receiving performance appraisal results challenges the assumptions of a manager; an exercise on values clarification challenges the assumptions of a graduate student. If the challenge is strong enough, the individual then may proceed to a stage of reflection; however, it should be noted that many challenges pass by—assumptions and values are strong, and we do not often pause to examine them unless pushed into the process in some way.

The reflection process begins with a new awareness of the assumptions that have just been challenged, ranging from a simple, "Oh, I never thought of it that way," to a crisis in the individual's life. Awareness of the assumptions may be followed by an examination of them—or making them explicit, thinking about them, and reflecting on them.

If the process is fostered by an educator (or if the learner possesses strong self-analytical skills), the next step will be to examine first the sources and then the consequences of the assumptions. Why do I think that? Where did it come from? Did my parents tell me? Did I learn it in school? Does it come from previous experiences? Was it a norm when I was growing up? Then the consequences are considered. What will happen if I continue to believe that? Will I be able to deal with this new situation if I keep that assumption? Would I be happier without it? Am I passing that assumption on to my children, to my friends? Will this assumption work in my changed circumstances?

This kind of reflection leads naturally to considering whether or not the assumptions are valid. The questioning of previously accepted assumptions comprises the process of critical reflection, and when an individual questions his or her own assumptions, it is critical self-reflection. It may well be that the individual concludes that the assumptions are valid, and stability returns. This can occur when a person is not yet ready to change; it may be that the person has undergone an unusual experience or interaction which is not likely to reoccur; it also may be that the original assumptions simply hold up under scrutiny.

Assumptions seen as invalid, however, will be revised. Transformative learning will occur. Changes in assumptions lead to changes in an individual's perspective, the way he or she sees the world. And that almost inevitably results in action based on the changed perspective. The woman in the evening course may go home and refuse to cook dinner the next night; the abused woman may call the number in the advertisement; the drinker may call a taxi; the teacher may plan a field trip; the manager may enrol in a workshop on resolving conflict; the graduate student may change thesis topics.

In Chapter 4, working toward self-directed learning is described as a potentially difficult emotional process that can produce anxiety, anger, and resentment. Assumptions about the role of educator and learner are challenged. In transformative learning, the challenges may be to any (and vital) assumptions that the individual holds. In an analysis called "The Doubting Journey," Keane (1987) writes, "... the most difficult challenges were at the nonrational level... Immersed in pain and confusion of my own and others' doubts I tried to understand what was happening within myself while cognitively

searching for patterns and relationships. Vague, confused and varied feelings, ranging from shame to anger, surfaced as I worked with the data.
Loneliness was enormous. I often had to cease transcription because my
emotions were stirred so strongly. The unconscious surfaced intensely in
powerful dreams, spontaneous images and fantasies and instinctual forces. I
became a powerful learner in this nonrational world. Images, feelings, intui-
tions, dreams and bodily sensings led me to a knowing which went beyond a
factual knowing and which I increasingly trusted and came to value" (p. 89).

The objective depiction of the process in Figure 5.1 does nothing to
convey the power of the description above. And, unfortunately, not enough
is known about learners' reactions to be able to incorporate them into a
model. However, every attempt will be made to maintain this perspective as
we explore transformative learning.

Before going any further, some terms will be clarified which will be used
in this exploration. An *assumption*, as we have seen, is simply something
taken for granted, a supposition. The manager *assumes* that his subordinates
will do as he tells them without question—this is taken for granted. The
woman *assumes* that she is responsible for cooking dinner, that no one else
can do it; this is taken for granted. A *perspective* is based on a set of
assumptions and determines the way we live in the world and understand
what we experience. The manager sees organizations as being more efficient
when subordinates are kept in line. *Values* come from assumptions and
perspectives—the social principles, goals, or standards accepted by the individual; the perception of something as worthy of esteem. If a woman takes it
for granted that it is her responsibility to cook supper (assumption), she may
also see that as a standard or a social principle and accept it as such (value).
That is, she values the role of women as homemakers and believes that
families are happier when this is the case. Critical reflection and transformative learning involve the examination of both assumptions and values. The
manager, for example, might be stimulated by an article on participative
leadership to question his basic approach.

Mezirow (1990, xvi) provides the definitions of the remaining terms to be
used here. *Reflection* is the examination of the justification for one's beliefs.
Critical reflection is the assessment of the validity of the presuppositions of
one's meaning perspectives. *Critical self-reflection* is the assessment of the
way one has posed problems and of one's own meaning perspectives.

Transformative learning is the process of learning through critical self-reflection, which results in the reformulation of a meaning perspective to allow a more inclusive, discriminating, and integrative understanding of one's experience. Learning includes acting on these insights.

The Process of Working Toward Transformative Learning

The prospect of challenging others to question the basic assumptions upon which their view of the world is determined is a daunting one for the educator. Many dangers and pitfalls are involved, perhaps the most dangerous being that of confusing indoctrination with education, as was discussed in Chapter 3 in conjunction with the reformer role. The educator does not impose his or her own assumptions or values on the learner, but rather sets up a situation in which the learner can critically reflect on assumptions. Even the educator with an apparently valid cause, such as the eradication of illiteracy from a sub-culture or the raising of consciousness of women, does not *impose*—instead, the learner is given the opportunity (and the power) to see.

The general steps that the educator takes include:

- recognizing the learner's assumptions that are acting as constraints in the situation;

- creating an environment, an activity, or an interaction which challenges those assumptions;

- providing an activity or the guidance to help the learner make those assumptions explicit;

- providing an activity or an interaction to explore the sources and consequences of the relevant assumptions;

- supporting and accepting the learner in this analysis;

- encouraging the learner to question the validity of the assumptions he or she holds;

- providing a psychological environment and relationship in which it is safe for the learner to do this questioning;

- providing guidance and support in the revision of assumptions (rejected assumptions must be replaced with acceptable assumptions);

- assisting in the process of integrating the assumptions into the learner's overall perspective, particularly in dealing with conflicts;

- creating the environment in which the learner can act on revised assumptions; and,

- supporting the action when it is transferred to another environment.

The ways in which this general procedure can be followed will vary, depending on the context in which one works. However, following through the steps, using a concrete situation as an example, may serve to illustrate the process. A clinical instructor of physiotherapy takes a small group of learners into their first practical experience with patients. The setting is a hospital gerontology ward. Two students seem reluctant either to interact with or to touch the patients. Near the end of the day, the instructor takes the group into a conference room in the hospital, on another floor. She asks the students to comment on their first day. During the discussion, the instructor hears students saying things like, "It all seems so hopeless, when the patients are that old." The next day, in the pre-clinical meeting, the instructor introduces a role-play activity, whereby two learners take on the roles of elderly patients and one learner takes on the role of a physiotherapist who does not like elderly people. In the discussion following the role-playing, it becomes clear that one student assumes that there is no point in working with such patients. The source of this assumption seems to be a social standard—older people are "put away" and not valued, in the student's experience. Over the next weeks of the clinical experience, this assumption is discussed in relation to specific patients whom the learner gets to know on the ward. The learner is encouraged to spend time talking to patients, as she works with them. She begins to revise her assumptions and feel less reluctance in working with them.

Similar examples can be found for many different groups, such as new immigrants learning a second language, nursing students, new college instructors, prison inmates learning a trade, incest survivors, etc.

A variety of approaches to encourage transformative learning will be described now, with an indication of situations in which they would be appropriate. The innovative adult educator will adapt these approaches to different situations and create others. If the learner is challenged or stimulated to become aware of assumptions, guided through the analysis of those assumptions, and supported while questioning and revising assumptions, transformative learning can occur.

Journal Writing

Journal writing, for some individuals, provides the key to critical self-reflection. Lukinsky (1990) writes, "Active journal writing jogs the memory, brings lost potentials to the surface, and instigates retrievals...connections and integrations occur to the writer; as the writing unfolds, new thoughts emerge and are written down" (219). There are as many different ways of writing a journal as there are individuals who write them—the writing may be rather structured, divided into distinct sections, or completely free-flowing. Regardless of the format, most learners will, over time and with educator feedback, become involved in critical self-reflection in their journals. There are, however, in the literature, a variety of suggestions which may be useful for educators working in different contexts. Lukinsky (1990) describes Progoff's (1975) *intensive journal process*, which includes various journal sections or components, and also describes several journal formats. These approaches will be summarized here, and, to some extent, adapted so as to be more applicable to learners working in diverse subjects.

A *life history* section can be a useful way to begin journal writing. This provides the learner with an opportunity to reflect on those past experiences or values most relevant to the present situation and most likely to affect assumptions about the present. If the educator is reading the journal, it gives him or her information about the learner that otherwise may not be made available in a group. The life history section can also be extended to include the present, with a log of learning events and how they are related to previous learning or to current applications of the learning. Again, the learner will be encouraged to consider the nature of the learning; contradictions with previous experiences will become more apparent when the events are described in writing. This journal section fosters awareness of the relationship between current and past learning and tends to highlight assumptions that need to be questioned.

In a *dialogue section*, this awareness can be extended. The learner chooses a person who played (or plays) an important role in past or present learning and writes a dialogue with that person. The dialogue allows the learner to look at two sides of an issue or to remember things that were neglected or avoided. It is rather like role-playing, a technique that allows an individual to see different perspectives on an issue. Progoff (1975) also suggests that the learner can write dialogue sections with fictitious or historical characters. The learner in psychology could write a dialogue with Carl Jung; the learner in religious education could write a dialogue with God. And the learner has the opportunity to compare his or her assumptions with those of other individuals or with the assumptions underlying certain events.

Depth-dimension sections may be related to life history or dialogue sections of a journal, or they may be written separately. Here, the learner develops metaphors for experiences, records and reflects on related dreams, meditates on images, considers spiritual histories or peak experiences. Jung would describe this kind of process as making the unconscious conscious. Clearly, a depth-dimension journal section would be suited to some learners, but not to all. When appropriate for an individual, it would provide an ideal means of making hidden assumptions explicit.

In a *life-study* journal, Progoff suggests that the learner write *as* another person. The learner in adult education could write as Malcolm Knowles or John Dewey. The process starts with writing from the "outside," then moving to the "inside" of the individual whose identity has been assumed. The learner encounters gaps in knowledge of the individual, then must reflect on what he or she would say, would think, would feel. Again, similar to role-playing, this approach provides the learner with the opportunity to see issues from another perspective and thereby challenges learner assumptions. It can be very provocative to write things that are the opposite of one's own beliefs or values.

Lukinsky (1990) also describes from the literature a number of journal writing methodologies, some of which will be reviewed here. Ranier (1978, cited in Lukinsky, 1990) discusses seven approaches, including:

- *lists,* which are clusters of ideas on a topic (e.g., things that irritate me, beliefs I have discarded);

- *portraits* or descriptions of people to whom one is drawn, including what one learns about oneself in developing the portrait;

- *maps of consciousness,* which are drawings of a state of mind;

- *guided imagery*, the recording of images or daydreams within a specific or predetermined context;

- *altered points of view*, developed through writing about oneself in the third person or about another person in the first person;

- *unsent letters*, which allow the learner to express thoughts impossible to say in reality (e.g., anger that cannot be expressed or things one would like to say to someone who is dead); and,

- *dialogues*, as described earlier.

Different approaches will obviously be more or less effective with different learners. The educator should provide a brief description of each technique to learners and indicate that any, or any combination, of these methods of keeping journals can be experimented with. Each one provides a slightly different strategy for triggering reflection.

Fulwiller (1987, cited in Lukinsky, 1990) provides another list of journal writing techniques as follows:

- a *dialectical notebook* in which the learner writes "as a way of knowing" (observations, memoranda, notions of all sorts, before and after learning) and returns to the writing to reflect and assess;

- a technique in which the educator *writes directly in* the learner's journal, commenting and clarifying and questioning;

- *draft sketches* for future writing and papers;

- *letters* from one fictional or historical or present person to another;

- *personal comments* written on facing pages with explanations of readings or events;

- *historical* interpretations and judgments and speculations;

- *music journals* written while listening to music which stimulates associations and fantasy;

- *dialogues* between educator and learner;

- *therapeutic* journals written during or after interactions; and,

- *team journals* in which every team member writes regularly in the same journal and reads what other members of the team have written.

The educator can select approaches to journal writing which are relevant for the learning context, and indeed it can be seen that some approaches will be more suited to some contexts than others. Learners, however, should always have a choice of approaches, and probably should also have a choice of whether or not they wish to write a journal. For some individuals, this can be a time-wasting, anxiety-provoking, and difficult task. Most often, suggesting that learners write journals in any format or style that suits them produces the most interesting (and effective) results. Many of the formats suggested in the literature will appear, and learners have the added benefit of independently determining what is best for them.

Although it is only mentioned as one approach, it is invaluable for the educator to respond regularly to the journal writing. Such a dialogue provides the opportunity for learner and educator to come to know each other; and most importantly for working toward transformative learning, it provides an opportunity to question or challenge assumptions that appear in the writing.

Case Studies

Case studies have long been used as a means of facilitating problem-solving skills, either individually or in groups. A case provides information about a simulated (or sometimes real) situation; learners respond to predetermined questions or develop an action plan or in some way "solve" the case. With very little adjustment, case studies can become an ideal means of encouraging transformative learning. If cases are developed so as to bring about a questioning of learner assumptions, and if learners are also provided with the opportunity to examine those assumptions in interactions with others, critical self-reflection will be fostered.

Boyd's (1980) guidelines from the *Training and Development Journal* will be summarized and adapted for working toward transformative learning. Boyd suggests that the development of a case begin with the selection of the *concepts* with which the learner will be working. The concepts, of course, are dependent on the subject in which work is being done and the characteristics of learners. They quite often involve such interpersonal relationship skills as resolving conflict or leadership or management techniques. However, in working specifically to encourage transformative learning, the concepts should also be based on an awareness of learners' assumptions and values. If, for example, the educator is working in the health professions, relevant issues might include conflicts of values between patients and professionals or, perhaps, such concepts of medical ethics as maintenance of life support systems and terminally ill patients' rights to terminate treatment. If there is any evidence that learners hold distorted assumptions (see the discussion of Mezirow's description of distortions in Chapter 2), then concepts can be selected to bring about an awareness of this.

A *situation* is then developed and described which focuses on the selected concepts. The situation should be as realistic as possible, with its characters and their roles and attributes described fully. Enough information about the context should be given to make the situation seem real to learners. If the case situation is similar to that of the learners, they will be more likely to identify with its characters and elements. Learners can play an important role in developing the situation for case studies: they can provide details of the context into which the characters are placed, or they can provide both context and characters that focus on the concepts selected. Learners may even wish to develop real-life case studies in which they are characters and have the case analyzed by the group; however, this requires considerable care. It is easier to analyze a fictitious character's behavior (even though that character may strongly resemble oneself). The situation must be close enough to home to allow learners to see themselves and question assumptions, but it also should protect learners' self-esteem.

Third, Boyd suggests that the major *influences* on people and events in the case be included. These may be social contexts, previous experiences, or cultural backgrounds. Again, to foster the questioning of assumptions, these influences should be such that learners can relate to personally. It may seem like an excuse or rationalization for the learner to say, "I think like that because of the way I grew up," but, in fact, examining the sources of assumptions and values is a critical component of reflection. The individual becomes able to separate unquestioned and possibly distorted assumptions from those which have been considered and accepted as valid.

The case study should include *questions* which will focus learner discussion and facilitate the exploration of the issues it contains. Questions can be developed that lead learners to recognize alternative solutions, consider contributing influences, and anticipate probable consequences. Learners can also be involved in developing their own questions for a case study, either in addition to or in place of educator-determined questions. It may be effective to have groups of learners develop questions, then exchange questions with another group and respond to the received questions. However, if learners are new to the process of questioning assumptions, at least some of the challenges should come from the educator.

Finally, Boyd suggests that case studies be *revised* and refined. This step in the guidelines may be more relevant to the traditional problem-solving cases than it is to transformative learning. At times, in the latter instance, cases can be reused with new groups; but most often, it is more effective to design cases based on the background, needs, and values of the current group of learners. To be effective, the cases must address individual issues; every individual and every group will be different. However, at the completion of a case study, it can be useful for the group to analyze the case and the process itself, suggesting improvements.

The case study provides a relatively nonthreatening way for learners to increase awareness of their assumptions and begin to question the sources and consequences of those assumptions. The closer the case is to the real lives of learners, the more threatening it may be, but also the more effective it may be in fostering reflection.

Critical Incidents

Critical incidents resemble personal case studies. The use of critical incidents was first introduced by Flanagan (1954) and has since been used in a variety of ways, including the collection of research data. A critical incident is simply a learner's description of a significant event in his or her life. The learner produces a detailed description of an event, related to a particular concept, which is then analyzed. In working toward transformative learning, the incident is explored for the assumptions that underlie the learner's behaviors during the incident and her or his reactions to the incident, both at the time and in retrospect.

Brookfield (1990a, 31–34) describes three ways of using critical incidents. Although he is using the technique as a means of becoming aware of how individuals experience learning, any other concept relevant to the situation or subject can easily be substituted. The approaches will be reviewed and adapted so as to be applicable to a variety of contexts.

In the first approach, learners are asked to respond to a ten-item *Critical Incident Questionnaire*. They think back over their last appropriate experience (any role descriptor; e.g., caregiver, discussion leader, person responsible for a decision, student nurse in the clinical setting, person in charge, student teacher on a placement). Learners then describe in as specific, concrete, and honest a fashion as they can, the following details of that experience:

- the incident that was the most exciting and rewarding, because it represented a time when something significant and important was happening;

- the incident that was the most distressing or disappointing, because it represented a time of despair or frustration;

- the characteristics and behaviors of others that were most helpful;

- the characteristics and behaviors of others that hindered the process;

- those times of feeling valued and affirmed in their roles and why this was so;

- those times of feeling demeaned and patronized in their roles and why this was so;

- the most important insights realized about the nature of effective functioning in their roles;

- the most important insights about the self in their roles;

- the most pleasurable aspects experienced; and,

- the most painful aspects experienced.

Brookfield suggests that learners analyze their responses with regard to: common themes emerging from the positive aspects of the experience; common themes emerging from the negative aspects of the experience; advice that the learner would give to a person who was entering that role on how to survive and succeed; and advice that would be given to others in the same context. The individual working toward transformative learning should add to the analysis (or replace the "advice" components with) assumptions that have been made that underlie the descriptions of positive and negative aspects of the experience and the sources of those assumptions. If learners share their critical incidents in small groups, it can be particularly useful for group members to question each other's assumptions—it is often easier to see someone else's assumptions than your own.

Brookfield also provides two shorter forms of the critical incident technique. In the first exercise, directions such as the following are given. "Think back over your last six months as a... (again, substitute the relevant role descriptor). At what point did you feel confident enough to write or speak an opinion that you knew contradicted the expert wisdom in your subject? Write a brief description of when this happened. Describe in detail where and when this occurred, who was involved (job titles or functions, not names) and what it was that gave you the confidence to challenge the experts." Again, as a way of encouraging critical reflection, learners can analyze the incident as to the assumptions underlying their behavior, the sources of those assumptions, and the consequences of acting on the assumptions. Ideally, learners should share their incident with others in the group and discuss the assumptions involved. It is also often useful for the educator to prepare and share a critical incident with learners—this provides a model for the process, a nonthreatening introduction to the analysis of assumptions (learners should question and analyze the educator's assumptions), and a means by which the educator can be "human" and thus encourage the learner to be open with the educator and with peers.

The second short form of the critical incident involves the examination of a negative experience. Brookfield titles this, "Critical Incident Exercise: Hitting Bottom." Directions such as the following are given to learners. "Think back to the last time you felt ready to give up trying to _____ (substitute any appropriate activity or skill)—a time when you hit bottom and said to yourself, 'Things can't get any worse than this.' Why did you keep on _____? What was it that stopped you giving up completely? Write down whatever you remember about the factor or factors that helped you through this low period in your life as a _____." Learners can analyze their assumptions, as before, and consider any revisions in assumptions that took place as a result of the negative experience. If the learner has gone through "hitting bottom" and has stayed in the same context, it is likely that some change in perspective (transformative learning) took place. Realization of this can be most useful in fostering further critical reflection.

Critical incidents can be used in many ways. Renner (1983), for example, describes a variation in which the incident is provided by the educator in the form of "A Day in the Life of a _____," and another in which the incident is simulated or acted out and learners respond in writing with what they would do as a character in that incident.

When using the critical incident technique, the educator should be pre-pared for emotional responses, conflicts within the group, and perhaps even individual withdrawal or rejection. Nobody likes to consider the possibility that they have been operating under invalid or distorted assumptions! If trust with learners has been built, and if the environment (including other learn-ers) is supportive, learners will develop an awareness of and a questioning attitude toward their assumptions from an analysis of significant events in their lives.

Repertory Grids

The repertory grid technique of Kelly (1955) is based on an early psycho-logical theory of how people behave, think, and feel in specific situations or roles. Unfortunately, Kelly's work did not gain recognition until the last fifteen years when it was seen to contribute to the trend toward qualitative research and the emphasis on understanding individuals within the context in which they live, work, and learn. And, interestingly, his theory provides a way of understanding individuals' assumptions and encourages transforma-tive learning. The theory will first be briefly summarized; then the use of repertory grids will be described.

Personal Construct Theory

Every individual, writes Kelly, has a different set of experiences and therefore every individual perceives reality in a different way. People's psy-chological reactions and responses are related to the ways in which people anticipate events. In other words, depending on what has happened to you, you have certain expectations of what will happen in the future. Kelly holds that individuals have personal systems of meaning. These systems consist of pathways or *constructs*, which are the person's guide to living. Through our constructs, we have predictable and regular expectations and ways of inter-preting experiences. Constructs are dichotomous—we take this path or that path, we do not set out into the unknown. For example, an individual may predictably take the conservative path or the risk-taking path or the safe path or the path that leads to being together with others or the path that leads to solitude.

In order to measure constructs, Kelly defines a construct as the way two things are similar to each other, but different from a third thing. When working with clients, Kelly presents them with three descriptors and asks them to give the similarity and difference. These responses then become two "poles" or ends of the construct (e.g., sociable vs. unsociable; smart vs. stupid; organized vs. unorganized). Once the construct is established, other people or events are then ranked along a continuum between the two poles. This becomes the repertory grid technique, which will now be described in relation to working toward transformative learning.

Repertory Grid Technique

Candy (1990) provides a clear example of the use of the repertory grid technique. This example will be examined and summarized. The hypothetical learner is one who wishes to understand her working relationships with colleagues; however, the issue can be any one which is relevant to the learning situation. The steps used in developing the grid are given below.

- The learner is asked to list, on separate cards, each of the people she regularly comes into contact with at work, using initials or some identifying characteristic.

- The learner is asked to identify the "best colleague I have ever worked with" and "the worst colleague I have ever worked with" and to write the identification on two cards. She writes her own name on a third card.

- The educator enters the initials from all cards at the head of separate columns across a pre-prepared form (see Figure 5.2).

- The educator, shuffling the cards and presenting three of them, asks the learner to describe in what way two of the people are similar to each other, but different from the third person. A word or phrase is asked for to make the differentiation, e.g., helpful versus obstructive. These descriptors are entered on the form, "helpful" in the left-hand margin and "obstructive" in the right-hand margin.

- Next, all cards are placed in front of the learner and she is asked to arrange the people along the continuum from helpful to obstructive. People who cannot be separated are placed at the same point on the line. A score is allocated to each person, from 1 to 7, with 1 representing "very helpful" and 7 representing "very obstructive." The learner, herself, is included in this arrangement, along with the "best" and "worst" colleagues.

- The process is repeated with another shuffling of the cards and another three being presented, with the question, "How are these two people alike, in a way that distinguishes them from the third?" And again, each individual is placed along the continuum that emerges from that question.

Figure 5.2. Sample Repertory Grid

	P.	E.	S.	R.	B.	T.	V.	W.	
Helpful	1	5	3	1	4	2	7	6	Obstructive
Specialized	3	3	2	7	6	1	5	4	Not specialized
Experienced	1	2	4	4	6	3	5	7	Inexperienced
Sociable	2	1	4	3	5	5	7	6	Unsociable
Tidy	4	1	7	5	7	2	3	6	Messy
Up-to-date	1	3	2	3	6	5	4	7	Out-of-date
Initiator	3	5	5	1	7	4	6	5	Follower
Plans ahead	2	1	1	4	7	5	6	3	Reacts
Writes well	1	2	7	3	2	4	6	5	Writes poorly

The results of this exercise produce a matrix, as is shown in Figure 5.2. The learner has provided the elements of the matrix (the people, in this case) and also the criteria upon which she distinguishes among them. These criteria form the *constructs* which determine the learner's expectations and ways of viewing reality. Clearly, the matrix provides the learner with considerable information which can be used to analyze assumptions about relationships with colleagues in the workplace. The learner can examine relationships among the constructs listed. (For example, is there a tendency to associate planning ahead with being an initiator, or being messy with being a good writer?) These relationships reveal assumptions about the way people behave—the person who thinks ahead is going to be an initiator; good writers are always messy. The learner can consider other characteristics of the individuals (or events) listed and determine whether the placement on the continuum is related to those characteristics. (Are women always considered "sociable," for example?) As the elements listed are people, and the learner has included herself, she can analyze her expectations of others in relation to her expectations of (and assumptions about) herself.

Note that learners can conduct this exercise in pairs; it is not necessary for the educator to lead the process.

For transformative learning, the advantage of the repertory grid is that the learner is the one to define both the constructs (the learner's own way of seeing the world) and the important events or objects which are seen. The educator has no opportunity to impose values or criteria—the process is descriptive only of the learner's perspective. The placement of events, people, or objects in the matrix will inevitably lead the learner to an awareness of connections, which in turn leads to an awareness of assumptions about how the world operates. Through an examination of the relationship among constructs, the learner can see that he or she assumes, for example, that a good mechanic is one who makes the most money; that a nurse who cares for her patients is also well groomed; that a manager who gets the job done is not necessarily a good communicator. These assumptions can then be questioned. Is it possible to be a good mechanic and make little money? Is it possible that a nurse who is sloppy cares for her patients? Is it possible that a manager who gets things done also communicates well?

Role-Playing

Role-playing is a powerful technique for encouraging learners to view situations or problems from perspectives other than their own. It is commonly used to give learners the opportunity to practise skills (e.g., interviewing) or interpersonal relations (e.g., dealing with conflict) in a safe environment where feedback can be provided. However, when participants are assigned to roles which are quite different from their usual roles, they are provided with an opportunity to examine and question their assumptions. The student physiotherapist who has played the role of an elderly patient, perhaps using a blindfold and earplugs, may revise an assumption about "cranky old patients." The manager who plays the role of a subordinate in a discussion of organizational procedures may revise an assumption about participative leadership being a "waste of time." The school board superintendent who plays the role of a principal receiving a performance appraisal results may revise an assumption about "telling it like it is" when giving feedback. We don't often "walk in the other person's shoes" as the saying advises, but role-playing effectively simulates this process.

On the other hand, role-playing is a difficult and anxiety-provoking technique. Inevitably the evaluations of a session with some role-playing will include comments such as, "No more role-playing *please!*" People are afraid of looking foolish; introverted types hate performing in front of others; no one particularly likes to have assumptions challenged. In addition, role-playing is often poorly managed by the educator, further increasing people's dislike of the technique. Role-playing must be carefully planned, facilitated, and analyzed afterwards. Here are some guidelines for these three phases of role-playing.

- As with the case study, a realistic scenario must be drawn up with enough information about the context and the situation available for individuals to draw on during the role-playing and with enough information about the players available for individuals to know how to respond. Too much detail, however, may prevent people improvising and thereby "living" their roles. Participants should not have the sense that they are reading a script. It is useful in the preparation of a role-play to use (and adapt) real situations or experiences for the background information.

- Each participant should receive, in writing, a description of the situation and its context, along with his or her own character description.

- The objectives of the role-play must be made clear. Ideally, the objectives have been developed by learners or by educator and learners together.

- It is best to have volunteer players, rather than assigning roles or asking individuals to play roles. Unfortunately, however, learners usually select those roles that appear closest to their own behavior, which tends to defeat the purpose of using the technique for transformative learning. Volunteers can be asked for, and then roles assigned. If this does not produce the right combination of individuals and roles, learners can be asked to participate, as long as it is made very clear that they can refuse. The exercise should be abandoned rather than forcing any person to participate.

- Observers' responsibilities should be made clear. They should have the information about the context and the situation, but not necessarily the role descriptions. They should know what to look for during the role-playing and be encouraged to take notes. In some circumstances, videotaping the exercise is very useful, but may further increase anxiety.

- The room and the furniture should be arranged so that the observers can clearly see all players and so that the players' "stage" simulates the real situation.

- The amount of time that the role-playing will continue should be stated in advance and adhered to.

- During the role-playing, there should be no interference (laughter, comments, questions, nonverbal messages) from the audience.

- Upon completion of the role-playing, the educator should review the factual events, beginning with the players. Players are asked to report on what happened, not how they felt. The observers should then also report. Observers can question the players about the actual events, but not make critical comments.

- After this review, players should move to rejoin the group and thereby leave their roles. They can then address how they felt when they "were that person." Again, observers should interact with the players, presenting their view of what took place and questioning the players. At this stage, they may also say how they would have played a role differently, or how they would have felt in a role.

- Finally, the group should discuss the assumptions that underlay the behavior of the players. These assumptions should be stated and compared to the assumptions that learners (including observers) hold in real life, and the validity of both the role-playing and the real life assumptions should be examined.

Used in this way, role-playing allows all participants (players and observers) actually to experience a different perspective and, quite often, to see the consequences of holding that perspective. The anxiety and emotional reactions often produced is typical of any technique which fosters critical reflection. However, with explicit objectives, careful preparation, and perhaps most importantly, with effective debriefing, the technique can yield dramatic change in individual perspectives. Years later, a learner will often still talk about the effect of a particular role-playing experience.

Biographies

People enjoy telling their life stories and listening to those of others. Learners who compose a biography of themselves as learners or in relation to their work, and discuss those biographies with others will be challenged to engage in reflection. Dominice (1990) describes "education biographies" as a technique used in conducting research on the process of adult learning; however, he also notes the extent to which transformative learning occurs during the development of a biography. Although Dominice is primarily interested in biographies of the learning process, he does indicate that the approach could be used in a variety of other contexts. In this section, we will examine the use of biographies as a general approach for stimulating reflection and transformation.

Remember the (sometimes dreaded) assignment of writing "How I Spent My Summer Holidays" every September? And yet, quite often the summer holidays seemed different as a result of thinking back over them and trying to compose an interesting essay. One thinks, oh yes, I had forgotten that day we had a picnic in the pasture, or the time that all the cows got out in the night and wandered into the vegetable garden in the morning. The very process of recalling and writing about the summer somehow changed the way it was perceived. And so it is with the biography. Learners can write histories of themselves as managers or social workers or mothers or spouses. Whatever the context, a biography exists. The process of organizing one's thoughts about the role in order to produce a biography leads to an awareness of assumptions. "It seems that I really became a nurse because my mother was a nurse." "I ended up in education because at that time girls who went to university became teachers, not veterinarians." "I chose to study computer science only because I saw that it would lead to a job immediately." Reading the biographies to other learners or sharing them in writing leads to discussion and further questioning of the assumptions. "You say you don't like working with people, yet it seems that you spend most of your time as a manager working with others." "Why do you say you weren't a good mother because your son didn't go on to university?" "Why do you believe you'll never understand how to use a computer?" On two levels, then, first in the development of the biography and second in the sharing of it, individuals will reorganize and transform their perceptions of their history.

Although Dominice (1990) suggests that learners should select their own format for composing their biographies, there are some guidelines which can facilitate the process.

- Learners should begin writing their biographies by recalling and describing *events* only. This step enables them to create a basic structure composed of what happened and "what happened next," without worrying about reasons for or any values or feelings associated with the events.

- The next step can be to go back over the biography and elaborate on each event or experience, particularly examining why the learner made the decision or behaved in a certain way, and how she or he felt about the event.

- From this description, a list of assumptions underlying the behavior can be made. Learners should also be encouraged to consider the sources of these assumptions and the consequences of holding them.

- In small groups (and only in an atmosphere of trust), learners should either read their biographies or share them in writing. The role of others in the group is to look for patterns or trends in the story and for hidden assumptions that seem to be motivating the individual's behavior in that role. The group discussion must be supportive and accepting, but assumptions and values also must be questioned and challenged. This is a difficult part of the process; the educator must be aware that conflict and emotional reactions may emerge and be prepared to work with them.

- After discussion, learners may want to revise their biographies by including some new perceptions gained from the group. In some situations, it may be valuable to hold a second discussion of the revised biography with the same people or a different group.

- If learners are interested in journal writing, the biography can evolve into a journal—a current history.

Educators who plan to use this technique should consider writing their own biographies as well, preferably before learners compose their stories. In some cases, it may be relevant to share these with learners, but if not, it is valuable to discuss them with trusted colleagues or friends. Embarking on the experience oneself is an important component of being able to guide others through it effectively.

The biography technique is similar to that of critical incidents in that both focus on significant events, and to journals, which contain reflections on current experiences. This technique is unique, however, in that it provides a general review and perspective on an aspect of one's life history. And this promotes an extremely valuable type of critical reflection—the questioning of one's earlier assumptions and the examination of their effect on the present situation.

Metaphors

That metaphors have a powerful influence is well known to advertisers. Cars called Mustangs or Rabbits or Colts spark specific images in the mind of the consumer. Suburban developments with names such as Woodland Retreat or Lakeview Acres (even without a tree or lake in sight) create an expectation on the part of the house buyer. And, apart from advertising, metaphors define the way we perceive our culture and our work. An organization that engages in strategic planning is using a military metaphor and influencing our perspective of that organization. A school board which uses the phrase, "a family of schools," is creating an image of warmth and friendliness that defines the workplace.

Likewise, an analysis of metaphors that learners use to describe various aspects of their experience can provide invaluable information about their assumptions, values, and perspectives. If I use the metaphor "desert" to describe my childhood, one would assume that I received little warmth or encouragement from my parents. If I describe my office as a "zoo," one would expect that I see my working environment as chaotic, noisy, and unpredictable. The use of metaphors is a freeing and often surprising experience for learners.

Deshler (1990) describes eight steps for facilitating metaphor analysis. These steps will be summarized and adapted somewhat so as to be applicable to a variety of contexts.

- Learners should first select a subject for metaphor analysis. Deshler lists three possibilities: personal, popular culture, and organization domains. However, what is most important here is that the subject be relevant to learners' experiences and the context within which they are learning.

- Learners then try to recognize several metaphors that are used in relation to that subject. If no commonly used metaphors come to mind, learners can create their own by attempting to complete a sentence such as: "My organization reminds me of a..."; or "Being a dentist is like being a..."; or "To me, mathematics is a..." Learners who have trouble at this stage will most likely be stimulated to create their own metaphors by the examples produced by others. The educator should participate in providing examples.

- Learners select one of the metaphors that they have selected or created and "unpack" the meaning of the metaphor. This is done by asking oneself what characteristics of the metaphor correspond to characteristics of the real subject or situation. This step is crucial in the analysis, as it reveals previously unexamined characteristics of the subject. The metaphors usually come quickly and intuitively; it is the "unpacking" of the metaphor that reveals the underlying assumptions. If, for example, I say that my marriage is a prison, I might discover that the similarity or common characteristic is that I am questioned closely about my activities by my husband or that I feel restricted or that I can't leave. If I describe my home as a haven, the common characteristics might be peacefulness, silence, or retreat—a sense of escaping from other activities I don't enjoy.

- The learner reflects on the values, beliefs, and assumptions that are embedded in the meanings of the metaphors. Although this can be done individually, discussion and questioning of the assumptions with peers is extremely valuable.

- The learner is now in a position to question the validity of each of the assumptions revealed in the metaphor. Questioning can involve comparisons with other experiences or with knowledge or value systems. Again, interactions with others is useful here. The sources and consequences of the assumptions can be examined, with individuals questioning whether or not they still hold the same assumptions.

- Most likely, learners will see some meanings in the metaphors with which they do not or no longer agree. They should create new metaphors which portray a changed meaning of the subject—one that they now hold or one that they would prefer to hold. The new metaphors and their meanings should be shared and discussed with other learners.

- Learners should consider the implications for action that can be derived from the new metaphors. For example, if I prefer to see my home as a haven rather then a hotel, I might decide to not issue so many invitations to friends and relatives. If I prefer to see my workplace as a family rather than a machine, I may decide to cultivate more social contacts with my colleagues.

- The analysis can be repeated either with other metaphors for the same subject or with metaphors for other, related subjects.

Metaphors, of course, do not need to be used in precisely this way. The interesting aspect of this process is that the metaphor reveals a way we have of thinking about familiar things which we often have not previously considered. Listening closely to our own (and others') metaphors, figures of speech, and cliches can provide.a remarkable amount of information about our values and our meaning perspectives. An *awareness* of the metaphors we use in speech will trigger reflection. Often, when learners have gone through a systematic metaphor analysis once, they will then report further awareness of their use and of the meanings of metaphors.

The X/Y Case

In Chapter 3, under the discussion of the role of reflective practitioner, the work of Argyris and Schon was briefly reviewed. These writers, in their work encouraging reflective practice, are engaged in fostering transformative learning. The process of becoming aware of the discrepancies between espoused theories and theories-in-action is also the process of questioning one's assumptions. In several books and articles, some of which are referred to in Chapter 3, the use of the *X/Y Case* is described as a technique for encouraging learners to see these discrepancies. In his 1982 book, *Reasoning, Learning, and Action*, Argyris applies this strategy to working with managers and executives, but also discusses its use in the classroom.

The X/Y case is simply a transcript of a communication from one individual to another (Y to X). The phrasing may be adapted to a particular context, but the content or meaning remains the same. Learners are asked to assume that the statement represents the entire range of *meanings* that Y communicated to X.

Figure 5.3. The X/Y Case

- X, your performance is not up to standard, and moreover you seem to be carrying a chip on your shoulder.

- It appears to me that this has affected your performance in a number of ways. I have heard words like *lethargy, uncommitted,* and *disinterested* used by others in describing your recent performance. Our supervisors cannot have these characteristics.

- Let's discuss your feelings about your performance.

- X, I know you want to talk about the injustices that you believe have been perpetrated on you in the past. The problem is that I am not familiar with the specifics of those problems. I do not want to spend a lot of time discussing something that happened several years ago. Nothing constructive will come out of it. It's behind us.

- I want to talk to you about today, and about your future in our system.

(Argyris, 1982, 29)

The steps in completing the X/Y case are as follows:

- Learners are asked to write a short analysis and critique of the way Y dealt with X.

- Learners make any recommendations or present any advice they would give Y to make his performance with X more effective.

- They are then asked to assume that Y came to them and asked, "How well do you think I dealt with X?" (They also are to assume that Y wants to learn.)

- Learners are asked to divide sheets of paper into two columns—on the right-hand side they write exactly what they would say and on the left-hand side they write any concurrent thoughts or feelings they would have, but not communicate to Y.

What inevitably happens in the analysis of the X/Y case is that learners will diagnose Y as ineffective. They will state that Y was not open, that he or she had hidden agendas and produced a counterproductive communication. Then, also inevitably, learners will produce the *same* counterproductive behavior in their proposed advice to Y. In other words, the way in which they say the situation should have been handled does not match the way in which they would handle it themselves. Argyris and Schon also recommend conducting impromptu role-playing sessions with participants (holding X/Y interactions). Again, learners will exhibit the same behaviors that they criticized in Y and will often remain unaware of doing so.

Argyris and Schon have developed a systematic procedure for the analyses of both the responses to the cases and the ensuing role-playing discussions. Unfortunately, these analyses take considerable time, not normally available to the adult educator, and are complex and difficult even for someone who is experienced with the technique. Nevertheless, the X/Y case, in itself, is a powerful way to create an awareness of underlying assumptions and see discrepancies with practice. A procedure such as that outlined below could be used to take advantage of the approach. Readers who are interested in pursuing Argyris' and Schon's analyses should consult any of the references given.

- The X/Y case should be slightly adapted to match the context of the learning environment. For example, Y could be an educator and X a learner; Y could be a dental hygienist and X a patient; Y could be a supervisor and X a worker. This leads to some adjustments in wording, such as "learning" for "performance"; "college" for "system." However, the educator should take care to leave the meaning of communication intact.

- The case should be completed as suggested by Argyris.

- If relevant in the context, the educator may conduct impromptu role-playing sessions as Argyris suggests. The most effective way to conduct this is to ask a learner to read their advice to Y, after which the educator says, "OK, I am Y; I would argue that..." (assuming the same stance as Y in the case). The role-playing should last no more than a minute or two and immediately should be discussed with the group. Observers most often will note the discrepancy between what the player of the role said he or she should do and what was actually said when in the role. (It is easier to see the discrepancies of others than one's own.) The process can be repeated with some or all learners in the group, and the educator's questioning can stimulate the awareness of discrepancies.

- Whether or not role-plays are conducted, learners should share the results of their cases in small groups. The educator should direct the groups to look for discrepancies between the right- and left-hand columns of the analysis (what was said and what was thought) and for similarities between Y's communication in the case transcript and learners' proposed interaction with Y.

- Either remaining in the small groups or working individually and then discussing the results, learners should list the assumptions that they have discovered were underlying their behavior. For example, a learner may see that because she did not want to hurt Y's feelings, she said something different from what she really thought—the assumption being, "If I say what I think, I will hurt someone's feelings." Or, a learner might realize that he did not give the patient information, because he thought that the patient would not understand—the assumption being, "Patients do not understand technical information."

- Learners can then question, as a group, the sources and consequences of the assumptions. Perhaps the assumption that saying what one thinks hurts others' feelings comes from childhood or from a relationship with a spouse or an experience with a colleague. And the consequence of holding this assumption is that constructive, honest feedback will not be given. The assumption that patients cannot understand technical information may come from a previous experience with a patient or with other individuals; the consequence would be that patients will not be informed about their own care.

- In groups or individually, learners then should question the validity of the assumptions revealed by the case.

- Rejected assumptions can be revised and a plan developed to act on the revision. For example, a revised assumption may be "I can say what I think as long as I address behavior and do not attack someone personally" or "I can say what I think as long as I include constructive suggestions for change" or "I can give information to patients as long as I explain it in a clear way."

In almost every instance in which it is used, the X/Y case produces a discrepancy between espoused theory and theory-in-action; Argyris and Schon have documented hundreds of applications in a variety of settings. It is this feature of the technique that makes it such a powerful tool for transformative learning. The last step of the procedure, including the action plan for the revised assumptions, should be emphasized.

Summary

Transformative learning produces elusive changes. Little research has been conducted on the process—quantitative research would be exceedingly difficult to do. Transformative learning is a long-term process. No one will undergo transformation in a one-day workshop (although the process might begin there and be continued by the learner). Changes in values cannot be expected in a short time. Transformative learning is an interactive process. It is difficult, and often impossible, to see one's own hidden assumptions, to determine where they came from and where they lead, and to question them. It may be simply the concern of a friend, a changing context, or the skilful questioning of an educator, but nearly always the challenge is an external one. No one wants to believe that long-held assumptions are invalid. No one wants to recognize that their perceptions have been distorted by culture, by family, by previous experiences. Anxiety, fear, hostility, or sadness at the loss of assumptions and values can result.

Transformative learning must include action. Mezirow (1990, 375) goes so far as to say, "Learning is not a desirable outcome or goal; it is the activity of making an interpretation that subsequently guides decision and action." And, "Praxis is a requisite condition of transformative learning" (356). Praxis simply means "putting into action," or the practical application of knowledge.

Transformative learning is also a vehicle for social change. Mezirow (1990) strongly presents the case that individual transformation precedes societal transformation. If individuals discover that their assumptions are based on cultural distortions (women can't be mechanics; men don't know how to do laundry; all Germans are ruthless; the poor cannot go to university) and if those assumptions are revised and acted upon, social change will be the next step.

6
What If...?

In Chapters 4 and 5, procedures have been described for the fostering of self-directed and transformative learning. The educator who is attempting to engage in these activities may encounter difficulties in either working with learner groups or in working within the constraints of educational institutions where more traditional approaches to teaching are expected. It is the purpose of this chapter to provide some practical approaches which can be tried when difficulties are encountered. However, two points should be kept in mind. First, these are techniques to be used *only* when difficulties are encountered (if it isn't broken, don't fix it); the educator's goal is student learning, not personal therapy. Second, this chapter is addressing those situations where learner self-direction and mutual educator/learner education are goals. This is *not* to say that instructor-centered approaches are inappropriate or that things do not go wrong when using them; many other books and resources deal with these situations (cf. Brown & Bakhtar, 1983; Renner, 1983).

As practitioners well know, there is often a discrepancy between how the education process is described and the way it really is. Actual practice usually needs to be adjusted to the situation. The reflective practitioner builds a theory of practice based on experience, a theory which can look quite different from the guidelines in an adult education text.

Conditions and/or problems affect practice. For example, what if learners do not get along? Learners working in groups do not always interact harmoniously to achieve mutual goals. People can be sullen, withdrawn, shy, or aggressive, and they may be struggling with important problems outside the group. Conflict can occur between individuals, strong dislike can arise

among group members, and competition for attention rather than coopera-
tion can prevail.

What does one say when students expect the impossible? Learner expectations may far exceed the possibilities of the situation, or the educator's
stated intent may be unrealistic. For example, a one-day workshop intended
to train college instructors to implement a self-directed learning program or
a half-day workshop intended to provide managers with the skills to interpret and use performance appraisal results clearly cannot achieve their goals.

What if the characteristics of learners are completely unknown? It is often
impossible for the educator to obtain information about a learner group. No
information may be collected about individuals who have signed up for a
professional development session. University students may register for
courses for a variety of reasons, including the evening on which the course
is offered and the location of the meetings.

What about learners who resist learning in the face of one's best efforts?
For example, what does one do with a group whose members have been
forced to attend a course or workshop by an employer or as part of a
government program? Everyone clearly hates to be there and hates you for
being there as well. Or, what if a learner is attending the sessions simply to
gain a salary increase?

What if the institution who employs the educator insists on having a
normal distribution of grades? Or cannot make resources directly accessible
to learners? Or does not have rooms with movable chairs for group work?
Or has a required curriculum? What if the educator expects a group of 25
and walks into a room containing 75 people? Or, when a large number is
expected, how does one assume a facilitator role?

The educator is, more often than not, faced with unpredictable situations
or situations which do not seem to work. At those times, none of the usual
advice is of much help. And yet our goal must be to cope with those situations and incorporate what we learn from them into our own philosophy of
education. The assumption that learners enjoy working in groups becomes
revised to learners generally enjoy working in groups, but when the atmosphere is all wrong, I can do this to help. Over time and with experience, the

educator builds a repertoire of "if _____ then_____" assumptions about the learning experience. A parallel may be found in learning to cook by following recipes which result in endless curdled sauces and fallen cakes and burned vegetables. Without an understanding of why the recipe was supposed to work (what difference does beating the egg make?), it cannot be adjusted. A cookbook that includes a chapter on "what if...?" (What if the sauce separates? What if you don't have milk when the recipe calls for milk? What if the fudge doesn't harden?) can lead to an understanding of the assumptions underlying the recipes. The cookbook remains invaluable, but the cook must develop the understanding that allows adaptation.

It is hoped that this chapter will serve the same purpose as the cookbook that answers "what if" questions. All unpredictable events or things that might go wrong cannot be included, of course. But difficult situations that commonly occur will be addressed, with suggestions as to how to "fix the sauce." The educator, with reflection and research, will discover many more ways of adapting and fixing.

Difficult Group Dynamics

Some guidelines for promoting effective group behavior were reviewed in Chapter 4. Nevertheless, group dynamics are complex and can easily go wrong. Any educator who has been confronted by an angry group (or group member) demanding that the group be disbanded can attest to the difficulties that may be encountered. First, we will briefly examine the psychology of small group behavior, then discuss ways of dealing with problem group dynamics.

Shaw (1976), in his book, *Group Dynamics: The Psychology of Small Group Behavior*, comprehensively summarizes the research on group behavior. Individual characteristics not only determine learners' behavior and their reaction to others, but also those behaviors and reactions in turn influence the reactions of others. If I am introverted and consequently dislike or am anxious about working in a group, I may behave in a withdrawn or even hostile way. That behavior may then result in others becoming more aggressive (thinking I am hostile) or more outgoing and friendly (thinking I need to be drawn into the group). Even in a group of four or five individuals, the combinations of behaviors and reactions are complex. However, most learners want the group to be effective and will make efforts to promote positive group dynamics.

Some of Shaw's summary statements about group behavior may be useful for our discussion.

- Individuals prefer smaller groups.

- The amount of participation in a group decreases with increasing group size.

- When a group is larger, there is more likely to be individual conformity to the majority opinion.

- A group leader is more likely to emerge when a group is larger.

- Emerging group leaders tend to be older than other group members.

- The individual with more experience related to the task tends to make more contributions and to have more influence on a group.

- There is more social participation when group members are older.

- Men tend to be more aggressive and competitive (e.g., interrupt more frequently, state opposing views more often) than women in groups.

- An individual who displays anxiety inhibits group functioning.

In addition, the concept of psychological type can shed further light on the nature of group dynamics. Similar types of individuals are more likely to work harmoniously in groups; however, their way of perceiving the task is limited by their type. Introverted types do not generally enjoy group work. Most extroverted types are effective group members, each serving different functions: the extroverted feeling type smooths over any conflict; the extroverted intuitive type sees all the possibilities for approaching the task; the extroverted thinking type organizes others and the task; the extroverted sensing type reminds everyone of the facts. Among the extroverted types, the "opposites" (thinking versus feeling; intuition versus sensing) may have trouble understanding each other, may annoy each other, and may come into conflict.

Similarly, groups with a similar learning style tend to be both harmonious and also limited by the sameness of their style.

Although effective group behavior is a prerequisite to learning in group activities, attention to the group process should not, of course, take over from attention to learning. Now, let's turn to some common group problems and suggested repairs.

Learner Conflict

What if a working group simply does not get along? They do not seem to like the each other; they complain about working together; they are not productive because they spend all of their time arguing or trying to outdo each other. The following suggestions may help.

- Observe the group together if possible. Talk to individual group members and ask for their perceptions of what is going wrong. Meet with the group as a whole and ask them to list the problems *and* possible solutions to each problem.

- If the group is able to generate reasonable and productive solutions, suggest that they put these into the form of objectives for the group and attempt to work toward those objectives as they carry on with their regular activities. They should then report back on how they are progressing.

- If the group is in so much conflict that they cannot produce objectives, or perhaps even discuss the problem objectively, suggest, based on your perceptions, some objectives that they might try to achieve in the next one or two meetings.

- If it is immediately apparent that the group will never work well together, or if the problem continues after they work toward objectives, consider disbanding the group. The difficulty here, of course, is that other groups will also be disrupted. The educator can simply say, "It's time people had a chance to work with others—we're going to rearrange the groups for our next meeting."

- In a one-day workshop or other short-term session, all groups should simply be rearranged for the next activity.

Group Disruption

What if it is clear that one individual is inhibiting group effectiveness? It can be a dominant group member, an aggressive individual, a withdrawn or anxious person, someone who interrupts or inhibits others, or argues incessantly. The specific problem behavior should be identified, but the repair process is similar regardless of the nature of the behavior.

- Through observation, the educator should attempt to determine any reasons for the behavior—perhaps the aggressive individual is hiding a lack of confidence; perhaps the withdrawn person is simply introverted; perhaps there is a conflict between two members of the group.

- The educator should then meet privately with the individual before or after a session. This must be handled with care. Making accusations, blaming the learner, or making evaluative statements of a personal nature will not be effective. The conversation must be directly related to the learner's behavior and also must be open. The educator should stress any positive aspects of the behavior or display an understanding of the behavior. For example, one can say something like, "I know it's hard to work in small groups, in fact, I have trouble with it myself, but I've noticed that you haven't said anything for the last two sessions, and I'm wondering if there's anything we can do in the group to make this easier for you"; or "It seems that there's some conflict in the group. This happens sometimes, but you seem to be responding in an aggressive way. I'm wondering how we can deal with this." Of course, the approach will depend on the individual and the behavior, but if these components can be included (understanding, direct, and open comment on the *behavior* and a positive or constructive perspective), the meeting will probably be more effective.

- Set up one or two specific (and achievable) objectives for the next group session. This may be as simple as, "I will make one contribution to the session"; or "I will make a contribution by writing down my ideas and then sharing them with the group"; or "When I feel like yelling at the group, I will write it down instead"; or "I will let one other group member say something without interruption after I've spoken and before I speak again."

- Through observation determine whether the objective has been met and, if needed, set a further objective.

- If this approach does not seem feasible for the individual in question, or if it does not work, the educator might consider assigning specific roles (perhaps temporarily) to group members. The withdrawn individual can be assigned the role of recorder; the aggressive individual can be assigned the role of summarizer or questioner. Of course, each other member of the group is assigned roles as well.

- If the difficulty persists or if these approaches do not seem right for the situation, the problem can be made a group issue. Here, the educator must take care to not make the one learner into a "problem person" or to attach personal blame to that person. Yet, the communication must remain open and direct. The educator can say something like, "Group work is not easy—everyone's behavior influences everyone else's behavior. It seems that this group is not as effective as it could be; what do you suggest we do to improve things?" If considerable anger is focused on one individual in the group, this approach is *not* a good idea, but usually the group will rally and make suggestions to change the nature of the interactions. These suggestions can be made into objectives, as before, followed by further observation.

- In a short-term session, this situation is more difficult to deal with. Many educators have experienced the one-day workshop that seems to be ruined by a dominant or aggressive participant. As soon as the behavior emerges, even if learners are working on a task, the educator should speak to the individual, saying, simply, "Could I talk to you for a minute?" and take the learner out of the room. The conversation should proceed along the lines discussed above, leading to an agreement for changed behavior for the remainder of the session.

- The educator must not view it as a personal failure if none of these strategies works. There are learners who are dealing with personal issues which cause them to exhibit inappropriate behavior in the group; there are values and personality conflicts that do not respond to rational objective setting. There will always be some sessions that are not as effective as others. The educator is only one individual within a complex set of relationships and their dynamics, and at times, he or she can do very little.

Lack of Progress

What if the group has a wonderful time but gets nothing done? People may know each other from the workplace and be happy to have an opportunity to visit. Or, they may discover common interests or friends, or simply enjoy each other's company. At the end of a work session, they may scramble to put together a few ideas, saying, "Oh we were discussing such and such, instead." Or, they may attend superficially to the content, while thoroughly enjoying each other's company. It is not that they find the content uninteresting or irrelevant; it is simply that they prefer more sociable conversation. This is probably the educator's most common fear in instituting group work—that learners will "goof off," and not get anything done. This is also one of the most difficult situations to handle for the adult educator who does not want to act as an authority. The educator with a philosophy of practice which assumes that learning is the learner's responsibility will find intervention against her principles and difficult to carry out. (They *choose* not to work, it's their responsibility.) Indeed, one could suggest that they go to the coffee shop or the nearest pub!

There are, however, some strategies to try in order to promote more productive group work.

- The educator can suggest that the group conduct an analysis of the functioning of their group. This can take different forms. Each individual can rate the group separately on items pertaining to task accomplishment. (Sample items include: I am satisfied with the amount of work we get done; Our group deals with tasks in a well-organized way; Our group comes up with innovative ideas and solutions to problems.) The content of the items varies with the learning context. Individuals then share and discuss their ratings. If learners are *unaware* of the group's lack of productivity, this exercise will often lead to change. Sometimes, learners may be aware of the situation, but not know what to do about it, or be enjoying themselves so much they have no interest in change. Their analysis can consist of an experiment which they design together in order to describe their group process. They can, for example, record the number and type of interactions among individuals, the amount of time spent on the task versus on other topics, and the nature of the other topics. This analysis, of course, takes place as the group is engaged in their usual learning activities. Individuals can assume various roles in the conduct of the analysis, then discuss the results. Since people in this kind of group are interested in each other and their own interactions, they usually enjoy this activity. In the process, they may realize what they are doing. It can be suggested that they develop objectives for changed performance, followed by a repeat of the analysis.

- If it is comfortable for the educator, more structure can be provided in group activities, with recommended times, assigned roles for group members, or a suggested format for the product of the work supplied.

- All groups can be re-formed, breaking up the group. This, of course, has obvious disadvantages, as it disrupts other groups and may well result in hostility on the part of the sociable group.

- One individual in the group can be selected (a thinking type, if the educator is aware of psychological type) to meet with outside of the group. The problem can be discussed, with the suggestion that this person assume a leadership role in keeping the group on task. The approach must also be discussed with the group as a whole in an open manner. For example, one can say, "I've observed, as I'm sure you have, that your great discussions are often not related to what we're doing here. I've just been talking to Leslie who has agreed to act as a task-leader for this session—do you think that might be a useful thing to try?"

- In a short-term session, there clearly will not be time for group analyses. The educator can again increase structure, e.g., suggested times, and perhaps advise one individual to act as leader. (However, often the educator does not know people well enough to do this skilfully.) Possibly the best option, depending on the context, is to leave the group as it is—to interfere may cause more damage than good. Something as simple as the educator joining the group for a while may change the behavior temporarily and yield involvement in the task.

Group interaction is common in adult education and is used with a variety of educator roles. It is also one of the most complex processes that the educator faces. It produces powerful responses from learners; it contributes to working toward self-direction and toward transformative learning; and it is invaluable in affective learning and complex cognitive learning. With practice, patience, and experience, most problematic group dynamics situations can be sorted out.

Unrealistic Expectations

There are several circumstances in which the educator deals with unrealistic expectations; perhaps the most common is the one-day workshop which is expected to inform fully or train participants in a complex area. Unrealistic expectations also occur in other areas, such as literacy education and job retraining, or simply, in situations where the learner is unaware of the scope of the activity he or she is undertaking. For example, a graduate student asks for a two-hour meeting so that she can "learn how to do her statistics" for her thesis. A college department requests a one-day professional development workshop to train all faculty to work in a self-directed program. I hope that an hour with the squash pro will provide me with the skills to do well in a local tournament. The educator is in a difficult situation. The learner is, most often, very motivated and enthusiastic. That enthusiasm should not be dampened, but this seems impossible to avoid, either at the beginning, by solemnly informing the learner that this is a *very* difficult area, or during the process, as the learner starts to perceive failure on the horizon.

Several examples of this kind of situation will be examined, with suggested strategies.

Too Much Material, Too Little Time

What if you are given a day to assist a group to master complex material? Expectations will be unrealistic. Usually, the educator will know neither the learners nor their backgrounds. There will be no opportunity for application to real-life situations or for reflection. Constraints of various kinds (learner time, resources, organizational finances) usually prevent a change in the one-day format. What can the educator do?

- The topic can be narrowed down. In discussion with the organizer of the session, or the learners if at all possible, the educator can make it clear that the expectations are unrealistic. ("We cannot turn people into self-directed learners or financial experts or leaders in one day.") A choice of more manageable topics can be offered, and it can be suggested that the organizer consult with the learners as to their preferences among these options.

- The educator should request information about the learners. A short survey given in advance to all participants who register for a session can be invaluable. It may turn out that individuals have some experience in the area and have already attended workshops, or that their interests and background can suggest ways to address the broader expectation.

- Once the topic has been narrowed and some information obtained about the group, the educator must then carefully design the session with realistic, achievable objectives and activities designed to facilitate meeting those objectives. At the same time, enough flexibility must be maintained so that learners can modify, change, or add to the plan.

- It is helpful, at the beginning of the session, to ask participants to give their expectations *before* distributing a prepared agenda. As this is done, the educator should be very clear about the possibilities of the session: "This fits in with what we can do"; "Good idea, I hadn't thought of that, we'll include it"; or "Given our time constraints, we can't manage that topic."

- The educator must be careful to not get involved in advanced or technical topics which may be of interest to one or two individuals, leaving all others behind.

- At the end of the session, people probably will feel that they have just scratched the surface, that they want to know more. Resources can be suggested, and participants can be encouraged to request follow-up sessions.

Lack of Learner Experience

What if the learner just does not have the experience, background, or knowledge to realize how complex or difficult the learning is going to be? The person who expects to learn to read by next month? Or speak a second language before being transferred to another country? Or be able to manage a new farm when the crops are ready in two weeks? Or win the next squash tournament? Or analyze thesis data for the department deadline next week?

The difference between this situation and the previous one is that the time constraint is a product of the learner's lack of experience rather than one imposed by the format of the session. The process, therefore, must be one of guiding the learner to a realization of the amount of time and effort required, or, depending on the context, encouraging the learner to modify the goal. Under no circumstances can the educator simply agree to "meet the learner's needs"—only disappointment and frustration will result.

- First, learner needs must be clarified. It is possible, for example, that "learn how to do statistics" means "be able to calculate means and standard deviations" or "be able to run the computer package that produces means and standard deviations." A learner who is being transferred to another country may need only the most rudimentary words and phrases in a second language if he will be working in English. If the learner's expectations are not as impossible as they first appeared, the educator can then work with the learner to prepare specific, manageable objectives. A time frame for achieving the objectives can be developed. The objectives, of course, may be modified at this stage or as the learning progresses.

- If learner goals are as broad, complex, or time-consuming as initially expressed, the educator should work with the learner to break the goals into a list of more specific objectives. (Usually, the educator contributes most of this information as the learner does not have the expertise.) The resulting objectives can then be arranged hierarchically, listing the simpler prerequisite learning first, or sequentially, in the order of performance of a complex skill. This process, though it may take an hour or more of time, gives the learner the opportunity to work with and develop an awareness of the nature of the goal. At this point, the individual may say, "I realize I was completely unrealistic—can we work on this part of it?" or, "Can you recommend a course for me?"

- If the learner wants to continue, time frames should again be estimated for the various components of the goal. The learner must be completely clear as to what is involved, and expectations must be realistic.

- If the process continues to be mutually agreeable, the educator is now in an ideal situation for working toward self-directed learning. In other words, handled with care, a difficult situation can be turned into an exciting one, because the learner has become *involved* in the process of untangling the expressed need.

Impossible Learner Goals

What if learners enroled in a course or program have unrealistic expectations about that course or program? The laid-off steel workers who expect the course to guarantee them a job? The new immigrants in an English as a second language course who expect to be able to enter the work force at the end of the semester? The abuse victims who expect to be cured? The functionally illiterate assembly line worker who expects a promotion to supervisor after the course? The graduate student in education who expects an academic position upon completion of the program? We no longer have to face the time constraints of the previous examples, or at least not the same time constraints. Rather, learners have attributed too much power to the situation. For the educator who views learning as a lifelong activity, this situation is potentially dangerous. The disappointed learners may blame the educator, the system, or their own efforts; they may lose self-confidence and see themselves as failures; they may react by rejecting all learning activities. Again, the educator must confront the unrealistic expectations and work with learners to facilitate their awareness of their own goals.

- The educator should, at the beginning of the course, have learners list expectations, assumptions, or values. This can be done as an exercise, with individuals working together in small groups or pairs. (The beginning of a course is usually not a good time to turn the spotlight on individual learners.)

- The list of expectations can then be analyzed by the group as a whole. This can parallel the analysis of assumptions discussed in Chapter 5. The educator must challenge unrealistic expectations if the group does not. This process may evoke anxiety, but the expectations need to be addressed. As in transformational learning, only the learner can go through his or her own process—the educator "telling" will not result in change.

- Expectations which are judged to be unrealistic by the group and the educator can then be revised. Learners should not be left with rejected expectations, without a replacement. This can be done individually, but is probably more effectively done as a group or in small groups. The original expectations can still remain anonymous if this seems important for individuals.

The educator first works with learners to make the expectations explicit, then fosters an understanding of the nature of the expectations within the constraints of the situation. Ideally, revised and more manageable expectations are created without a loss of interest and motivation.

Unknown Learners

In many educational settings, the educator is unable to obtain any information about incoming learners. He or she may have a generalized sense of the nature of the group based on previous experience with a particular program or group—first year trades students, physicians in a continuing education workshop, dental hygienists in a clinical setting—but this often provides nothing more than educational background. Groups within any one category can be as different as they are across disciplines or professions. Ideally, the educator conducts a needs assessment prior to the session to collect information about learners' backgrounds, interests, and expectations. However, a variety of institutional or organizational constraints may prevent this. Registration procedures are often carried out by others. Registration lists may not be available until the day of the meeting, the first day of a course, or even a week or two after sessions have begun. Regulations which guarantee confidentiality of information will also restrict the educator's ability to collect information. And in some settings, such as professional or management development sessions, or general interest courses, people do not register.

The educator, then, must select strategies, decide on appropriate roles, collect resources, and perhaps even submit an outline or agenda to an administrative body with only the most superficial knowledge of the learner group. After years of experience with the same type of group, this problem is lessened, but for most of us, it is a dilemma. Some strategies will be suggested and discussed, first for a longer term setting (say, four sessions or more), then for shorter term situations. Any of these strategies should be used before an agenda or course outline is discussed with the group.

No Learner Information Available: Several-Session Situation

What if you have agreed to work with a group over several sessions, but have virtually no information about the individuals in that group? You may know that they are nursing students, chemistry students in their first course, graduate students in your discipline, or people who are interested in improving their tennis game. Depending on the context, useful strategies might include one or more of the following.

- In some form, in the first session, collect information about what people do, what they expect, how they see themselves. The form will depend on the group. A survey can be administered (either with educator-constructed questions or open-ended questions), but *not* if the group is anxious or is likely to associate this procedure with evaluation. Learners can introduce and talk about themselves, but again *not* if there is any anxiety. Learners can form pairs, interview each other, and then introduce their partners to the rest of the group. Or, learners can immediately form small groups, discuss their backgrounds and expectations with each other, determine commonalities, and then introduce themselves as a group.

- Another approach is to use a game, or as it is often called in the literature, a warm-up exercise. For example, learners can be given a list of possible descriptors of individuals in the group, some serious and some not so serious: "I haven't been in a classroom in more than five years"; "I am an enthusiastic gardener"; "I've read more than two books in the area of this course"; "I'd rather not be here"; "I have a thing about chocolate"; "I'm a Gemini." Individuals then circulate and question others in the group to find out the names of people who fit the descriptors, recording the names beside the statements. The educator participates as an equal member of the group. People will relax, have fun, get to know each other, and the educator will also learn about the learners.

- In some groups, providing information makes people feel threatened, mostly by the educator (e.g., "I don't want him to know that I'm nervous"; "If she finds out I've been out of education for six years, I'm in trouble"). If this appears to be the case, the educator can first model self-disclosure. Learners can immediately form groups to think of as many questions as possible to ask the educator. These questions can be serious or not-so-serious, and a couple of examples should be given: "What other courses do you teach?" "Are you married?" "Do you like dogs?" "Will we have examinations in this course?" The groups then select their four or five top priority questions and interview the educator. Following this, it is easier to move into another group activity where learners provide information about themselves.

- Learners who are more confident, particularly those who have had some experience with self-directed learning, can form groups to work on suggested topics for the sessions. These suggestions can then be used to make an outline or agenda, or integrated into an existing outline. In this way learners' backgrounds, interests, and expectations will have a direct influence on the nature of the sessions to follow. Of course, this technique can only be used when the educator has the flexibility to use the suggestions and when learners have the knowledge or experience to make suggestions (as was discussed in Chapter 4).

- In some situations, it will be possible to administer a psychological type test or a learning style inventory to learners. Any group who may be anxious about evaluation or testing should not be subjected to this in a first session, but it may be possible in a second or third session. The educator gains valuable insight into the nature of the learners.

No Learner Information Available: One-Day Session

What if it is a one-day workshop (or less) and there is no information available about the participants? Even if there are two or three shorter sessions, the educator justifiably hesitates to use time in activities designed to obtain information about learners. However, regardless of the length of the session, even if it is only for an hour or two, the educator *must* take some time to learn about the learners. This can be done in different ways and must always be done before a prepared agenda is distributed. Nothing stops an open expression of interests faster than a carefully organized agenda which contains no trace of what one hoped to learn! Again, different techniques will be appropriate in different contexts.

- The session can be started by posting a blank sheet of flip chart paper with the heading "Issues and Concerns" or "Expectations" written at the top. The educator can say, "I do have a proposed agenda for the day, but it is only proposed. First of all, I want to hear from you, and I am prepared to work with the issues or expectations that you have." Typically, there will be a prolonged silence, some shuffling of feet, and surreptitious glances among participants. The workshop leader should *sit down*, near the chart paper, marker in hand, and wait. Someone will speak, even if only to break the silence. Once ideas start coming, they will trigger others. Each should be recorded, with a comment that both reinforces and indicates whether or not the issue can be included in the session: "Good idea! We'll talk about that this afternoon"; "I find that really interesting, it might be too complex for us to address fully today, but we'll touch on it"; "I know that's a problem, I haven't resolved it yet myself, I think it's outside of our time available, but I have an article I can suggest you read." The suggestions received must be acted on; they must be included in the agenda or an explanation must be given as to why they cannot be included.

- A quick "getting-to-know-each-other" exercise can be included within almost any time period. For example, participants can be asked to write a few alternative completions of the sentence "I am...": e.g., I am a dictitian; I am a mother of four boys; I am a stamp collector; I am interested in working with people. These "I am" statements can be posted, with the participants' names, on the wall. People should also be wearing name tags or have their names taped to their tables. It is interesting to see how often group members (and the educator) look to the "I am" statements as people talk during the day.

- A warm-up exercise which focuses more on the content of the session may be appropriate in some situations. For example, the educator can prepare a set of controversial statements related to the content and write or type each on an individual filing card. There should be at least twice as many cards as participants. The cards are shuffled and randomly distributed to group members. Each learner is asked to exchange cards with others in the group until cards are obtained that he or she agrees with. If the group is relatively anxiety-free, individuals can read out the cards they accepted; otherwise, the educator can circulate with the group and discuss the cards being accepted and rejected. Often certain cards are rejected by everyone, providing more invaluable information to the educator.

No matter what the context or the constraints of that context, the educator can give some time to determining the characteristics of the learners. This may be as simple as asking the group to express their expectations or as time-consuming as assessing psychological type and conducting a needs assessment.

Resistant Learners

The learner who directly and overtly resists learning poses a difficult challenge for the educator. This individual may reject working toward self-directed learning without understanding the concept; the learner may not participate in activities, or promise to hand in a project or paper but never do so; the learner may have been forced to attend a session by an employer or an agency and be resentful and determined to resist involvement; the person simply may not seem to change, learn, or develop; or the individual may drop out of the course or never return after the morning coffee break in the workshop. The educator usually feels responsible for doing something about the resistant learner, sometimes even at the cost of spending less time with more eager learners. There are times when a certain strategy will be effective, but there are times when overcoming the resistance is beyond the control or the power of the educator.

Brookfield (1990b, 150–154) provides an excellent analysis of the reasons why people resist learning. His points will be summarized.

- Individuals may have a poor self-image as learners, usually based on previous unsuccessful educational experiences.

- Learning is change, and change is disturbing and painful for many people; routine, habit, and familiarity are preferred. Brookfield refers to this as "fear of the unknown," and describes it as "perhaps the single greatest cause of resistance to learning" (150).

- Sometimes apparent resistance to learning is simply the person's normal rhythm of learning. He or she is "taking a break" from learning.

- If learners are unsure as to what is expected of them and how they will be judged, they may mistrust the educator and display this as a resistance to learning.

- At times the resistant learner has a personal dislike of the educator, based on personality differences, values, or background. Learners may perceive educator statements as racist or sexist; they may see or think they see favoritism, discrimination, arrogance, or lack of caring.

- The individual's learning style may be in conflict with the educator's style. Some people hate group work and discussion; others have no patience with listening or reading, but prefer to "do" (see Chapter 2).

- If the learning activities appear to be irrelevant to the learners' interests and concerns, they will resist learning. For example, adults who have immediate practical work-related issues to deal with will have no patience with theoretical analyses.

- People have a fear of looking foolish in public. Most of us prefer to do things that we know we can do well, and trying something new and difficult in a group or in front of the educator can provoke considerable anxiety. Reactions to this situation may appear to be a resistance to learning.

- Some cultures and sub-cultures do not value learning or education. The learner with this cultural background may risk a loss of cultural identity by accepting too much change and prefer to withdraw or drop out.

- The level of learning may be inappropriate due to either the educator's misjudgment of learner readiness or the learner's mistake in selecting the course or session.

Brookfield (1990, 154–162) goes on to describe a variety of approaches aimed at overcoming resistance to learning. Many of these approaches are techniques used by any effective educator (e.g., involving learners in educational planning, providing feedback, encouraging peer interactions). Brookfield's suggestions are integrated into the discussion below. The reader who is interested in the details should consult *The Skilful Teacher*.

There are two situations which may have quite different causes and therefore may require different strategies: the individual resistant learner in a group which is otherwise doing well; and the group or sub-group of learners which is resisting learning.

The Resistant Individual Learner

What if one learner in a group is resistant or appears to be resistant to learning? This person may refuse to participate, begin to read or work on projects or papers, become hostile, aggressive, or withdrawn, or demonstrate no change or learning. The educator can take some or all of the following steps.

- The first step must be to attempt to determine the cause of the resistance through an individual meeting with the learner, with care being taken to not further aggravate the problem. If the learner is keeping a journal, this may provide a valuable source of information. Other techniques described in Chapter 5, such as critical incidents, metaphor analyses, or biographies, also can help the educator sort out the cause of the resistance. Sometimes it is advisable to have the whole group carry out one of these activities, rather than to single out the resistant learner (the information from others will also be valuable).

- If the learner's culture or background is a possible contributing factor, the educator can ask about it. In some cases, a discussion with the learner about his or her background will have the additional side benefit of demonstrating an interest in the learner as a person.

- If the cause cannot be determined, the educator's options are limited. Sometimes, suggesting that the learner work with another individual in the group on a project will be effective. Or, a simple variation in style or methods will draw the individual into the activities. It also may be the case that the individual prefers to withdraw (an introverted type) or that the circumstances are beyond the control of the educator. At this point, considerable energy should *not* be devoted to the resistant individual. Energy spent to no avail can be used much more effectively with others, but this is the route to follow only when there is reason to believe that the educator is not responsible.

- If the cause is determined, the action to be taken depends on that cause. The individual with low self-esteem will benefit from positive feedback and by engaging in activities in which success is ensured. The individual in whose culture the educator is an authority figure will benefit from more initial structure and guidance. The introverted individual may just need to be left alone and not be expected to participate in role-playing or larger group discussions. If the level of learning is wrong for a person, they may be counseled to change to another session, or perhaps provided with alternative activities, depending on the context. If there is a mismatch of learning and teaching styles, the educator can vary his or her style and also provide alternative activities for the individual. Most often, determining the reason for resistance will indicate a clear course of action.

The Resistant Group of Learners

What if an entire learner group or the majority of a learner group resists learning? They may display hostility, cooperate only reluctantly, demonstrate no notable change or learning, complain to other educators or to the administration, grumble amongst themselves at breaks, etc. The educator can analyze the situation in one or more of the following ways.

- Based on notes, handouts, activities, outlines, and agendas, the educator can analyze the roles he or she has played, the amount of responsibility that learners have for their own learning, the degree to which learners' experiences are incorporated into their work, the clarity of expectations, and the amount and type of feedback they receive. During this analysis, other components of the educative process not listed here also may appear to be relevant and should be examined as well. The educator may wish to take notes on this analysis. It may also be useful to observe one session and record what takes place.

- Information about learners' characteristics can be examined, including background, related experience, cultural variables, values, psychological type, and learning style. If little information has been gathered up to this point, it now should be done.

- The educator can analyze the match between what is taking place in the learning situation and learners' characteristics, and make a hypothesis as to the nature of the problem. Examples might include: learners' prior experiences are not being considered; learners want practical information, but the content has been theoretical; learners are not ready for self-directed learning; or the difficulty level of the readings is inappropriate for the group.

- The issue can be discussed with learners. With concrete hypotheses and observations, the educator can facilitate an open and constructive session. It may begin with statements such as, "It's become clear to me that we're not doing something right, here. Nobody seems happy. We have to make some changes, but first I would like to hear from you...."

- In some contexts, a discussion with the whole group can be held. In other situations, the educator may want to suggest that learners work in smaller groups to discuss the problem. The educator should listen and observe closely, not become defensive, but where appropriate explain why certain decisions were made.

- Following discussion, the educator can suggest that the group come to agreement on specific changes to be made. Suggested changes can be listed on chart paper, as everyone should be clear as to what is being said. If some suggestions are impossible due to institutional constraints (for example, changing to a pass/fail system or changing the number of sessions), this must be made clear. If some suggestions contradict each other, the group should try to reach its own compromise or solution. The educator should facilitate the process by clarifying or questioning. If some differences are irreconcilable, the educator can suggest that different subgroups can work in different ways, as long as this is feasible.

- When the changes are agreed upon, the educator must, of course, act on these suggestions. It is usually advisable to put the changes in writing, including a revision of outlines and agendas, if this is appropriate. This information should then be distributed to all learners and checked with them to ensure that it is what they have suggested.

- In a shorter term session, such as a one-day workshop, it is difficult to follow this procedure. However, a mini-version could be conducted. The educator might simply stop the proceedings and remark that things do not seem to be working, asking for advice on how the workshop might be revised at this point.

People cannot be forced to learn. The resistant learner has, for him or her, a valid reason for resisting. This reason may have to do directly with the educator's behavior, in which case, once it is discovered, it can be changed. The reason may have to do with system variables, some of which can be changed and some not. Or, the reason may have to do with the learner as a person, or the learner's personal or work life. Sometimes the educator can adjust to better meet the needs of that learner, and at other times this is outside of the scope of what the educator can do.

Mandatory Attendance

In one sense, in our culture, there is no mandatory attendance for adult education classes: the worker can refuse the promotion or give up the job rather than attend the training session; the physiotherapy student can drop out of physiotherapy rather than take the anatomy course; the laid-off worker can apply for unemployment insurance rather than enter the retraining program; the secretary can switch jobs rather than take the word processing course. However, most people view situations requiring attendance as mandatory. These situations pose yet another type of challenge for the educator. Learners who must attend courses or workshops are sometimes resistant, as described in the previous section, and they have a valid reason for being so. Or some learners simply put in time, going through the motions, meeting the requirements, and picking up their certificates or letters of completion at the end. Sometimes, when faced with mandatory attendance, learners will be hostile and challenging, become angry with the educator, or try to prove that they do not need to be there. Primarily, the educator must build a relationship of trust with the group, respecting the legitimacy of learners' reactions to the situation. Some strategies will be suggested for sample situations.

Minimum Effort

What if learners are putting in time, trying to get through the workshop or course with a minimum of effort and inconvenience? This is a common reaction to mandatory attendance. "Since I have to go, I'll go, but don't expect me to put any extra time into it." This reaction is also sometimes displayed by learners who have chosen to attend, but only in order to earn salary increases or promotions. The educator has to work hard to make the experience interesting and fun, to build rapport with the group, and to draw individuals into the learning process. In different contexts and with different groups, some of the following suggestions will be appropriate.

- The educator must acknowledge that learners have not chosen to attend or that they have chosen to attend for reasons unrelated to learning. This acknowledgement should not be made in a confrontational or challenging way, but openly, directly, with understanding. If the educator has undergone some similar experience (even attendance at department or committee meetings may qualify), this can be relayed to learners as an indication of understanding. The educator can then follow this acknowledgement with a statement of his or her own philosophy, including the belief that any learning experience can be turned into a meaningful event in a learner's life. It may be appropriate for the educator to say that she considers it her responsibility to work toward this goal.

- It is unlikely, of course, that after such an introduction learners immediately will begin the first activity with enthusiasm. It is important to establish a trusting relationship with the group. Brookfield (1990b, 164–175) provides several good tips on building trust, some of which include: make sure that your words and actions are congruent; be ready to admit your errors; reveal aspects of yourself unrelated to teaching; take learners seriously; and realize the power of your own role modeling. The educator must demonstrate consistently his belief in the learners and the value of the learning experience. Consistent respect for learners and belief in what they can do, coupled with being oneself, will almost inevitably lead to a trusting relationship.

- One aspect of building trust and respecting learners is valuing their experiences and lives outside the learning environment. Although this is always important, it can be an essential "hook" for learners who must attend sessions. If people see that the sessions will really be of benefit, relate to what they do, and help them to do a better job, interest will pick up. For this to happen, of course, the educator must become familiar with learners' experiences and work lives, and must learn about what they need and want to learn. Techniques from Chapter 5, such as the use of biographies or critical incidents, can be extremely useful here.

- The experience must be enjoyable for learners. Since most people like to talk and get to know others or visit with people they already know, opportunities should be provided for social interaction. Many people enjoy games or simulations which involve moving around and interacting with others. The physical environment should be made as comfortable and cheerful as possible, including the provision of coffee and snacks. If food is not available, it is worthwhile suggesting that learners take turns bringing muffins or cookies for the break, and even bringing your own coffeemaker. The planning of this kind of activity will increase learner involvement and enjoyment.

- Where it is appropriate or possible, moving a mandatory attendance group out of the classroom can work miracles. Sometimes the new setting can be directly related to the learning, such as a visit to a field site or attending a concert, lecture, or play. A professional development session can be held away from the building, perhaps at a hotel or retreat center. Even suggesting that the group move out to the lawn on a summer day can have a dramatic effect on learners' perceptions of the experience.

Learner Hostility

What if the group which is forced to attend is angry and hostile? This reaction may occur if, for example, a change is being introduced by management in an organization and people are forced to attend training sessions, or if performance appraisal is mandated and individuals must learn about the process. Anger and hostility also will occur if a session or series of sessions are planned to cover material which participants feel they do not need or already know. What does one do when faced with twenty or thirty pairs of hostile eyes?

- As before, the situation must be acknowledged openly and directly. Almost the only way to begin such a session is to give people the opportunity to state how they feel. Blank flip chart paper should be posted, and learners should be invited to state their concerns. The educator should only record responses and not enter into arguments or defend the value of the session. Even if the session is a short-term one, perhaps a part of a day, participants need to express their feelings at the beginning of the session.

- When it becomes clear that everything has been said, the feelings expressed must be acknowledged. The educator should indicate an understanding of why learners have reacted in this way, and again, if possible, relay some personal experience which is similar.

- It is then time to turn the energy to a more productive use. In either small groups or a large group brainstorming session, the educator should suggest that people devise alternative solutions to the problems posed. As no criticism or judgment of wild ideas is permitted in a brainstorming, this technique is usually preferable. Participants can then make the transition from blocking to solution by providing some "angry solutions." In a large group session, the educator should act as recorder, and in small group sessions, only listen and observe.

- At the end of this activity, the educator should clearly indicate which options are possible or feasible and which are not. Often in a mandatory attendance situation, restrictions on content and timing are imposed by the institution or organization, so some suggestions may not be possible.

- Out of the remaining possibilities, learners should select the most palatable. Obviously, the educator must act on the ideas provided by learners.

- The educator then can use the strategies discussed above for building a relationship of trust with learners and creating an atmosphere of enjoyment.

The group of learners who do not want to be there is one of the most difficult situations for an educator. And yet, with consistent belief in and respect for learners and their reactions, the educator can turn such an experience into a meaningful one.

Institutional Constraints

A wide variety of institutional or organizational constraints can influence learning situations. Constraints within the *physical environment*, such as room size, furniture, lighting, room temperature, and availability of appropriate resources or equipment, can plague the educator who is attempting to create a comfortable working atmosphere. *Administrative* constraints, such as requirements for examinations, required grading distributions, scheduling, multisectioned courses, deadlines, and registration procedures, can severely inhibit working toward self-directed learning or transformative learning.

Curriculum constraints, such as required textbooks or course outlines, pre-set evaluations, and the use of prepackaged materials, can restrict self-directed learning. *Financial* constraints which lead to extremely large groups, restrictions on materials or photocopying, outdated equipment, sharing of equipment, or restrictions on the use of field sites can limit the effectiveness of the educator's work.

Some constraints are simply a part of the learning context. For example, training and professional programs have required skills or competencies which comprise a mandatory curriculum. The educator must work within this framework, providing opportunities for learners to take responsibility in ways other than curriculum choice. Other constraints are out of the educator's control. For example, group size, scheduling, and financial resources are usually the responsibility of administrators. Here, the educator must still work within the constraints, but can be more innovative in overcoming them. Still other constraints can and should be opposed, with a view to changing the system. Institutions which inappropriately expect a certain distribution of grades, for example, should be questioned.

As can be seen, dealing with constraints is a varied process which depends on the nature of the constraint and the situation within which one is working. Not all issues can be discussed here, but a few constraints will be examined in greater detail. Overall, the educator should determine what the constraints are, then whether or not they should or can be changed, and finally, how to work within them or how to work to change them.

Physical Constraints

What if the physical environment is inappropriate for the session? A hot stuffy room. Desks bolted to the floor in rows. A room that is clearly too small. An intolerable noise level from the neighbouring machine shop. Twice as many learners as computers. Some suggestions follow.

- The educator must first determine whether and how changes can be made. This may involve contacting the organizer of the workshop, the person in charge of room scheduling, or the person in charge of the program and its facilities. Even if learners are actually assembled, the educator can say, "We cannot work here; we'll have to see about a change." In some circumstances, such as an on-site workshop for an organization, the participants can become involved in helping with the change. This can be a bonus—the educator is immediately able to give participants the opportunity to assume responsibility for their learning environment. If learners are just as lost and bewildered as the educator, they can still be asked for suggestions and advice, or take on some responsibility for investigating what to do. At worst, they can go off to the cafeteria or the nearest coffee shop and get to know each other while the educator works on changing the room. For an evening session, when all personnel responsible for physical facilities are unavailable, the educator can search out an unlocked room or apologize and say that the problem will be worked on for the next session.

- There are times, however, when changes are *not* possible. There are simply no other rooms available, no other arrangements that can be made. Now, the educator must work within the physical constraints. This can be posed as a problem to be solved mutually with learners; in fact, groups formed under adverse circumstances, which are given responsibility for dealing with those circumstances, will often turn out to be strong and cohesive learning units. Learners can engage in a brainstorming session or a general problem-solving discussion to produce alternatives. Feasible alternatives will depend, of course, on the context, but might include: using unassigned space, such as a lounge; bringing in chairs from other rooms and working at the front of the large lecture hall; meeting elsewhere (a learner may have access to a room at his or her place of work); meeting in someone's home; working outside (weather permitting); or dividing into subgroups and working in several locations, such as the cafeteria or a large office. While such solutions are not ideal, any improvement is worthwhile. And learners will enjoy coming up with the alternatives.

Administrative Restraints: Grading

What if administrative requirements, such as a normal distribution of grades or a pre-set final examination, are inappropriate for the situation and the learners? Among the most troublesome constraints are procedures and regulations related to the evaluation of learning. The issues involved will be described briefly.

There are two primary purposes of evaluation. One is to make comparisons among individuals, to rank them, or to select the best and the worst, or the above average and the below average from any group or population. The second is to provide feedback to individuals on the extent to which they are achieving or have achieved their goals. The comparative type of evaluation is called *norm-referenced*, as people are being compared to a norm or an average. The second type is called *criterion-referenced*, as individuals are being compared to criteria (set by themselves or others). No comparison among people takes place in criterion-referenced evaluation.

Norm-referenced evaluation produces a distribution of results which is ideally "normal." That is, most people are in a middle range (around the average), and fewer people receive results at the extremes of the distribution (very high and very low).

Many colleges, universities, certification boards, and other organizations and institutions accept a norm-referenced model of evaluation. First of all, it is the most common way of thinking about evaluation. If we are evaluating models of Rototillers with a view to buying one, we want to rank them and choose the best one. There are legitimate reasons for using the norm-referenced model: employers want to know who the best graduates are; the institution wants to reward the best students; graduate school selections rely on rankings; professional school selections rely on rankings; and certification boards want to ensure that the poor practitioners are sorted out and not certified.

However, in any one group of adult learners, there would be no reason to expect the same distribution of measures of learning as in the general population. More importantly, the purpose of evaluation of learning in most adult education settings is to determine the extent to which learners have achieved objectives rather than to compare or select individuals. When the teaching and learning process has been effective, the educator and learners expect that this will be reflected in high grades.

What can the educator do when conflict arises?

- The educator should first determine the nature of the constraint. Through discussion with a department head, registrar's office, or other administrative personnel, one can see whether the requirement is flexible. Some organizations will have an overall requirement, but will be quite flexible in individual cases.

- If the requirement turns out to be flexible, the educator can work within that, but may still choose to work toward change within the organization.

- If the constraint of submitting a normal distribution of grades appears to be inflexible, the educator can:

  — ask for a clear statement of policy;

  — ask for clarification of the reasoning behind the policy;

  — respond to the policy with a clear statement of the purpose of the evaluation of learning in his or her own setting; and,

— offer to work with others to revise the policy for situations in which it is not appropriate.

Administrative Constraints: Mandated Curriculum

What if part or all of the curriculum is mandated? In many adult education settings, particularly in professional education, professional development, and training programs, the skills, competencies, and even values to be learned are prescribed by others. In other situations, materials, resources, books, and techniques for evaluation of learning are pre-selected by others. In many cases, these constraints *are legitimate* (nursing students must learn how to administer medications). The educator's job here is to sort out real constraints from those which interfere with learning or are inappropriate.

- Based on professional and subject expertise, the educator should carefully examine the extent to which the curriculum is mandated. In many professions or trades or technologies, there are essential skills to be learned and these must be treated as givens. Even in these contexts, however, there are often nonessentials that are treated as "essentials"—learners of mechanics who must learn about engines that are no longer in use; students of statistics who must learn how to prove various theorems mathematically; learners of computing skills who must learn how the computer's hardware operates. Each required goal and objective should be questioned.

- Required books and materials should also be treated with skepticism. Even when the nature of the discipline determines many of the topics and objectives, learners can assume some responsibility for how they reach objectives.

- Evaluation procedures, as was discussed in the previous section, are often a product of misguided thinking about the purposes of evaluation. Naturally, when the subject contains essential competencies, it will be required that learners be evaluated on those competencies before certification or employment. But this does not mean that regular anxiety-provoking, norm-referenced evaluations need to be carried out.

- When the educator has determined which components of the curriculum constraints are legitimate and which are not, he or she should work toward change within the system.

- Given legitimate constraints, the educator's next step is to determine what remaining aspects of the learning experience are flexible, and how individuals' responsibility for learning can be fostered within those aspects. For example, most often, the methods by which learners reach prescribed objectives need not be constrained. The educator can work with learners to determine appropriate methods for specific groups or individuals. The steps that can be taken depend greatly on the context, but the adult educator can introduce considerable learner self-direction in almost any situation.

Financial Constraints

What if organizational financial constraints adversely affect the conditions under which the educator works? One common scenario is large group size—the group must be large to "pay for itself"; or "we can't afford to hire more educators" to reduce group size. In the face of large numbers, many educators will decide that they have no choice but to use an instructor-centered lecture approach. How can one do otherwise with groups of 50 or 100 or 600? Common in university undergraduate settings, this situation also occurs in almost any setting: the workshop where no limit is put on registration; the professional development day for teachers; the one trainer who is responsible for all employees in the organization. What does the educator do?

Large groups have several effects, including, among others: inhibiting interaction among learners; making it difficult for the educator to establish rapport with individuals; creating problems in the management of self-directed or individual learner projects; and making it difficult for learners to receive comprehensive feedback on their work.

Some strategies that can be used with large groups for a variety of contexts include:

- Groups of up to 50 or 60 (whether for one day or a full course) can be permanently divided into working groups. Groups can work on activities, problems, or cases, reporting periodically to the larger group. The educator rotates among the groups, joining and interacting with each. The group activities can be learner-directed or preplanned by the educator, depending on the context. This strategy has the advantage of providing for maximum interaction among learners, but does not allow for extensive individual learner interaction with the educator.

- Groups of any size can discuss an issue, solve a problem, or question each other in pairs. Although the noise level in a lecture hall containing 300 people may seem excessive, learners will appreciate the opportunity to talk to each other. This technique can be used intermittently with an instructor-centered approach in a very large group, perhaps every 15 minutes or so (about the length of the average learner's attention span for listening).

- Peer teaching can be effective in large groups that are heterogeneous in experience or educational background. Individual learners can choose and prepare topics which they "teach" to a partner or a small group. If physical facilities permit, several rooms can be used for these sessions, with the educator dropping in on each session.

- Large groups in clinical or field settings present a unique problem to the educator who cannot observe much of learners' work. In these settings, learners keeping journals, notes, or anecdotal records of what they did, how they felt about it, or what they wished they had done can be extremely useful. The educator can frequently and regularly review these records and provide feedback on performances that were not observed. Learners may begin such an exercise by writing what they think the educator would like to hear, but with time, when they come to realize that the purpose is to obtain positive and constructive feedback, most learners will report events honestly.

- In some contexts, simulations can be useful with a large group. Learners might simulate marketing research, parliamentary procedure, organizational behavior, procedures in the hospitality industry. Parts can be assumed by fairly large numbers of individuals; a committee (of learners) can be set up to orchestrate the simulation. Activities can take place (in some subjects) outside of the classroom with individuals actually collecting data from the field for the simulation. As everyone becomes involved, both interaction and experiential learning take place.

- Panel discussions, to a lesser extent, provide an opportunity to involve all learners in a large group. In most subjects, a controversial issue can be found for debate. Volunteer learners prepare for the debate—six or eight can be a part of the debating panel—and the audience can vote or present awards to the winning side. To further increase involvement, a committee of learners can organize the event.

- The critical incident technique described in Chapter 5 can be a useful strategy for groups working in clinical or field settings. It can provide a valuable means for the educator to get to know learners when direct contact is insufficient due to the group size.

With these beginning suggestions, the creative adult educator can devise a variety of strategies for increasing interaction among learners and between learner and educator within the constraints of a large group size. This is not to say, of course, that a large group size always should be viewed as a constraint. A well-organized and dynamic lecture to a large audience is an efficient means of conveying information.

Summary

There are dozens more "what if?" questions that could have been included in this chapter. The practising educator develops ways of dealing with adverse conditions and with "things gone wrong," and the reflective practitioner incorporates these strategies into a theory of practice.

One purpose of this chapter was to acknowledge explicitly that we all have bad days and bad groups and impossible situations to deal with. Such situations are not often transformed into exemplary practice by a twitch of the felt marker, but can be learning experiences for both learner and educator. It can be infinitely valuable for the educator to analyze such situations and consider his or her own behavior. It can be just as valuable for the educator to analyze these situations *with* learners, to foster their involvement in the process by looking back at what was done and why. There is almost no better way to begin to give learners responsibility for the learning experience than to involve them in dealing with difficult situations.

The second purpose of this chapter was to provide some specific and practical strategies for dealing with difficult situations. It is hoped that these sample strategies will stimulate further ideas in different contexts.

7

Developing a Theory of Practice

It has become clear, in the recent literature, that educators cannot define their practice simply as the selection of the right technique for a specific situation. Rather, the educator should develop a broader view of professional practice, including an awareness of his or her own philosophy and beliefs about working with learners. Brookfield (1986) writes: "Technique is, after all, only a means to broader ends. When technique is worshipped to the exclusion of the human or social purposes it is meant to serve, then it is easy for us to become dazzled by the convolutions of the latest shaman of procedure..." (289). We cannot hope, in other words, that if we only can find *the* right technique, all will go smoothly. The educator who discovers group work or introduces computers into the classroom or has a polished lecture series must still think beyond the technique. Why do I assume that students will learn more in groups? Do computers really facilitate learning, or am I just intrigued by computers myself? Why do I prefer to lecture?

It is the intent, in this book, to encourage educators' development of a theory of practice upon which decisions about the teaching and learning process can be made. In the first three chapters, the broad array of theoretical foundations, learner characteristics, and educator roles are described. Chapters 4 and 5, working toward self-directed and transformative learning, present theories of practice advocated in the adult education literature. Techniques are required (e.g., journals or critical incidents), but they are a means to a broader end, the process of self-directed or transformative learning. The overall theory guides the choice and use of techniques. Following the theory of practice, Chapter 6 includes guidelines for some situations in which the process does not work. An educator who has a different theory of practice may approach these situations in another way; however, the educator who has little awareness of a theory of practice is more likely to simply try another technique.

In this chapter, the development of theories of practice will be examined in more detail and illustrated by two case studies. The chapter will conclude with a look at the practical and research implications of the theories of practice that guided this book.

A Theory of Practice: The Process

A theory of practice can be defined simply as a set of assumptions, beliefs, and values about education. These assumptions are based: on past experience as both an educator and a learner, on observations of others' behaviors as educators and learners, on reading and learning about educational practice, and on reflection on one's own practice. Every educator has a theory of practice, a set of assumptions about his or her work with learners. Many educators, however, are not conscious of their theory and consequently do not use it to make consistent and informed decisions about their teaching.

Theories of practice are likely to be context-bound, as most of us work within specific situations, subjects, and cultures. Theories of practice are also likely to be person-bound, as most of us are constrained by our own personalities, values, backgrounds, and cultures. Schon (1983) presents evidence that professionals do make decisions, in practice, that are based on their theory-in-use, this theory being quite different from the espoused theory (e.g., taken from the literature). However, most individuals are not aware of the discrepancy between the theories that they use to make decisions while "in action" and the theories that they espouse. An educator who is conscious of his or her assumptions and beliefs about working with learners can make informed decisions about practice, as well as explain the approach to students.

The development of a theory of practice can be described best as a process of becoming aware of one's beliefs, akin to consciousness raising. It need not be a time-consuming process, but it must be one of self-reflection. As such, it includes the steps of:

- making explicit the assumptions about education;

- considering the sources of those assumptions;

- observing and considering the consequences of the assumptions;

- questioning the validity of the assumptions;

- revising assumptions that do not hold up under scrutiny; and,

- acting on the revised assumptions.

Although such techniques as journal writing or producing a biography can foster this type of reflection, they are not essential to the process. It is helpful, if at all possible, to discuss one's thoughts about practice with a colleague: another person's perspective often encourages the challenging of one's own beliefs.

Two case studies, each from different contexts, will be used to illustrate the nature of theories of practice, as well as the process of becoming aware of one's beliefs about educating.

Case Study # 1

Mark grew up and still lives in a small, relatively isolated East coast community. The educational and income levels in this area are quite low, but education is valued as a way out of the poor community. Parents tend to encourage their children to finish high school and go on to college, though the attrition rate in both high school and college is higher than average. Many young people drop out of school to earn money. But quite a high proportion of adults eventually return to educational settings after ten or more years in the workforce.

Mark is in his late 30s, married, and has three young children. His wife works as a receptionist and typist for the local car dealership. Mark and his wife own a house, but must struggle financially.

Mark worked for 10 years as a marine mechanic before applying for an instructor's position at the local college in the Marine Trade and Technology Program. Accepting the position meant a decrease in salary, but Mark shares his community's respect for education and sees this step as a positive one for himself and his family.

The new position was probationary for the first two years, with permanent full-time status being contingent upon successful completion of an Instructor's Training Program. Mark was required to complete one summer session of training before he started to teach, followed by work with a teaching consultant during his first year of practice, and then a second summer session. He had mixed reactions to this requirement. He never considered himself a good student, but he was interested in learning how to teach. His first summer session was difficult and anxiety-provoking. There was a lot of reading to do and he was required to write papers, neither of which he had done for many years. Mark feels he did not learn much that first summer; he was trying simply to survive the experience.

Mark is now finished his first year of teaching and is in his second summer session. During this year, his work with a teaching consultant included her observations of his work with students, the collection of feedback from students, several informal discussions with the consultant, and the preparation of a videotape of his teaching to bring to summer school. When asked to describe his approach to teaching, Mark's response included the following statements:

> I know my trade, I think that's one of the most important things. I also know the type of guys that are going into the trade. They mostly grew up around here, and we speak the same language.

> When I first started teaching, I thought that that's all I needed, to know my trade. I didn't get much out of summer school, writing objectives and all of that, because it seemed to me that I would just show the students, and explain things, and they would learn. I didn't count on having to motivate students, and I didn't realize that they wouldn't always understand things after I had shown them. It was very frustrating, particularly during the first semester. Maybe I would have quit altogether and gone back to earning more money in my trade, but my consultant was very supportive. She gave me several little things to do differently; for example, having the students work in pairs and help each other in the shop, rather than everybody listening to me all the time. It still makes me nervous though— there's a safety factor involved, and some of these students just have a bad attitude towards safety. I don't know what a teacher can do about bad attitudes.

> I know more about teaching though, after my first year, and working with my teaching consultant. I realize that teaching is a subject, too, and that I have a lot more to learn about it. I'm very interested in what I still have to learn.

I still see myself as the expert; I rely on my experience in the trade. I know all the kinds of things that can happen and go wrong, and my students just don't have this experience. I know the importance of the safety regulations and even just things like taking care of your tools. Also, in this field, there's a lot of content, a lot of technical information. I have that information and I can help my students to understand it. But I also see that people learn in different ways and are in the course for different reasons. I have found, this past year, that when I give the guys more responsibility, *expect* them to be more independent (don't watch over them all the time in the shop, for example), things go better. Not for all of them, I guess, but quite often that's true. I don't know if I could take this idea any further, but I really don't think so, not in the area that I'm teaching in. For example, they tell us in summer school that you shouldn't take attendance or mind about people coming in late, that it's demeaning for adults. Well, my students won't last long on the job if they don't show up or show up late. I can see that I have to think through all these things and see what applies to me and what is better for, say, the academic instructors. It's still frustrating. I wish the answers were clear, like they are in my subject.

Analysis

Mark's assumptions and beliefs about teaching include:

- education has an intrinsic value;

- being an educator is a valued profession;

- being an expert in one's subject is essential to being an educator;

- the nature of the subject determines the role(s) that the educator assumes;

- the instructor's job is to share his knowledge and expertise with learners;

- one can learn more about teaching (teaching is a subject, too);

- different students learn in different ways;

- giving some students more responsibility facilitates learning, but this is restricted by the subject; and,

- different teaching techniques and principles apply in different situations.

Likely sources of Mark's assumptions include:

- the values of his community and family;

- his own experiences as a student of his trade;

- his experience practising his trade;

- his work with his teaching consultant; and,

- his first year of teaching experience.

There is evidence, in this case study, that this instructor has seen some of the consequences of his assumptions ("I didn't realize that they wouldn't always understand things after I had shown them") and has done some questioning and made some revisions ("I have found...when I give more responsibility...things go better"). It is also clear that his theory of practice is not yet fully explicit and that it is still likely to change with further teaching experience.

The beliefs of this instructor are ones which lead him to instructor-centered roles, including those of expert, demonstrator, and guide. The theory is specific to the context and subject within which the instructor works. If this individual remains an educator within the same context, his theory (perhaps with some refinement) is likely to remain valid and useful in guiding his decisions about his practice.

Case Study # 2

Beverly grew up in a farming community in the mid-west. The educational level in the community is very low, but the income level is high, with most farmers running large beef cattle operations. In general, education is not valued; a negative attitude is common, as continuing in school sometimes "takes away" the children from the farm. Although the majority of young people do complete their studies at the local high school, only a very small percentage go on to college or university.

Beverly is in her mid 40s, divorced, and has one child who is living on his own. She now lives in an urban center.

Beverly was certified as a secondary school teacher, but rather than practise in that profession, she went on to complete master's and doctoral degrees. She was very successful as a student, earning high grades and enjoying her studies. She liked reading, writing, and working on her own; she carefully avoided all courses which had a reputation for including group projects.

With her doctorate complete, Beverly accepted a position as a university professor in a faculty of education. She was very anxious about teaching, having had no experience and seeing her early teacher training as having little relevance to the university level. That she was to be teaching teachers seemed particularly intimidating.

For the first few years, Beverly taught as she had preferred to learn as a student. There was very little interaction among students in her classroom; each session was a carefully prepared lecture followed by a question-and-answer period. Over time, this approach evolved into one in which considerable group work and interaction among learners was incorporated. The change was not deliberately planned, but was based on discussions with colleagues and feedback from students.

Beverly is now in her 16th year of teaching. When asked to describe her approach, Beverly's response includes the following statements:

> As is true of most educators in higher education, I had little experience with teaching. In my first faculty position, as a new member to the department, I was given a course that no one else wanted. It was called General Methods in Special Education. At least I had taken one psychology course, but I knew absolutely nothing about Special Education. Learners were experienced teachers, an average of 10 years older than I was. I faked it!

> I was never comfortable with telling others what to do, with being an authority, with enforcing things. Still, it took considerable time to grow into the role that I now assume with learners.

> Now, I am more of a learner than a teacher. We work in groups, and I learn from the products of the group work. My learners have so many ideas of their own—they are experienced, creative, innovative. They know what they want to learn. I am, in a way, just another member of the group. I have never been able to revert to an "expert" role. Maybe this is because I started out with that first frightening experience where I was truly not an expert.

> I do provide a lot of the structure, particularly at the beginning of a course. And I provide most of the resources throughout the courses. As time goes by, though, the students take over, so to speak. They like to lead sessions where they present to the others what they've been I would say that all learners, regardless of the level at which one is teaching or the discipline, have experience that is relevant to the learning and have ideas about what they want to learn that should be incorporated into the teaching. Of course, I realize that many disciplines have heavy content requirements, and that's a limiting

factor, but I still believe that when people make their own decisions
they are more interested in the outcomes of the decisions.

Analysis

Beverly's assumptions and beliefs about teaching include:

- education has an intrinsic value;

- as an educator, one can "grow into" new roles;

- educators are learners as well as teachers;

- interaction among learners is valuable;

- learners are resources for group learning;

- learners are to be valued for their experiences, ideas, and contributions;

- the educator has responsibility for providing structure and resources,
  though this may change over a course;

- given opportunity and guidance, learners will become self-directed; and,

- all learners should make some decisions about their learning.

Likely sources of Beverly's assumptions about teaching include:

- her experience as a learner, including that of being a university student;

- personal characteristics or preferences ("I was never comfortable
  with...");

- the nature of her first teaching assignment;

- her interactions with colleagues and students;

- feedback from colleagues and students; and,

- continued experience with different types of student groups.

It is clear that for this instructor consideration of the consequences of the
assumptions has led to considerable change, though this does not appear to
have been done in a deliberate or systematic manner. If her current roles
have evolved or grown, it is likely that this change has been the product of
gradually experimenting with different techniques and obtaining positive
results. Over time, she has developed a fairly explicit theory of practice.

The beliefs of this instructor are ones which lead her to roles such as
facilitator, resource person, and co-learner. The theory is not seen to be

specific to the context, though there is an indication that it would be modified in other contexts ("...I realize that many disciplines have heavy content requirements..."). The instructor appears to be aware of and confident of her theory of practice at this stage.

Summary

It is the intent in these case studies to provide illustrations of quite different theories of practice which are valid for those educators employing them. However, each educator is in a unique situation. The social context, learning environment, educator characteristics, and learner characteristics interact in complex ways in an individual's practice. The adoption of others' theories of practice is similar to an acceptance of espoused theory. Each of us must engage in critical reflection on our practice, and through that process develop an informed theory.

Some Implications of Theories of Practice

An educator who reflects on his or her work with learners and becomes aware of a theory of practice often then discovers that this process leads to further questions. These may be practical questions; for example, in the first case study, Mark wondered what to do about safety issues after deciding that students should have more responsibility. These also may be research questions; in Case Study 2, Beverly's belief that "when people make their own decisions they are more interested in the outcomes of the decisions" leads naturally to such an inquiry. We will examine some of the questions and implications that arise from the approaches presented in this book.

Practical Implications

The ideas presented here lead to a questioning of the instructor-centered approach employed in higher education (colleges and universities, as well as other settings). Instructor-centered roles are seen to have appropriate uses, but can be considered more valid for use as a beginning point with dependent or inexperienced learners. The educator then has a responsibility to move toward turning over responsibility to learners. How does one reconcile this with current practice in higher education? Could the approach taken by institutions of higher education be changed? Would they change? How could this be advocated? Implemented? With what effects?

In Chapter 4, the process of working toward self-directed learning is discussed. The assumptions are made that not all learners are able to accept self-direction, and that the process of becoming self-directed needs to be carefully facilitated for all learners. If these assumptions are accepted, there are several practical implications for self-directed courses and programs. Most self-directed programs have little, if any, preparation for either educators or learners. What may be required is one-half to one year of working towards self-directed learning. This can, of course, be done within the context of the discipline and not detract from learning the subject. But, on the other hand, considerable educator expertise is also required, which means that providing professional development for educators is necessary. Is this possible, feasible, or likely? If not, what is the fate of self-directed programs? If so, what would be the content of the professional development activities? How would they be implemented? Should the process begin much earlier, with the fostering of self-direction among children and adolescents?

Another aspect of the discussion of self-directed learning is the concept of felt learner needs (or expressed needs) versus real needs. The meeting of expressed needs only is assumed to be inappropriate; acceptance of this assumption implies that learners do not necessarily know their real needs. Several questions arise. Who does know the real needs? How can the educator determine them? How can learners be persuaded that these are their real needs? How does the educator deal with learner-expressed needs?

Transformative learning is relatively new in the adult education literature, particularly in its application to practice. Mezirow's theoretical description of the process has been with us for about 15 years, but often has not been viewed as a goal of adult learning or as a responsibility of the adult educator. There are several implications of assuming that transformative learning is a responsibility of the educator. When should transformative learning be fostered—in which situations, with which learners? How can the educator encourage learners to explicate their beliefs and assumptions? What is the best way to encourage questioning of beliefs without harming learners' self-esteem or confidence? How can the educator avoid imposing his or her own beliefs?

Skills-training courses or programs have long been in conflict with the theories of practice advocated in the adult education literature. Programs which include minimal essential competencies or skills as required curriculum leave the educator with seemingly little room for either self-directed learning or transformative learning. The learner in mechanics must be able to clean the carburetor; the student chef must be able to prepare a white sauce; the dental hygienist must be able to clean teeth. Training in psychomotor skills seems to be a particular problem, as these skills must be repeatedly practised until they are automatic—not only the objectives, but also the approach to learning seem to be dictated by the subject. An implication of accepting the assumptions pertaining to the value of working toward self-directed learning and transformative learning is that the educator must examine ways of resolving this conflict. To what extent can learners become designers of their own instruction in training programs? How can the educator ensure that essential competencies are obtained? What methods could be used to impart technical information? How can one turn over decision making to learners without sacrificing too much program time?

Recently, as a result of the work of educators such as Mezirow and Brookfield, we are returning to an earlier notion of education as social change. Social change is inherent in transformative learning: individuals question distortions in their assumptions and values; groups, sub-cultures, and cultures who ask these questions are involved in changing their society. Accepting the assumption that transformative learning is valuable leads the educator to accept social change as a goal. Who determines the direction of change? Who determines what is a distorted value? How can the educator determine whether his or her own values are distorted? How can learners be encouraged to act on the basis of their revised assumptions and values? How far does the educator go in advocating social change?

The idea that there are principles of adult education has long been a component of the adult education literature. However, the complexity of the educator/learner interaction within a learning environment and a social context leads to the questioning of general principles. Principles that are not grounded in theory are not likely to hold up in practice. We have said that the adult educator must develop a theory of practice based on his or her critical reflection on experience and the literature, and in light of the context within which he or she works. However, adult educators do not have the same opportunity for training and professional development as do other professionals. We do not expect medical doctors to practice on the basis of ten principles of medicine. We do not expect elementary school teachers to enter the classroom with their eight principles of teaching. Other professionals are involved in professional training and thereby come to realize the complexity of their chosen field. There are several implications for practice. Should we have more professional education programs for those who work with adult learners? Should there be associations that regulate such programs and control certification procedures, as there are in other professions? Given the diversity of contexts, is this possible? Would adult educators choose to participate? What would be the content of such programs?

Research Implications

All educators can be researchers, as discussed in Chapter 3. The academic adult educators might embark on larger scale systematic studies of the characteristics of adult learners, or the process of implementing a self-directed learning program, and it is this work which will eventually strengthen the theoretical foundations of our practice. However, every practitioner also can formulate hypotheses, collect information in a systematic way, and come to conclusions which are generalizable to his or her practice. And this is the definition of research. Theories of practice lead to research questions for both the academic researcher and the practitioner/researcher.

The model presented in Chapter 1 has several implications for research. To what extent do educator characteristics, such as psychological type, developmental phase, and cultural background, influence educators' choice of roles, activities, and methods? To what extent do learner characteristics affect learners' roles, activities, and degree of change? To what extent do these characteristics interact to influence the nature of the overall process? What factors enhance educator change? What factors, or what interaction of factors enhance learner change? How does the learning environment influence these processes? How does the social context influence these processes?

Psychological type is introduced in this book as an important educator and learner characteristic (Chapter 2). One can predict from type theory a variety of learning preferences and group interaction styles. How is type related to self-directed learning? How is type related to transformative learning? How does educator type influence the education process? How does learner type influence preferred approaches to learning? How does learner type influence group dynamics?

In Chapters 2 and 4, the concept of self-directed learning is discussed, both as a product of growth and development, and as a process. It is possible that the ability to be self-directed can be predicted by other learner characteristics, such as psychological type, learning style, and various cultural and educational background variables. What learner characteristics predict success at becoming self-directed? What is the process of becoming self-directed? Are there identifiable stages in that process? Do individuals with different characteristics go through that process in different ways? Are there better ways to assess a learner's readiness to be self-directed? How can we determine when a learner is self-directed?

Adult educators play a variety of roles, and the use of these roles varies in different contexts. Many practical guidelines advocate the selection of different roles for different situations; however, these guidelines often are not based on research evidence or theoretical foundations. How are learner characteristics related to learner preferences for educator roles? How are educator characteristics related to preferred roles? How do learner characteristics and educator roles interact to affect learning? What influence do learning environment and social context have on the effectiveness of educator roles? How do subject and educator roles interact to affect learning?

The process of working toward transformative learning is described in Chapter 5. However, very little is known about how people actually go through that process. Are there stages that a learner typically goes through? Is the ability to engage in transformative learning related to other learner characteristics? Do people with different characteristics go through the process in different ways? How can we assess whether transformative learning has taken place? What educator roles or behaviors facilitate transformative learning?

It is assumed throughout this book that both self-directed learning and transformative learning are valuable undertakings. Do people learn more or better or faster or differently when their learning is self-directed? How do individuals change as a result of transformative learning? Are the learning outcomes different with transformative learning? With self-directed learning?

In Chapter 6, it is acknowledged that adult educators often work in difficult situations and within practical constraints. Yet there is a lack of research on the effect of these constraints on learning. How do educators usually behave under such circumstances? What effect do these situations have on learning? What process do educators go through in dealing with constraints? What effect do these situations have on educators' values or theories of practice? What process do learners go through in working under constraints?

In this chapter, the process of developing a theory of practice is examined and illustrated with two case studies. The process of educator change and development has not been addressed by research. How do educators learn their skills? How do educators develop a theory of practice? What assumptions underlie educator practice? What are the discrepancies between espoused theories of adult education and theories of practice? What effect does critical self-reflection have on educator practice?

Summary

The purpose of this chapter was to encourage educators to make their theory of practice explicit. An awareness of one's assumptions about practice can stimulate consideration of where those assumptions came from and what they lead to. The educator who undergoes this reflective process is then able to identify distorted assumptions, revise them, and deliberately develop a conscious and informed approach to practice. Education becomes much more than simply selecting the "right method" for next week's class.

Of course, the educator will also find that developing a theory of practice leads to many more questions than it answers. Examples of practical questions and research questions have been given in this chapter; individuals will generate their own such list. Through this process, reflective practitioners will create and maintain enthusiasm and passion about education throughout their careers.

References

Argyris, C.

1982　*Reasoning, Learning, and Action: Individual and Organizational.* San Francisco: Jossey-Bass.

Argyris, C. and D.A. Schon

1974　*Theory in Practice: Increasing Professional Effectiveness.* San Francisco: Jossey-Bass.

Ash, C.R.

1985　Applying principles of self-directed learning in the health professions. In S. Brookfield, ed., *Self-Directed Learning: From Theory to Practice.* New Directions for Continuing Education, No. 25. San Francisco: Jossey-Bass.

Aslanian, C.B. and H.M. Brickell

1980　*Americans in Transition: Life Changes as Reasons for Adult Learning.* New York: Future Directions for a Learning Society, College Board.

Beder, H.W. and G.G. Darkenwald

1982　Differences between teaching adults and pre-adults: Some propositions and findings. *Adult Education, 32,* 142–155.

Bligh, D.A.

1980　Methods and techniques in post-secondary education. *Educational Studies and Documents, 31,* Paris: UNESCO.

Boud, D., R. Keogh and D. Walker

1985　*Reflection: Turning Experience into Learning.* London: Kogan Page.

Bowers, R.D.

1977   Testing the validity of the andragogical theory of education in selected situations. Unpublished doctoral dissertation, Boston University.

Boyd, B.B.

1980   Developing case studies. *Training and Development Journal*, June, 113–117.

Brookfield, S.

1985   Training educators of adults: A comparative analysis of graduate adult education in the U.S. and Great Britian. In G.J. Conti and R.A. Fellenz, eds., *Dialogues on Issues of Lifelong Learning in a Democratic Society*. College Station: Texas A & M University, 59–78.

1986   *Understanding and Facilitating Adult Learning*. San Francisco: Jossey-Bass.

1990a   *The Skillful Teacher*. San Francisco: Jossey-Bass.

1990b   Using critical incidents to explore learners' assumptions. In J. Mezirow and Associates, eds., *Fostering Critical Reflection in Adulthood*. San Francisco: Jossey-Bass.

Brown, G.A. and M. Bakhtar, eds.

1983   *Styles of Lecturing*. Loughborough: Loughborough University Press.

Brundage, D. and D. Mackeracher

1980   *Adult Learning Principles and Their Application to Program Planning*. Toronto: Ontario Institute for Studies in Education.

Candy, P.

1987   Evolution, revolution or devolution: Increasing learner control in the instructional setting. In D. Boud and V. Griffin, eds., *Appreciating Adults Learning: From the Learners' Perspective*. London: Kogan Page.

1990   Repertory grids: Playing verbal chess. In J. Mezirow and Associates, eds., *Fostering Critical Reflection in Adulthood*. San Francisco: Jossey-Bass.

Cohen, P.

1981   Student ratings of instruction and student achievement: A meta-analysis of multisection validity studies. *Review of Educational Research, 51*, 281–309.

Cranton, P.A.

1989   *Planning Instruction for Adult Learners*. Toronto: Wall & Emerson.

Cranton, P.A. and R. Knoop

1990   *Psychological Type and Learning Style*. Beamsville, ON: Professional Effectiveness Technologies.

Cranton, P.A. and R. Smith

1986   A new look at the effect of course characteristics on student ratings of instruction. *American Educational Research Journal, 23,* 117–128.

Cronbach, L.

1957   The two disciplines of scientific psychology. *American Psychologist, 12,* 671–684.

Cronbach, L. and R. Snow

1977   *Aptitudes and Instructional Methods*. New York: Irvington Publishers.

Cross, P.

1981   *Adults as Learners*. San Francisco: Jossey-Bass.

Danis, C. and N. Tremblay

1985   Critical analysis of adult learning principles from a self-directed learner's perspective. *Proceedings of the Adult Education Research Conference, No. 26*. Temple: Arizona State University.

Deshler, D.

1990   Metaphor analysis: Exorcising social ghosts. In J. Mezirow and Associates, eds., *Fostering Critical Reflection in Adulthood*. San Francisco: Jossey-Bass.

Dewey, J.

1916   *Democracy and Education*. New York: Macmillan.

1933   *How We Think*. New York: Heath.

1938   *Experience and Education*. New York: Collier Books.

Dominice, P.

1990   Composing education biographies: Group reflection through life histories. In J. Mezirow and Associates, eds., *Fostering Critical Reflection in Adulthood*. San Francisco: Jossey-Bass.

Fierrier, B., M. Marrin and J. Seidman

1982   Student autonomy in learning medicine: Some participants' experiences. In D. Boud, ed., *Developing Student in Learning*. London: Kogan Page.

Flanagan, J.C.
1954   The critical incident technique. *Psychological Bulletin, 51,* 4.

Freire, P.
1972   *Pedagogy of the Oppressed.* Harmondsworth: Penguin.

1974   *Education: The Practice of Freedom.* London: Writers and Readers.

Fuhrmann, B.S. and R. Jacobs
1980   *The Learning Interactions Inventory.* Richmond: Ronne Jacobs Associates.

Fulwiller, T., ed.
1987   *The Journal Book.* Portsmouth, NH: Boynton/Cook. Cited in J. Lukinsky, Reflective withdrawal through journal writing. In J. Mezirow and Associates, eds., *Fostering Critical Reflection in Adulthood.* San Francisco: Jossey-Bass.

Gagné, R.
1975   *Essentials of Learning for Instruction.* Hinsdale, IL: Dryden Press.

1977   *The Conditions of Learning, 3rd ed.* New York: Holt, Rinehart and Winston.

Gagné, R.M. and L.J. Briggs
1970   *Principles of Instructional Design.* New York: Holt, Rinehart and Winston

Geis, G.
1987   Adult education and instructional design. Paper presented at the Annual Meeting of the Canadian Society for Studies in Education, Hamilton, Ontario.

Gilligan, C.
1982   *In a Different Voice.* Boston: Harvard University Press.

Gorham, J.
1984   A current look at "modern practice": Perceived and observed similarities and differences of the same teachers in adult and pre-adult classrooms. *Proceedings of the Adult Education Research Conference, No. 25.* Raleigh: North Carolina State University.

Guglielmino, L.M.
1977   Development of the Self-Directed Learning Readiness Scale. Unpublished doctoral dissertation, University of Georgia.

Hart, M.

1990   Liberation through consciousness raising. In J. Mezirow and Associates, eds., *Fostering Critical Reflection in Adulthood*. San Francisco: Jossey-Bass.

Herbeson, E.

1990   Psychological Type and Self-Directed Learning. Unpublished Master's thesis. St. Catharines, Ontario: Brock University.

Hilgard, E.R. and G.H. Bower

1966   *Theories of Learning*. New York: Appleton-Century-Crofts.

Jaques, D.

1984   *Learning in Groups*. London: Croom Helm.

Jarvis, P.

1983   *Adult and Continuing Education; Theory and Practice*. London: Croom Helm.

1987   *Adult Learning in the Social Context*. London: Croom Helm.

Jung, C.

1971   *Psychological Types*. Princeton: Princeton University Press.

Keane, R.

1987   The doubting journey: A learning process of self-transformation. In D. Boud and V. Griffin, eds., *Appreciating Adults Learning*. London: Kogan Page.

Kelly, G.A.

1955   *The Psychology of Personal Constructs*. 2 vols. New York: Norton.

Keirsey, D. and Bates, M.

1987   *Please Understand Me: Character & Temperament Types*. Del Mar, CA: Gnosology Books.

Knights, S. and R. McDonald

1977   *Adult Learners in University Courses*. Perth, Australia: Educational Services Resources Unit, Murdoch University.

Knoop, R.

1990   *Working in and with Groups*. Beamsville, ON: Professional Effectiveness Technologies.

Knoop, R. and P.A. Cranton

1990   *P.E.T. Type Test.* Beamsville, ON: Professional Effectiveness Technologies.

Knowles, M.

1975   *Self-Directed Learning: A Guide for Learners and Teachers.* New York: Association Press.

1980   *The Modern Practice of Adult Education.* New York: Association Press.

1984   *The Adult Learner: A Neglected Species,* Revised. Houston: Gulf.

1984   *Andragogy in Action: Applying Modern Principles of Adult Learning.* San Francisco: Jossey-Bass.

Knox, A.

1987   *Helping Adults Learn.* San Francisco: Jossey-Bass.

Kohlberg, L.

1969   Stage and sequence: The cognitive-developmental approach to socialization. In D.A. Guslin, ed., *Handbook of Socialization Theory and Research.* Chicago: Rand McNally.

Kohlberg, L. and E. Turiel

1971   Moral development and moral education. In G.S. Lesser, ed., *Psychology and Educational Practice.* Glenview, IL: Foresman.

Kolb, D.A.

1976   *The Learning Style Inventory: Technical Manual and Self-Scoring Test and Interpretation Booklet.* Boston: McBer.

Kolb, D.A.

1984   *Experiential Learning.* New Jersey: Prentice-Hall.

Kulik, J.A. and C.L.C. Kulik

1979   College teaching. In P.L. Peterson and H.J. Walberg, eds., *Research on Teaching: Concepts, Findings and Implications.* Berkeley, California: McCutcheon, 70–93.

Leacock, S.

1914   *Arcadian Adventures with the Idle Rich.* Toronto: McClelland and Stewart.

Lindeman, E.C.

1926   *The Meaning of Adult Education.* New York: New Republic.

Little, D.

1979   Adult learning and education: A concept analysis. In P. Cunningham, ed., *Yearbook of Adult and Continuing Education, 1979–1980*. Chicago: Marquis Academic Media.

Loevinger, J.

1976   *Ego Development: Conceptions and Theories*. San Francisco: Jossey-Bass.

Luker, P.A.

1987   Some case studies of small group teaching. Unpublished Ph.D. Dissertation, University of Nottingham.

Lukinsky, J.

1990   Reflective withdrawal through journal writing. In J. Mezirow and Associates, eds. *Fostering Critical Reflection in Adulthood*. San Francisco: Jossey-Bass.

Marsh, H.W.

1987   Students' evaluation of university teaching: Research findings, methodological issues, and directions for future research. *International Journal of Educational Research, 11,* 253–388.

Maslow, A.H.

1968   *Towards a Psychology of Being*. New York: Van Nostrand.

McKeachie, W.J.

1970   Psychological characteristics of adults and instructional methods in adult education. In R.G. Kuhlen, ed., *Psychological Backgrounds of Adult Education*. Syracuse, NY: Syracuse University Publications in Continuing Education.

Mezirow, J.

1977   Perspective transformation. *Studies in Adult Education, 9,* 100–110.

1981   A critical theory of adult learning and education. *Adult Education, 32,* No. 1.

Mezirow, J. and Associates

1990   *Fostering Critical Reflection in Adulthood*. San Francisco: Jossey-Bass.

Moore, A.B.

1982   Learning and teaching styles of adult education teachers. *Proceedings of the Adult Education Research Conference,* No. 23. Lincoln, NB: University of Nebraska.

Nemiroff, G.F.

1989   Beyond "talking heads:" Towards an empowering pedagogy of women's studies. *Atlantis, 15,* 1–16.

Pavlov, I.P.

1927   *Conditional Reflexes.* New York: Oxford University Press.

Perry, W.G. Jr.

1970   *Forms of Intellectual and Ethical Development in the College Years.* New York: Holt, Rinehart and Winston.

Progoff, I.

1975   *At a Journal Writing Workshop.* New York: Dialogue House Library.

Ranier, T.

1978   *The New Diary.* Los Angeles: Jeremy P. Teacher. Cited in J. Lukinsky, Reflective withdrawal through journal writing. In J. Mezirow and Associates, eds., *Fostering Critical Reflection in Adulthood.* San Francisco: Jossey-Bass.

Renner, P.F.

1983   *The Instructor's Survival Kit,* 2nd ed. Vancouver: Training Associates Ltd.

Riechmann, S. and A. Grasha

1974   A rational approach to developing and assessing the construct validity of a student learning style scale instrument. *Journal of Psychology, 87,* 213–223.

Rogers, C.

1951   *Client-Centered Therapy.* Boston: Houghton-Mifflin.

1969   *Freedom to Learn.* Columbus: Charles E. Merrill.

Schmidt, S.D.

1984   Examining the learning styles of returning adult students: Emerging elements of best practice with implications for teaching styles. *Proceedings of the Adult Education Research Conference, No. 25.* Raleigh: North Carolina State University.

Schon, D.A.

1983   *The Reflective Practitioner: How Professionals Think in Action.* New York: Basic Books.

Selman, G.

1989   The enemies of adult education. *Canadian Journal of University Continuing Education, 15,* 68–81.

Sharp, D.

1987   *Personality Types: Jung's Model of Typology.* Toronto: Inner City Books.

Shaw, M.E.

1976   *Group Dynamics: The Psychology of Small Group Behavior.* New York: McGraw Hill.

Skinner, B.F.

1953   *Science and Human Behavior.* New York: Crowell-Collier and Macmillan.

Taylor, M.

1987   Self-directed learning: More than meets the observer's eye. In D. Boud and V. Griffin, eds. *Appreciating Adults Learning.* London: Kogan Page.

Theil, J.P.

1984   Successful self-directed learners' learning styles. *Proceedings of the Adult Education Research Conference,* No. 25. Raleigh: North Carolina State University.

Thorndike, E.L.

1898   *Animal Intelligence.*

Thorne, E. and J. Marshall

1984   Managerial development at General Electric. In M. Knowles, ed., *Andragogy in Action: Applying Modern Principles of Adult Learning.* San Francisco: Jossey-Bass.

Tough, A.M.

1979   *The Adult's Learning Projects: A Fresh Approach to Theory and Practice in Adult Learning.* Toronto: Ontario Institute for Studies in Education.

Ume, T.

1990   Personal communication. St. Catharines, Ontario: Brock University.

Western Report

1990   *5,* No. 50, 1. Edmonton: United Western Communications.

Wilcox, S.

1990a   Instructor Support for Self-Directed Learning in Higher Education. Unpublished Master's Thesis. St. Catharines, Ontario: Brock University.

1990b   *Planning for Learning: A Self-Directed Strategy.* St. Catharines, Ontario: Instructional Development Office, Brock University.

Zerges, R.A.

1984   Instructional behaviors valued by adult continuing education students related to student personality type. *Proceedings of the Adult Education Research Conference,* No. 25. Raleigh: North Carolina State University.

Index